Conquering *my* NeMEsis

What others say

My curiosity was piqued by the way NeMEsis is written. This book poignantly highlights how we become our own saboteurs. The alignment between author and reader is established early on, because we all have a ne*m*esis of our own to conquer. The author recognises the power inherent in every individual who is, or aspires to be, an inspirational and exemplary leader. This thought-provoking read offers a journey of possibilities for self-discovery and refreshing insights.

What I liked is the simple truth: If you want to emerge as your best self, then you need to rescue yourself through heightened awareness, being goal-oriented, having a positive outlook, and honouring yourself. I enjoyed the creative mix of biographical and research content, which promotes, enhances and expands the world of self-leadership.

The author's wide research for this book combines his rich experiences with peppered wisdom from various authors to produce a resounding leadership philosophy. The valuable tips and practical tools encourage curiosity and introspection. It's definitely a worthwhile read that takes the reader on an epic journey of wisdom, insight and learning, through to self-mastery and overcoming obstacles with resilience, hope, optimism and a commitment to improvement.

I would recommend this book to anyone who is leading, or aspiring to lead, and who is ready to commit to conquering their setbacks and emerge as their best self.

Prof Mala Singh
Executive Coach and Executive Director – People and Culture
North-West University

Dr Hekkie van der Westhuizen has become a thought leader in the field of self-leadership, or leading yourself. With fad-free insight, he has managed to zero in on the basics with remarkable clarity. His book discusses the fundamental practices of leadership and leading oneself, the commitments these practices embody, as well as the day-to-day steps it takes to be a successful leader of oneself. Without this, one cannot be a successful leader of others.

At a time when words like "inspiration", "profound" and "influencer" are sometimes used in embarrassing contexts, Hekkie restores these concepts to their rightful place – at the core of the successful leader. The author displays compelling insights and practical experiences, which empower people to find and nurture their own self-leadership.

I have no hesitation in recommending *Conquering my NeMEsis* to you as an excellent approach to leading yourself.

Mark Peters
Strategy and marketing expert and consultant

Once you start reading it, Hekkie's 'real-life novel' is hard to put down. There are nuggets of wisdom on every page and in every paragraph. The book pours out power quotes that offer sage wisdom and guidance to both young and old, especially on how to take charge of your life, at any stage or phase. It can help you to take charge and makes you realise that you are in charge. The use of Hekkie's own story is a powerful illustration of the value about which he writes. It is both empowering and inspiring at the same time, while challenging us to do more and be more than we are.

If you are not yet in charge of your life, this book will kick you on the backside and challenge you to step up. It offers many tools to help you gain control. The powerful message in this book deserves widespread circulation and must be translated into multiple languages. It has the potential to transform and empower global youth and, help grow servant leaders everywhere. Go right ahead – confront your ne*m*esis. Start in front of the mirror. Can you handle it? Hekkie did, and he conquered. You can, too. Start within. Start now. Read this and you will flourish. I dare you to try it.

Dr Dumisani Magadlela
International Executive Coach, Team Coach, Ubuntu Intelligence Coach

Conquering my NeMEsis is a well-researched, principle-based book that explores the concept of self-leadership. The reflections provided, along with contextual interpretations and rich insights on important conversations on the topic, are a real inspiration. It offers us pragmatic advice and a set of tools and approaches to elevate our understanding of self-leadership for the modern age. As an experienced practitioner working inside and alongside organisations, Hekkie gives us an opportunity to think in a more connected way about self-leadership, which will, without doubt, help us to expedite the emergence of authentic leaders.

Prof H.B. Klopper
Executive Dean – Research and Institutional Partnerships
The Da Vinci Institute

Conquering my NeMEsis is one of those books that you cannot easily put down. Not only is it easily written for anyone to understand, but the author also uses personal examples throughout that resonate with the reader. As the book unfolds, he brings you close, into his personal life, helping you to understand his feelings around the fragility of life and about his self-leadership journey.

Hekkie offers an insight into the pitfalls that can derail one's life, business and career, together with clearly illustrated strategies to escape them and, of course, ways to avoid them altogether. The personal goals scorecard tool presented in this book helped me to realise that a balanced scorecard approach is not only a corporate concept for businesses – it can be applied in our everyday lives, too. I cannot remember any other book in recent times that has ignited the fire within me to be the best I was born to be.

I recommend this book as a valuable aid to both the young and the old, and to those individuals who, with enthusiasm and aspirations towards progress, recognise their personal nemesis and want to conquer it!

Reverend Muzi Radebe
Pastor and businessman

Conquering my neMEsis is all about self-leadership and self-improvement. If you are stuck in a rut, or you would like to improve as a person while also improving your output or performance and contribution in a work environment, then this book is a must-read.

The chapters cover many areas of personal behaviour, including, among others, self-motivation, self-confidence and being well organised. They provide all of the tools necessary to evaluate yourself, work on and improve on each aspect, while allowing you to measure and track your progress.

This book is, in my opinion, very well written, and can, and should, be used as a textbook for future referral. Following the advice and guidelines in this book will help you to perform better as a self-leader, which is paramount to your ability to successfully lead others. This, in turn, will help you to become a more productive, positive and happier person, whatever your starting point, and will go a long way to helping you become the best You, that you can possibly be.

Dr Philip Theron
Businessman and entrepreneur

This book is an informal read, yet it reflects the seriousness, experience, depth and insights the author wants to convey to his intended audience of anyone over the age of 16, on how to shape their own journey towards self-leadership.

Hekkie's pleasant and subtle sense of humour is evident throughout his writing. Lightheartedly presented, at times it surprises the reader and makes one realise that life is also about humour, and that humour serves as an important stepping stone to mastering self-leadership – being able to laugh not only with yourself, but also at yourself, and to learn from that.

The use of supporting quotes throughout the book, which the author uses to shape his thoughts, decisions, and journey towards mastering his own self-leadership, is serious food for thought for the reader. Practical tips and suggestions provided, using the author's own life as an example, aid the reader to write and score his or her own self-leadership charter throughout their self-leadership journey, which is a plus.

A feeling of "I can do this" is created within the reader, leaving the reader motivated and inspired. In my mind, this book fills a gap in current literature on the 'how to' aspect of being able to achieve self-leadership, and what that actually means.

Truly a must-read, and a thought-provoking book for each person who wants to live a full, productive and quality life.

Prof Lia (Magda) Hewitt
Associate Professor – Department of Industrial Psychology and People Management
University of Johannesburg

Over the last decade, and particularly during the current COVID-19 pandemic, a significant failure, or weakness, in leadership across international, national, regional and corporate levels has been exposed. Against this backdrop there has been increased interest in self-leadership as an alternative to traditional leadership models, which have been found wanting in addressing the need for leadership at various levels.

Enter this useful contribution by Hekkie van der Westhuizen on self-leadership. His formula is to go wide rather than deep, and hence the scope of topics with regards to self-leadership is wide, but nevertheless relevant. His use of one-liner quotes from celebrities and icons, such as Elon Musk, Nelson Mandela, the Dalai Lama, Mother Teresa and others, is most effective, and in some cases, inspiring.

To illustrate his approach and content, he uses well-chosen mini-biographies of prominent business and other celebrities to make his point, complemented by anecdotes and stories from his own life. This lends to the authenticity of the book. Also included are short definitions of concepts to aid understanding by the average non-academic reader.

In conclusion, this book, which is an easy read, is a most valuable resource for anyone wanting to enter the self-leadership journey, either as a primer, or as a reference book.

Tony de Gouveia
Clinical Psychologist and Resilience Coach

Conquering *my* NeMEsis

Stepping Stones to
Successful Self-leadership

HEKKIE VAN DER WESTHUIZEN, PhD

Published by Quickfox Publishing
PO Box 50660, West Beach, 7449
Cape Town, South Africa
www.quickfox.co.za | info@quickfox.co.za

Conquering My NeMEsis: Stepping Stones to Successful Self-Leadership
ISBN Print: 978-1-776-32988-5

First edition 2021

Copyright ©2021 Hekkie van der Westhuizen

All rights reserved

The right of Hekkie van der Westhuizen to be identified as the author of this work has been asserted by him in accordance with sections 77 and 78 of the Copyright, Designs and Patents Act, 1988.

All rights reserved. No part of this book may be reprinted or reproduced or utilised in any form or by any electronic, mechanical, or any other means, now known or hereafter invented, including photocopying, and recording or in any information storage or retrieval system, without permission in writing from the author: hekkie@saldati.com

Edited by Michelle Bovey-Wood
Book and cover design by Vanessa Wilson
Production by Quickfox Publishing
Printed by Tandym Print, Cape Town, South Africa

ACKNOWLEDGEMENTS

First and foremost, I would like to thank God for blessing me with life and the opportunities to love, lead, share and to influence positively.

I would also like to express my sincere gratitude to the following people:

Marilé, my wife, my rock and my best friend. Thank you for your support and also for teaching me about life when I occasionally lose perspective.

Henri and Chris, my sons, who make me extremely proud. You bring joy to my life and I cherish our times together.

Mom and Dad. Your love, support and deep friendship have laid the foundation in my life. I can't thank you enough for this.

My sister, Rosa. You are my oldest friend, and for a better sibling I could never have asked. Although you are more than 16 000km away from me, distance will never change my love and appreciation for you.

Jenny Hoggarth. My executive coach for many years. You are like my older sister. You always said that I don't need to be fixed because there's nothing wrong with me. Well, I am finally at a point in my life where I do feel fixed and where all of your work – and mine – has paid off.

Steve Farrar. When I read *Finishing Strong*, while isolating after testing positive for Covid-19, it inspired me to both write this book and to finish strong in life.

Lou Tice of The Pacific Institute®, Norman Vincent Peale and Leo Buscaglia. Each of you passed on many years ago, and although I have never had the privilege of meeting you, I would like to thank you posthumously for your legacy and for making such a positive contribution to my life and my self-leadership journey.

All of the leadership gurus who taught me so much and to whom I look up. I have quoted you in this book to acknowledge you and your teachings.

Michelle Bovey-Wood, Vanessa Wilson and Adele Wilson. For partnering with me to make this book project a success.

Contents

From the Author 15
Preface 22
CHAPTER 1 Taking Charge 28
CHAPTER 2 Planning for Success 38
CHAPTER 3 Scripting Your Self-leadership Charter 45
CHAPTER 4 Avoiding Time-wasters and Distractors 71
CHAPTER 5 Living a Disciplined Life 82
CHAPTER 6 Refusing to Make Excuses 89
CHAPTER 7 Getting through Tough Times 94
CHAPTER 8 Becoming more Resilient 106
CHAPTER 9 Being in Charge of Your Emotions 122
CHAPTER 10 Living in the Present Moment 135
CHAPTER 11 Improving Self-confidence 142
CHAPTER 12 Choosing to be Positive 150
CHAPTER 13 Stepping out of Your Comfort Zones 159
CHAPTER 14 Learning and Living Good Habits 172
CHAPTER 15 Controlling Personal Finances 200

CHAPTER 16	Valuing Personal Brand Equity	211
CHAPTER 17	Cherishing Relationships	226
CHAPTER 18	Investing Time to Reflect	240
	Reflection Summary – Chapters 1-18	250
CHAPTER 19	Embracing that it is Never too Late	252
CHAPTER 20	It is Ultimately Your Choice	258
	Conclusion	265
	References	269
	About the Author	278

From the Author

"The first and best victory is to conquer self."
PLATO

When I arrived back at the Marriot Hotel in downtown Orlando, Florida, it was just before 3pm. It was 8 April 2012 and I had just returned from the Harley Davidson dealership where I had handed back the Fat Boy Lo motorcycle I had rented for three days while travelling east to Cape Canaveral and then heading down the A1A coastal road, through Palm Beach, to Miami, and then back on the interstate.

I had been in town on business to attend a plastics trade show, which had ended the previous Thursday. As an ex-biker who wanted to get back into motorcycling, the idea of not heading home for the Easter weekend, but spending some solo time on two wheels sounded like a great one. The fact that I also needed to clear my head after recently being served divorce papers made the idea just that much more appealing.

Having spent hours travelling under the Florida sun, I was tired. The plan had been to watch some television before taking a nap to recover from my time on the road. I'd had so much fun on my trip that I'd totally forgotten that my fellow South Africans were playing the final day of the Masters PGA Golf Tournament in Augusta, Georgia.

To my surprise, when I flicked through the television channels I saw Louis Oosthuizen and Bubba Watson playing the second hole, and very quickly my afternoon plans changed as I zoned into the golf. Armed with a yard-wide pizza and a couple of Cokes that I'd ordered from room service, I started to virtually support Louis as best and as hard as I could. When Bubba finally beat him to the green jacket and all of the excitement eventually died down, I settled back into my own thoughts, all alone in my hotel room.

While lying on my bed, a couple of serious thoughts unexpectedly crossed my mind. There I was, having just completed 854km (534 miles) across Florida, all on my own, after not riding a motorcycle for more than two decades. What if I'd had a bad accident in the middle of nowhere? What would have happened to Henri and Chris, who were aged nine and six at the time? For some unknown reason, I started to think about where I found myself in my life. I asked myself if I was satisfied with what I had achieved thus far … The unfortunate answer was a resounding: "No." My mind then leaped to the next question: "Why was I feeling that way?"

When I started to unpack things a bit further, I arrived at two answers: (1) I had not nearly achieved my full potential yet, as a father, son, brother, businessman or a leader, and (2) for so many years, I had been my own worst enemy – for probably more often than I had been my own best friend. This was evident in the way that I doubted myself, in the way I spoke to myself, and in the way that I pulled myself down from achieving great things. I realised that I could not live a full life unless I dealt with that enemy.

My last thought before I went to bed that night was: "What a sad day it would have been if I'd never got to address these issues before switching this life for the one hereafter, here, on two wheels, 13 000km away from home."

The start of my self-leadership journey

Before I get back to that special day of reflection in Florida in the spring of 2012, I would first like to take you back to where my self-leadership journey began. I come from a small, but close-knit and caring, middle-class family. Dad was a teacher and later became a school principal for most of his working career. Mom, a trained nurse, excelled in her career and became an Executive Member of Health Management in Limpopo province.

Our parents consciously focused on raising us in a loving home. They were always there for us, and together they were a formidable tag team who spent enough time with us to impart a love for life and much wisdom, too. That laid the foundation for my sister, Rosa, and I to confidently live the lives with which we were blessed. With their parenting came many of their own mottos about life, which they repeated enough times to have stuck with me – in a good way. To this day, they still come in handy.

Some of Dad's sayings that made the biggest impression were: "Make use of every single opportunity that you get in life"; "There is no better time than NOW to get something done" and "There's only one way of doing something in life, and that's the right way."

Mom used to say: "Each one of us needs to live his own unique life"; "Only dead fish swim with the current" and "As long as you did your best, then you have done well enough."

I have no doubt that growing up in a religious home and being exposed to my parents' wisdom made it easier for me to try to figure out life and how to live it. However, my journey of self-discovery and that around self-leadership really started as a teenager when, at the age of 16, I bought two Norman Vincent Peale books, *The Power of Positive Thinking*[1] and *Why some Positive Thinkers get Powerful Results*[2]. Then, when I was 17, I saw a video of a lecture given by Leo Buscaglia to the sales staff of the Ford Motor Company, called: "Only you can make the difference". Even at that young age, the content of those books and that video raised many questions in my mind around leadership, and specifically around my self-leadership, or personal leadership journey, although at that time, I did not know the terminology.

The burning desire to conquer myself

Although I have essentially been on a self-leadership quest since high school, taking stock of my life in a hotel room in Orlando that Sunday was a turning point in which the process of conquering myself was elevated to the next level. I realised that I didn't want to die one day feeling the same thing that I had felt on 8 April 2012. I told myself that I could be so much more – for my sake and for the sake of everyone around me. Two talks that I listened to prior to that important day have been top of my mind ever since:
- Brian Wegerle, 'Mr Harley-Davidson in South Africa', and the man who brought The Pacific Institute® to our country, gave a sermon before he died tragically in 2007. It was called: "One life to live, live it well".[3]

- Leo Buscaglia's talk, to which I referred earlier, "Only you can make the difference". In it, he made a statement, which to summarise, said: "Don't let God come back to Earth and ask: 'I have given you so much, but why did you achieve so little?'"

"Don't be afraid your life will end; be afraid that it will never begin."
Grace Hansen

The reality is that our lives are precious and we can either waste them in mediocrity or invest in greatness.[4] Another reality was that I was still far from greatness. Like all of us, I had so much untapped potential. I knew I had a lot of work to do, though, if I ever wanted to get close to greatness … The more I analysed myself, the more the words of Brazilian poet Floriano Martins started to resonate with me: "*The deeper I go into myself, the more I realise that I am my own enemy.*"

"It's not the mountains we conquer, but ourselves."
Edmund Hillary

When I finally realised that the sky is not the limit, but that *I am the limit*, it hit me like iced water in the face: The only person holding me back from achieving greatness was me! The personal Everest that stood between me and the best version of me, was *me*.

> **Nemesis**: The person or thing that causes somebody to lose their power, which cannot be avoided.[5]

I realised that I was my own ne*m*esis. As a priority, I needed to conquer that enemy within me, which kept pulling me back into feelings of doubt, low self-esteem, negativity, poor emotional intelligence, a lack of self-discipline and a fear of exploring opportunities – just to name a few.

"If you do not conquer self, you will be conquered by self."
Napoleon Hill

What gave me peace and hope, though, was that I was clearly not the only person who felt that way. If there were famous people, like those I have mentioned, who struggled with the fact that they, too, had to conquer themselves, then there were many more people out there who felt the same way.

Still, I wondered: "What if I can't conquer the n*em*esis – myself?"

"Well, if I can't conquer my n*em*esis, then I must at least learn to control it, or it will keep on controlling me, and it might ultimately destroy me," I told myself.

In theory, those were all great and noble intentions, but I had one question that needed to be answered first: "How?"

Answering the "How?"

I realised that the only way I could conquer, or at least control, my n*em*esis, was to work hard on my self-leadership success in order to achieve what I wanted to achieve in life, without holding on to something that kept slowing me down.

Upon reflection I could see that, by and large, whenever I was unhappy, unsuccessful, or experienced hardship in my life, it was because my self-leadership journey was not on track. There was a direct correlation between my self-leadership success and those issues I had faced at different times in my life.

After spending some time analysing that fact, I came to the conclusion that: If I have control over the process of leading myself, then, and only then, will I be able to achieve the following:

1. *Being the best that I can possibly be.*

    People who are successful at leading themselves are more content and live more fulfilling lives. The reason for this is actually quite straight forward: They feel more in control, and they achieve their goals in life. They understand that we have one life to live on Earth and that we need to live it well. It is indisputable that *we* are responsible for leading every single moment of our lives. It is important that we do this well, as not only do we only have one life, but we also only have one 'self'.

2. *Successfully leading others.*

    Self-leadership is a path towards more effectively leading others.[6] Let's use an analogy to explain this point: My family comprises myself, my wife, Marilé, and our two sons, Henri, 18, and Chris, 16. When I take them on our annual trip down to our holiday home on the KwaZulu-Natal South Coast, I first ensure that I am in good shape to achieve our goal of driving (or 'leading') them on our journey. The ultimate goal is to arrive safely at our destination 700km away from our Johannesburg home.

I cannot be successful in this leadership role if I haven't first checked a number of things:
- Am I buckled into my seat, well-rested and focused?
- Am I comfortable that my car is in good shape?
- Am I motivated to achieve the goal of having a safe trip that everyone enjoys?

I need to check these things first, before checking if my passengers ('team members') are okay to embark on the journey. Is it selfish to do the self-checks first? No, I am simply being responsible. If I am not in the right shape, or if I don't have the right mindset, then I can't lead my family to achieve our goal.

Here is the flipside: If I decide to finish a bottle of red wine and then watch a movie until midnight, ahead of our scheduled 5am start to our trip, then I would be demonstrating poor self-leadership and I certainly would not be in the right shape or frame of mind to safely lead my team of family members to our destination. Whether in a family context or any other, at some point in our lives, we lead other people. To be successful in this role, it is imperative that we are first successful in leading ourselves.

"He who cannot establish dominion over himself will have no dominion over others."

Leonardo da Vinci

This book is a celebration of finally having conquered *me*. I am grateful to be free from the bondage of being the 'lesser me', and I am well on my way to becoming the 'best me'. After a relentless pursuit over many years, I have finally figured out my life in terms of what works and what doesn't work for me as a successful self-leader. However, I do not, for one second, profess that I have everything under control all of the time, but I do have it under

FROM THE AUTHOR

control most of the time. I can confirm that the content of this book works, and that it will make you a better version of yourself – if you focus on it. It is my pleasure and privilege to share this book with you, and I trust that the content will assist you to become, or remain, successful at self-leadership.

Preface

Defining self-leadership

If we are to understand the crucial role of self-leadership in our lives, it is important that we properly define what it is that we are trying to achieve.

> Defined broadly, self-leadership is the process of influencing oneself.[7]
>
> It is important, though, to look at more detailed definitions:
> - *Self-leadership is the practice of intentionally influencing our thinking, feeling, and behaviours to achieve our objectives.*[8]
> - *Self-leadership is having a developed sense of who you are, what you can do and where you are going, coupled with the ability to influence your communication, emotions and behaviour on the way to getting there.*[9]
> - *Self-leadership specifies a collection of intra-individual strategies that provide explicit behavioural and cognitive prescriptions that can be used to achieve greater personal effectiveness.*[10]

Self-leadership includes:[11]
- Self-awareness;
- Setting goals for ourselves;
- Honouring ourselves;
- Actively rejecting pessimism;
- Being the change that we want to see in the world.

Self-leadership allows individuals to live more authentic and fulfilled lives. It is also important for organisations, as self-leaders are more motivated, productive and creative than other employees.[12] The biggest challenge of self-leadership is developing individuals to behave like leaders.

By mastering self-leadership, we are able to set direction in our lives, identify our needs and work more effectively.[13] Self-leadership often involves making choices that allow us to successfully navigate challenges and opportunities in life.[14] Therefore, self-leadership promotes performance.[15] Fortunately, we don't have to be born self-leaders, as self-leadership can be developed.[16]

The compound effect

Self-leadership needs to be part of our being; our very existence. It is not something that we can just switch on at work and then switch off again at home; or switch on today when we are with family, but then off again tomorrow when we are with friends. If we commit to self-leadership, then we need to be serious about constantly leading ourselves.

You may think that it is possible to keep your self-leadership process under control only part of the time, but I can tell from personal experience that if you try that, you will very quickly fall back into your old ways of being the lesser you, and only half of the person that you could potentially be. Still, that is the easy part … The difficult part is dealing with the regret of taking all of your hard work and progress and flushing it down the toilet.

We need to be aiming for a compound effect in which all of the hard work we put into our thinking, feeling and behaviour, and the benefits that we experience as a result, never ends. At the very least, we need to maintain it, but first prize is to keep building on to it, until we get to a point where we are successful self-leaders who reach our personal goals in full, on time, every time. The more we work and focus on developing our self-leadership, the more we will reap the benefits.

That voice in your head

When did you last tell yourself something, but then not listened to yourself? Can you remember a time when your inner voice spoke to you, but you decided to do something else instead?

The concept of self-leadership suggests that a single individual can act as both the leader and the follower.[17] So, my main aim as a successful self-leader is to ensure that the leader in me is a good, strong leader, and that the follower in me follows the leader at all times.

The follower and leader within us always need to be aligned. Only then will we reap all of the rewards and benefits in our lives from the leader and follower working together within us. It is only then that we will experience a truly successful self-leadership journey in which our behaviour, feelings and thoughts are perfectly aligned with achieving our personal goals. Then we will never have to regretfully admit: "I knew the right thing to do, but for some reason I didn't do it …"

When the follower is aligned to the good, strong leader that we have created within us, we can finally claim that we have conquered ourselves. The stepping stones in this book will guide you to that point.

"If a little voice in your head is telling you something is up, maybe you should listen."

Sara Shepard

Who should read this book, and why?

"Anyone," is the short answer. I would suggest, though, that any woman or man of 16 years of age or older should read this book. I have picked this 'threshold' starting age simply because that is when my self-leadership quest started. It is also typically the age when young men and woman start to think about and analyse life. It does not matter how rich or poor, able or disabled, or how motivated or demotivated you are, there is within each of us a deep desire to become greater and to be more successful.

If you consistently implement the self-leadership principles I am about to share with you, I have no doubt you will not only become a better self-leader, but that you will be more successful in whatever occupies your time. My liberal use of quotes from well-known and successful people across the world is a reminder that, to some extent, everyone battles with the same issues. We can also learn from their wisdom, which can assist us in overcoming our personal challenges.

> "Continuous effort – not strength or intelligence – is the key to unlocking our potential."
>
> Liane Cardes

How much potential do you think you have?

You need to think of yourself as having endless potential for development and growth, because only then will you do yourself justice by not placing any limits on yourself. Only by being able to successfully lead yourself will you be able to reach your full potential as a leader of others, too.

If we are not successful at self-leadership, we are making life exceedingly difficult for ourselves. If you want to live to your full potential, or to live a life that is easier – although maybe not initially, but certainly once you've mastered self-leadership – then this book is definitely for you.

After 35 years of self-discovery and working hard on my self-leadership, I have finally been able to document practical self-leadership interventions, tips and tools that have worked for me. I see no reason why they could not work for you, too. It is my pleasure to be able to share my self-leadership journey with you.

> "When nothing is sure, everything is possible."
>
> Margaret Drabble

I am writing this book at a time of unprecedented global chaos caused by COVID-19. This book is not a 'corona-virus-coping mechanism tool' though, because I believe we will see many more COVID-19-type challenges in our lifetime, although we have to believe that similar future events will be on a smaller scale.

The current pandemic is a stark reminder to us all that life might become increasingly difficult or challenging (even though my optimistic nature would kick against this statement). Amid all of this, you might ask me how the content of this book could help you if you have lost someone; if you have lost your job; or if you have been diagnosed with a terminal disease. If anything, I hope that this 'non-fiction novel' will give you the right perspective into your unique situation, and that it helps to improve your self-efficacy in overcoming your circumstances.

> "Self-efficacy is the belief in one's capabilities to organize and execute the sources of action required to manage prospective situations."
>
> Albert Bandura

We can't predict the future, but I can guarantee you that the stronger we are as individuals, from a mental health and emotional wellness perspective, the greater the probability of us surviving psychologically and being able to cope in these tough and volatile times. If I learn to better lead myself, I also don't entertain feeling sorry for myself. I then create the right mindset to face my challenges in life and to make the best of it. This creates hope in a sense, and hope is what we need when we increasingly face uncertainty.

We owe it to ourselves and to those around us to do whatever it takes to cope better with life. If this sounds appealing, then this book is also for you. I cannot promise you a quick recipe to sustainable success or happiness because that does not exist. However, I have no doubt that if you are serious about becoming the best version of yourself and about enjoying the resulting fruits in your life, then the content of this book will guide and assist you in achieving this important personal goal. There is one proviso, though: You must be willing to consistently put in the effort and work to become a better self-leader. The end result is that you will be more content and more at peace as a human being. That feeling is priceless.

When we reflect upon our lives one day …

What do we want to achieve in life, and how do we define success?

These answers are as unique to each one of us as our DNA and fingerprints. They are part of what distinguishes us from one another. I believe, though, that the only measure of personal success is if we can one day look back at our lives and honestly say with fondness that we are satisfied with what we see and with what we have achieved. Over our lifetimes, will we be satisfied with the way we acted; the thoughts we entertained; the impact we made; how we were as leaders; how we interacted with others, and with what we stood for?

In conclusion, you may still be wondering about the second part of the title of this book …

> **Stepping stone**: A raised stone used singly or in a series as a place on which to step when crossing a stream or muddy area.[18]

The content of this book summarises all of the things that helped me to conquer myself and to move from a point where I was my own worst enemy to the point where I am now: Satisfied, content and at peace with myself, my circumstances and my environment.

May the stepping stones within this book help you to cross the streams and muddy areas of your life, especially in the volatile times in which we are living, and help you reach where you would like to be. Most of all, I hope that it makes a positive and lasting impact on your self-leadership process, and I trust that the content will help you to live a life that you can look back on one day and smile with satisfaction and gratitude.

In the movie *Braveheart*[19], William Wallace (Mel Gibson) says to Queen Isabella (Sophie Marceau) after being jailed: "Every man dies, but not every man really lives." In this life there are two extremes available to us: We can lock ourselves in a room and only breathe, until we die – effectively imprisoning ourselves until the end of our days – or we can experience the total magnificence of life and truly live it. My wish is that this book is one of the many experiences in your life that will help you to 'really live'.

Chapter 1

Taking Charge

"Until you take charge of your own life, things don't happen."
SUZANNE BRAUN LEVINE

"I am the master of my fate, I am the captain of my soul."
William Ernest Henley

As the last two lines of the *Invictus*[20] poem so clearly remind us, we alone have control over our feelings and our destinies, regardless of our circumstances. If we want to choose our final destinations, we need to place ourselves in the driver's seat of our own lives. Taking charge of our lives is the most important step we can take on our self-leadership journey. When we do so, we finally become self-reliant and have the autonomy to make decisions for ourselves.

Oprah Winfrey, the American talk show host, television producer, actress, author, and billionaire philanthropist, was born into poverty in rural Mississippi to a teenaged mother and then initially cared for by her grandmother. She later moved to inner-city Milwaukee where she was raised by her mother. As a child, Oprah wore potato sacks because her family could not always afford clothing.[21] She was raped for the first time at age nine, and suffered repeated sexual abuse throughout her childhood and early teen years.

At age 14, Oprah was sent to live with her father, Vernon Winfrey, in Tennessee. At the time, she was already pregnant. Fourteen days after giving birth, her baby died.[22]

Life with her father was strict and focused on her academic progress. Oprah secured a job in radio while she was still in high school, and at age 19 she became a co-anchor on the local evening news. Partly owing to her spontaneity and warm personality, Oprah was transferred to the daytime talk show arena.[23] All of these events happened early on in her life before she became famous.

Each of us creates the life that we get to live,[24] but if we can learn from Oprah's story, we need to take on board the statement: We can only create the life we want if we make the conscious decision to take charge.

What a truly remarkable woman Oprah is. Amidst all the turmoil in her life, she must, at some point, have decided that she was finally in a position to create the future life that she wanted to lead. Despite her upbringing, Oprah triumphed and made a huge success of her life. Why? Because at some point she said: "No more," and she decided to take charge. While in a dark place, she made that important decision. I would like to think that she put into practice some of the things that I am about to share with you.

Make tough decisions to take charge

You might argue that taking control of your life is not that simple, and that your circumstances won't, or don't, allow you to make the necessary changes. I haven't walked in your shoes and I don't know your circumstances, but perhaps it's time to do something about them. Think about Oprah: Moving in with her father radically changed her life. She then made the decision to follow her passion for broadcasting at a young age, which opened up a world of opportunities for her. Taking charge of your life may require a tough decision.

> Ask yourself the following question:
>
> "In all probability, will my life be better if I stay where I am, or will it improve if I take charge of my life and go live somewhere else?"

You'll find that I use the term: "Whatever it takes" several times in this book. I honestly believe that when it comes to the fundamentals in life, we have no choice but to do what is necessary. If you need to break out of your current circumstances, and there is even a remote chance that this is possible, then take charge and break out. Do whatever it takes to give yourself the best possible chance of living a better life.

Be intentional

"There is great advantage in being intentional in what you do, and in taking initiative to make life happen, instead of merely letting life happen."

David Kraft[25]

To me, it's simple: We either decide to live with intent and purpose, or we live life on autopilot and drift in the ocean, like a wine cork. Like Oprah, sooner rather than later, we need to draw the proverbial line in the sand and say: "No more. Going forward, I am taking charge." Choice is one of the greatest assets we have in our lives – and it's all ours. It's actually as simple as that.

Being in the driver's seat gives us the freedom to live our lives our way. If you are religious and believe in a Higher Power, I can assure you that God also wants you to take charge of your life and to live a life of purpose and intent. Having said this, I don't think that understanding the importance of, and making the conscious decision to take charge of your life, has anything to do with your religious convictions. Although, if you have faith, life is easier, you can handle life's challenges better, and you'll know that you are not alone. But that is a topic for another book …

What happens without intent?

For more than three years of my life I had a brilliant executive coach who is now a friend and sibling figure. Jenny is a sage, and she played a key role in the success of my self-leadership story. During every coaching session in her office I would look at a large quote on her bookcase by Gary Lew. It read: *"This is your world. Shape it or someone else will."*

If you live without serious intent and don't want to take charge of your life, you will become a slave to someone, or to something else. Unfortunately, I have seen this happen to too many people in my lifetime – people who don't get that they, and only they, are responsible for designing their own future. If your life feels out of control, as if someone or something else is controlling it, then chances are, you're in a dark and uncertain place.

John Atkinson Grimshaw was a self-taught English artist who is today considered one of the great painters of the Victorian era. To the dismay of his parents, in 1861, at the age of 24, he left his job as a clerk for the Great Northern Railway to become a painter.[26]

When Grimshaw died, he left behind no letters, journals, or papers. His reputation and legacy are based on his townscapes and a jewel of a quote that he left us: "If you don't run your own life, somebody else will."

In this chapter we have looked at two examples of two different people who chose to live with intent. They illustrate that the struggles you and I face in attempting to take charge of our lives are not unique. If we haven't done so already, it is in our best interests to immediately put a stake in the ground and make a decision to take charge. If we don't do this, we will become vulnerable, and both the people around us and our environment will influence us more than we influence them.[27] That would be a mistake. Obviously, we have the option to choose not to live with intent or to take charge of our lives, but that would be sad. That would mean choosing to lead a lesser life.

Live your own life, no one else's

One of the key principles of successful self-leadership is the fact that we can only live our own lives and only we can be in charge of living our own lives. Nobody else on this Earth can do it for us. As Bill Gates points out, we are not in competition with anyone else but ourselves, and our goal should be to continuously improve ourselves.

"Our time is limited, so don't waste it living someone else's life."
Steve Jobs

Most importantly, our focus should be on taking charge of improving the leadership of ourselves, as part of the process of continually improving as individuals. If we want to compare ourselves, the only comparison we should be making is with who we were yesterday – not to who anyone else is today.[28] Only ever compare yourself to your own best possible self. Besides, as Will Smith reminds us, when we start comparing ourselves to others, we start losing confidence in ourselves. This is an important subject to which we will return later in this book.

"You are the only you ... You are the best you. You will always be the second best anyone else."
Leo Buscaglia

Keep your own bundle

Among my family members and friendship circle, we often refer to someone's 'bundle'. This is the sum of all the stuff with which he or she needs to deal in their lives. If we allow our mind to drift towards comparing our life to that of another, then our perception of their life, or the bundle they have to carry, is typically skewed by a touch of jealousy. In reality, though, we have no clue what's going on in anyone else's life. From the outside, it may seem that many people to whom we look up, like celebrities, have perfect lives. Later, we may be disappointed to discover that's not the case. The lives of Napoléon Bonaparte and Helen Keller illustrate this point perfectly.

French Emperor Napoléon Bonaparte lived a life that most men of his era envied, and if given the opportunity, many men would still swop theirs for his. Yet Napoléon declared while at St Helena that he never knew six happy days in his life. Despite all of the glory, power and riches, he was not a happy man.

Helen Keller, on the other hand, declared that she had found life to be beautiful, even though she was blind, deaf and dumb.[29]

From the outside, most of us would probably have chosen the life of Napoléon, but considering what we now know, I would rather have had the peace that Helen Keller felt in her life than have lived an unhappy, albeit heroic and limelight-filled, life of an emperor.

If we only knew the true story and had all of the facts about the lives of the people whom we envy, we'd probably be content just living the lives with which we've been blessed. Unfortunately, though, each of our bundles includes baggage. I personally came to the conclusion long ago that since I am the one who has control over my own journey, I need to be content with choosing and rather dealing with my own bundle.

You make your own luck

> **Luck**: Success or failure apparently brought by chance, rather than through one's own actions.[30]

I don't believe in luck, but I do believe in making my own luck. As Gary Player always said: "The more I practice, the luckier I get." The same applies to life: The more we take charge of our lives and live with purpose and intent, the 'luckier' we seem to get. If we rely on luck, we are like those people who rely only on winning the Lotto to change their lives so that they can live happily ever after. Perhaps in Fantasyland that works, but in real life, it's just not the case.

"Luck is the dividend of sweat. The more you sweat, the luckier you get."
Ray Kroc

To rely on luck is an unsustainable, short-term solution. Many people who won millions in the Lotto years ago cannot show a thing for it today. If we are waiting for luck to make the change that we think we want or need in our lives, then we will wait a long time, and ultimately we will be disappointed. On the other hand, to work hard and to take charge of our lives and ourselves is not necessarily easy, but I have no doubt that it is the right starting point for successful living.

Where is your locus of control?

I am not fond of 'consultant speak', which is quite ironic, considering I consult to organisations in the field of leadership development. I like to keep things simple since sometimes, we can end up sounding too clever for our own good. However, when it comes to the coined phrase 'locus of control', no other term describes it better. Please bear with me.

> People with a strong **internal locus of control** believe that events or incidents in their lives happen as a direct result of their own actions. They believe that their behaviour is guided by their personal decisions and efforts. For example: If I am late for a meeting and I acknowledge that it is my fault and that I should have left my home earlier, then I have an internal locus of control.
>
> People with a strong **external locus of control** look outside of themselves for sources of blame. Their behaviour is guided by fate, luck, other people and circumstances. For example: "The traffic and a faulty traffic light are the reasons I am late for the meeting. How could that possibly be my fault?"

It is critical that we each develop an internal locus of control. When we do that, it is a sign that we are taking charge. If we attribute the cause of our actions to factors outside of ourselves, we certainly won't have a successful self-leadership journey.[31]

John Burroughs summarised it well when he said that we can fail many times, but we are not a failure, until we begin to blame somebody else.

I suggest asking yourself the following questions:

> When something bad happens:
>
> "Do I own up to what happened as a consequence of my actions, or do I blame someone or something else?"
>
> When something good happens:
>
> "Do I, with humility, take the credit for what happened as a consequence of my actions, or do I allow the praise to go to someone else who doesn't deserve it?"

Be accountable

> **To be accountable**: To be required or expected to justify our actions or the decisions that we make.[32]

Mrs Sue de Villiers was my English teacher in grades 11 and 12. She always told us: "If you make a decision in life, you have to carry the consequences." That phrase is engrained in my mind because she said it so often – and I'm glad she did. It is a profound, fundamental principle in life, and it's a key part of being accountable and having the guts to own up. Only we can be accountable for our own actions. Nobody else can do it for us. I can't expect someone else to justify my actions or decisions, or to have to bear those consequences. If I am successful at self-leadership and at leading others, I have no option other than to be accountable.

You are always in charge

I believe that it is possible to be in charge of our lives at least 99% of the time. Of course, if, for example, we are diagnosed with an aggressive type of cancer, then we might not be in charge of that 1% of our lives. Or can we be? Can we not reduce that 1% over which we feel powerless by changing our attitude and mindset towards, for example, fighting cancer, regardless of the prognosis? By doing that, the 1% becomes 0.5% over which we are not really in control. So then, if we actually take charge of our lives 99,5% of the time, imagine how much we can achieve! This is our reality, and it is within our grasp. We simply need to exercise the choice to take charge of our lives as much as we possibly can.

Don't worry about what other people think

David Icke, the controversial English conspiracy theorist, former footballer and sports broadcaster, is also famous for saying: "The greatest prison people live in is the fear of what other people think." This is so true. Who gave other people the right to judge what we do with our lives?

Arnold Schwarzenegger put a more entertaining spin on this when he said: "If I would have listened to the naysayers, I would still be in the Austrian Alps yodelling."

If we worry about what other people think, then we cannot entirely take charge of our own lives. Yes, we need to consider what others say, but to give them the power to take charge of our lives in this way, instead of us taking charge and being focused on chasing our dreams, our life purpose and our personal goals, would be a colossal mistake and certainly to our detriment.

REFLECTION ON THE CONTENT OF THIS CHAPTER – TAKING CHARGE

Consider the topics that we have covered:

- Make tough decisions to take charge
- Be intentional
- What happens without intent?
- Live your own life, no one else's
- Keep your own bundle

- You make your own luck
- Where is your locus of control?
- Be accountable
- You are always in charge
- Don't worry about what other people think

Please rate your current overall level of success in Taking Charge as a percentage score:

_____%

This exercise will be repeated at the end of each chapter and summarised in Chapter 18 as a tool for continuous self-leadership improvement. In asking you to reflect on the content that we cover in each chapter, the assumption is made that you agree that your mastery of these areas will assist you in improving your self-leadership.

Chapter 2

Planning for Success

"Success without planning, is luck."
MIKE DENNIS

The water-soaked corpse of a British Royal Marine was found floating off the coast of Spain in April 1943. The dead marine had a suspicious-looking attaché case chained to his wrist that caught the attention of the German army, who colluded with pro-Nazi elements in the Spanish military to secretly gain access to its contents. Inside the briefcase they found a surprising letter to a British officer in Tunisia that outlined a secret Allied Forces plan to stage an invasion of Sardinia and Greece in the coming weeks.

The dead man's documents would have been a major intelligence coup for the Nazis, and a mini-victory, but unbeknown to them, the documents were all fake. As part of a plan dubbed Operation Mincemeat, the British had dressed the body of a deceased tramp and disguised it as an Allied courier named William Martin. The audacious plan had been masterminded by two British intelligence officers, Charles Cholmondeley and Ewen Montagu, with a little help from future Bond creator Ian Fleming. After the corpse's briefcase was stuffed with false military plans, a Royal Navy submarine secretly deposited the body off the coast of Spain, in the hope that it would fool the Nazis.

The result was the perfect ploy. Not only did the Germans intercept what they believed to be crucial information about where the Allies would attack the Mediterranean, but they were convinced they had done so without the British realising it. Fooled by Operation Mincemeat's hoax intelligence, Hitler diverted some of his tank divisions and other personnel to Greece, instead of Sicily, only to be caught off guard when the Allied Forces invaded Sicily in July 1943, and thereafter the whole of Italy with some 160 000 troops.[33] That helped change the course of World War II.

The amount of planning that went into Operation Mincemeat cannot be underestimated, and it was certainly not a matter of luck that the operation was a success. Some of the details of the plan involved finding out where pro-Nazi elements were operating in Spain; calculating where the body with the briefcase needed to be dumped to end up in the right area; ensuring that the false documents looked authentic; and ensuring that the tramp looked like a marine soldier.

Operation Mincemeat is a great example of how a detailed yet simple plan, successfully executed, can have a massive impact and deliver significant results. It is also a good illustration of Stephen Covey's quote: "Make time for planning: Wars are won in the general's tent."

Why bother to plan?

"Failing to plan is planning to fail."

Allen Lakein

We may not be able to predict it, but the future relies, to a large extent, on our ability to plan. I would like to use some short-term planning examples to explain this point:

If, within the next week, I fail to take my car to the garage for its overdue service, or I fail to change my route to work and forget to fill up with fuel at a service station, then there is a probability that, sometime over the next week, I won't make it to work. My life could potentially be disastrous in the short term because I might then miss an important new client meeting or an annual performance review with my manager as a result.

If I am not planning in the short term, at some point I will have a problem. I would also suggest that if we omit to do medium- and long-term planning, the potential impact on our lives will be even greater. This is simply because the things that we would like to achieve over longer periods, which will require more thought, and therefore more planning, are typically important events that will have a significant impact on our life journey. For example, if I would like to compete in the Olympics, get an MBA degree and one day own a business, this requires serious planning.

To list or not to list?

I am a planner – I love to plan. Sometimes, I plan years ahead, and I am not keen to change this part of my life because I think it's important. I even plan what I would like to complete, or *achieve*, over the next weekend. I also make lists of all of the tasks that I would like to complete in the short term. One of the ways I do this is by making voice recordings on my phone while I am driving.

Like many people, I get 'aha' moments in the shower or just before I fall asleep. I then quickly record these on my phone to use later. If I don't, I find that I forget what I wanted to record, or I lie awake all night trying to remember what it was that I didn't want to forget. Needless to say, this type of micro-planning works for me, and it helps me to not drop the proverbial ball by omitting anything. It might also work for you.

"Write down the thoughts of the moment. Those that come unsought for are commonly the most valuable."

Francis Bacon

Plan: A detailed proposal for doing or achieving something.[34]

I am of the firm opinion that plans are not plans unless you put pen to paper – otherwise, they are only ideas. By documenting plans, I obviously don't mean detailing routine things, like brushing my teeth or plugging my phone into its charger. Documented plans refer to the non-routine aspects of our lives – things that are complex enough, and that we are serious enough about, that we would like to document to reduce the risk of us failing to successfully implement them.

When documenting plans, we must not only reflect on what needs to be included in a plan, but also ensure that nothing is excluded from it.

For example, when planning my family's annual vacation, I typically list all of the things that we need to remember, because the reality is that we will forget something if it is not added to the list. We then tick them off just before we get into the car at the start of our trip. I have found that a documented plan, regardless of the area of my life, reduces my stress levels and helps me to execute endeavours successfully.

What is your definition of success?

Success means different things to different people. For some people, it is money; for others, it is power; some believe it to be qualifications, while still others define it by how many children they have. There are many such examples.

> **True success**: John Maxwell defines this as knowing your purpose, growing to reach your maximum potential, and sowing seeds to benefit others.[35]

Maxwell's definition resonates with me. I think the true test of success is being able to look back at your life one day and smile with satisfaction that you have achieved all that you wanted to achieve.

So, why are we still talking about success in this chapter on "Planning"? The answer is quite simple: Our plans need to align with our definition of success.

"Define success on your own terms, achieve it by your own rules, and build a life you're proud to live."

Anne Sweeney

You might have a different definition of success from what John Maxwell and I believe, and that's okay. It's important that you don't let anyone else's definition of success become your own. We each have our own unique definition of success, and at the start of the planning process, it's important to define what success looks like to us, as individuals. If we have taken charge of our lives, then we cannot let anyone else influence or determine what our definition of success should look like.

> Your definition of success needs to be authentic. It will form the basis of the planning process for your life. Otherwise, all of your plans will be in vain.

When we have executed plans without defining upfront where we are heading, we will have missed the mark and ended up in a place that does not even remotely resemble our picture of success.

Plan for the resources you need

Resource-requirement planning is critical in business – particularly in production planning. It is also vital in our personal planning, and to the success of our self-leadership story. We need resources to support us in achieving our goals.

> **Resources**: Everything that we might need – including time – to achieve our personal goals.

It is important that we identify our resource needs. If we don't have all of the necessary resources to execute our plan, then we have no other option than to first plan how we will acquire these resources before we can finalise the planning process.

The value of personal scenario planning

Scenario planning focuses on an outlook for the future. It is normally used by governments, businesses and other organisations, but there is no reason why we can't use it as part of our self-leadership process to plan for future events.

Doing scenario planning is like training in a flight-simulator. We, as the drivers or pilots of our lives, have to work out plans to survive when we are confronted by both predictable and unpredictable events. It prepares us for whatever plays out in our lives.

"One thing that makes it possible to be an optimist is if you have a contingency plan for when all hell breaks loose."
Randy Pausch

Ideally, we should not be spending many hours doing personal scenario planning, but it allows us to at least think of different scenarios that might unfold in the different areas of our lives by tapping into the creative part of our brains. At the same time, it offers us some comfort that we already know, to an extent, how to deal with a situation before it actually happens.

We may have the best intentions to achieve our personal and professional goals, but life happens and we need to be able to make adjustments to stay the course. Personal scenario planning is a great way to get a head-start when this happens.

Plan to have options in life

Options in life give you peace of mind; they make you 'richer' and life easier, simply because you have more than one thing to offer this world. The simplest way of creating options, is to either get more qualified in some area that is in high demand, or to learn a skill that will offer you the potential to make a living, or a better living.

Getting employed, or becoming employable, is based on the supply of people versus the demand for a specific skill or profession in the economy. For example, if you become a sweeper and you have the skill set to be able to sweep properly, that is fine – if you like to ensure that areas are clean. But if you have no ambition to advance your career beyond that point, you are likely doing yourself a disservice and you might not be living up to your full potential.

So, assuming you would like to stay in the same field, studying to gain supervision skills or a supervisor qualification will give you the option of being a sweeper and/or a supervisor of a cleaning team. If you then take it one step further and also enrol for a certificate in Business Management, then another option becomes available to you: Being able to own your own business, or to run someone else's cleaning business. If, for argument's sake, there are lay-offs of cleaners as a result of a downturn in the economy, then you still have the option of being a supervisor or managing a cleaning business, because you have additional skill sets to offer.

"Wealth is not about having a lot of money; it's about having a lot of options."

Chris Rock

It is important that we work towards having more options in life, but this unfortunately takes time. When we want or need alternative options and we don't have them available to us, it is then too late to plan for them. We'll find ourselves stuck. We need to have planned ahead to have options available now, in line with where our interests lie. Creating options in life must be included in our personal goals, which we'll explore in the next chapter.

REFLECTION ON THE CONTENT OF THIS CHAPTER – PLANNING FOR SUCCESS

Consider the topics that we have covered:

- Why bother to plan?
- To list or not to list?
- What is your definition of success?
- Plan for the resources you need
- The value of personal scenario planning
- Plan to have options in life

Please rate your current overall level of Planning for Success as a percentage score:

_____%

Chapter 3

Scripting Your Self-leadership Charter

> *"It's not enough to have lived. We should be determined to live for something ... Each of our acts makes a statement as to our purpose."*
> — LEO BUSCAGLIA

2020 was my son Henri's matric year. Everyone at school was looking forward to it, as it was their school's centenary year and there were a number of exciting celebratory events planned to mark the milestone. The school choir had started the year with a weekend camp. Unbeknown to us all, a national lockdown would be announced six weeks later.

Henri was the chairman of the choir, and, since the campsite was close to our home in Johannesburg, I offered to fetch him when the camp ended around noon on Monday, 10 February. The plan was to take him for lunch before he needed to be back at school the next day. Otherwise, he would have taken the bus back to Pretoria to enjoy a boarding-school lunch. Hostel food versus restaurant food – and time with his dad – was a no-brainer ...

Over lunch, we had a good discussion about his camp experience and what he was looking forward to in his matric year. At that point, I was slap-bang in the middle of working out my notice period for the company for which I worked as General Manager. I had decided to complete my PhD on a full-time basis rather than not complete it at all. As I enjoyed a spaghetti carbonara at our favourite restaurant, Henri threw a question at me from left field: "So, Dad, what are you going to do with the rest of your life?"

Fortunately, I had to finish chewing my pasta, which gave me a couple of seconds to think about my answer. Somehow, I thought to myself, the answer of wanting to take a sabbatical to finish my studies would not suffice. He expected more from me.

"Well, I am seriously thinking about starting my own business in leadership development and training because that is where my passion lies. It's where I have also been involved in corporate life, and it's what I'm busy researching," I replied.

Before I share Henri's response, I need to say that he was a November baby, for which he blamed me for many years. He would be the last in his class to get his driver's licence! That day we had lunch was a couple of months after he had turned 17. Still, despite his young age, he had read almost as many business and motivational books as I had read at that time.

I will never forget his response to my answer: "Dad, life is actually quite simple ..."

"Okay. Why is that?" I asked.

Then came the words that I never expected to hear from someone his age: "You see, I figured out that in life you have to achieve three things, and in this order. First and foremost, you need to *make an impact* on this world and its people. This has to be your priority in life. Secondly, you need to *love what you do*, because life is too short to not enjoy what you do for a living. Thirdly, which is the least important, but should automatically come your way if you get the first two priorities right, *you need to make enough money* to provide for you and for us, as your family."

At that point in our conversation, I was relieved to not have any spaghetti in my mouth, because I am sure I would have choked. His reply astonished me.

My lunch with Henri was a defining moment in my life. It made me realise that up until that point, my priorities had not exactly been on track. It also made me think that, given the sabbatical that I was taking, I was in an ideal position to fix those priorities: Impact first; followed by a love for what I do; and then money as a consequence of all of that.

You may argue that this new way of thinking was easier for me to adopt because I had saved enough from working hard enough for long enough in the corporate world, but I really don't think that makes much of a difference. I believe that if I had come to that realisation earlier in my life, I would have aligned my priorities sooner to what they are today.

From 10 February 2020, I had a clear idea of my purpose in life: To make an impact in people's lives through a business, which would also be my passion, and to also make a difference in this world outside of the business environment.

"The two most important days in your life are the day you're born and the day you find out why."

Mark Twain

"The main aim in life is simply to become all you're meant to be. Actually, even more important than who we are becoming as people is focusing on the difference we are making as leaders. Contribution is the ultimate purpose of work – and life."

Robin Sharma

I would like to introduce you to a simple starting point for successful self-leadership: Scripting your own self-leadership charter. This chapter is perhaps the most critical in the entire book, and the content of all of the subsequent chapters aligns to this one.

Before we get into its detail, I would like to share with you some important thoughts to consider in your personal goal-setting process.

It's perfectly okay to dream

"Give yourself permission to dream."

Randy Pausch

Dreams are simply our aspirations or ambitions in life. Most of them just make us feel good, but then there are some dreams that just don't want to disappear. I believe that it is those persistent dreams that we need to chase with everything that we've got.

Since my mid-20s, I have dreamed of owning my own business. Not only have I thought and dreamed about it, but I have been vocal about it, too. It is a desire that has always been there; sometimes stronger and sometimes weaker, but it has persisted.

"If your dreams don't scare you, they're not big enough."
Ellen Johnson Sirleaf

Consider first

Before deciding which dream to chase, it is important to think about the following:

- *Our abilities:* If I had a dream of becoming a successful golf professional, then I would never have been able to make that dream a reality. I simply don't have enough ball sense! It doesn't matter how much time I spent on the driving range or with a coach, that dream would never have taken flight.
- *Available resources:* I believe that nothing is impossible, but if I, for example, dreamed of building a people-transportation system to Mars, I frankly wouldn't have had the resources to do it – and never will have those resources. I will leave that to Elon Musk.
- *Impact on others:* Whatever dream we are chasing, we cannot pursue it if it is going to negatively impact on others, or have an adverse effect on our relationships with others – especially those close to us. If your dream is to start a massive gold mine in the Amazon Jungle that will wreak havoc on the ecosystem by dumping tons of mercury into the Amazon Basin every year, then you should probably reconsider that dream based on the adverse impact it might have on others.
- *Be authentic:* If your dreams are not your own, but someone else's, you will probably fail before achieving them, or you will be miserable when they become a reality. They were not authentic dreams in the first place. Choosing a career to please others, like becoming a doctor because your dad was one and said that you needed to become one, too, is a classic mistake that many people make.

If we don't consider these factors, we might end up feeling disappointed when our dreams don't become a reality.

The newspaper exercise

A book by Vasudha Deming, *The Big Book of Leadership Games*[36], sits in my leadership development library. It comprises 50 quick, fun activities to improve communication, increase productivity and bring out the best in leaders.

One of the exercises in the book is called "All the News". It requires leaders within an organisation to mock-up a newspaper that covers future predictions of various aspects of the organisation. My wife, Marilé, then adapted this exercise to apply to individual leaders as part of a leadership development programme in her company. I would like to share it with you here. It is a good way to document the dreams about which you feel strongly enough, as the first step towards making them a reality.

"People become successful the minute they decide to."

Harvey Mackay

Imagine that you have fast-forwarded to the last year of your life. What would you like to see on the front page of your personal newspaper? If your name is Jane, then call your personal newspaper *The Jane Times*, or *The Jane Daily Mail*. Your newspaper should feature your professional career and your private life. You are going to write your own future.

If you had to write down the highlights that you would like to see on the front page of *your* newspaper, what would those highlights be?

I suggest that you actually take a piece of paper and complete this exercise. Take the first step towards making your ambitions a reality: Put pen to paper.

Have vision and translate your dreams into goals

MasterChef Australia was probably the most exciting reality series that Marilé and I have watched together. I am useless in the kitchen, but fortunately, she is a great cook, although she always reminds me that I need to refer to her as a 'chef'. Apart from the excitement of the series, I really enjoyed watching her getting so much pleasure out of it. World-renowned chef Marco Pierre White guest-starred in a number of episodes in the series.

In April 2016, we watched an episode from the 2015 season. In that specific episode, Marco made a statement to the remaining contestants that was so inspiring that I had to write it down: "If you have a dream, it's your duty and responsibility towards yourself to make it come true. Otherwise, you are just a dreamer."

A self-leader with vision possesses a clear picture of what she or he wants in the future.[37] Such a person has the ability to think about or plan the future with imagination or wisdom.[38] We need to decide what we want our lives to look like in one, five, 10 and 20 years from now.

"Everyone's dream can come true if you just stick to it and work hard."
Serena Williams

We need to have vision to achieve our dreams, and the way to make our dreams come true is by breaking them up into bite-sized chunks and translating them into personal goals.

> **Goal**: The object of a person's ambition or effort; an aim or desired result.[39]

Achieving a dream typically requires reaching more than one personal goal in support of that dream. My dream of starting my own business did not simply rely on achieving only one personal goal: I needed to be able to tick off a number of personal goals before I could take that leap.

"What we give our attention to, grows."
Kenneth Blanchard

As self-leaders, we need to be clear about what we want in our lives, and then get ourselves into the best possible position to achieve our dreams.

This requires setting personal goals. Verbalise these goals and put them in writing, too. You will be surprised how much focus they add to your career and private life. Goals are key ingredients in generating hope and positive energy.[40]

"A goal should scare you a little and excite you a lot."

Joe Vitale

Living life without goals means not taking charge

So, if we decide to not set ourselves personal goals, what is the risk? Without goals in life, we live on autopilot, we become floaters, and the danger is that we end up in a retirement village one day, feeling empty because we have not achieved enough in life.

I know people who started living on autopilot in their 40s, who are not willing to celebrate and experience life up to their last day on Earth. Please don't do that to yourself.

"If you aim at nothing, you'll hit it every time."

Zig Ziglar

Live a life of significance

"Chase the vision, not the money, the money will end up following you."

Tony Hsieh

Most of us are wired from a young age to believe that success lies in money, and only in money: The more money we have, the more success we have achieved. I bet that if we asked the wealthiest people in the world, almost all, if not every one of them, would agree that money is a means to an end, and that the end is to make a positive impact and to do something of significance.

Our focus ought to be on living a life of significance – the money will follow. Even if money then does not follow, at least we will have found joy in the impact that we have made in the lives of others, as opposed to sitting with loads of money and not making a meaningful difference. If we let financial success be our main driver, then the other good things in life may not be there in the end. Perhaps not even financial success.

"Success is not about how much money you make. It is about the difference you make in people's lives."

Michelle Obama

It is extremely important that our actions are a reflection of our purpose in life.[41] I am by no means a saint, nor would I attempt to portray myself as a perfect example, because I'm not. After that lunch with Henri, I realised, though, what my purpose in life needs to be, and that my main focus has to be making a positive impact on the lives of others. Even in my business, alongside the work in which I make a living by consulting to and partnering with organisations to develop their leaders, I do pro-bono work that focuses on youth leadership development.

Not everyone's careers will lend themselves towards being able to do this, but nothing stops you from using some of the financial wealth that you generate, or your time outside of work, to make a difference in the lives of others.

"A life is not important, except in the impact it has on other lives."

Jackie Robinson

Your fire of burning ambition

Peter Fuda claims in his book *Leadership Transformed* that while "*fear may provide the initial spark for action, aspiration is a far more important motivator. Sustainable change requires the fire of a burning ambition.*"[42]

> **Aspiration**: A strong desire to achieve something high or great.[43]

Aspiration is reportedly the top trait in successful people. The second is drive.[44]

> Ask yourself the questions:
>
> - "How hungry am I to achieve my goals, to live my dreams, to achieve my purpose?"
> - "Do I have a burning ambition to align everything to the vision that I have for my life?"
>
> In my experience, if we are not hungry enough, then our flame of aspiration will at some point die.

The mistake of playing it safe

There is a danger in picking the safe options in life …

In the film *Con Air*,[45] Cameron Poe (Nicolas Cage) told Garland Greene (Steve Buscemi), a serial killer of 37 people, not to talk to him, because he and the likes of Dahmer, Gacy and Bundy were insane. Greene's response was: "Now you are talking semantics … What if I told you insane was working 50 hours a week in some office for 50 years, at the end of which they tell you to piss off … Ending up at some retirement village, hoping to die before suffering the indignity of trying to make it to the toilet on time … Wouldn't you consider that to be insane?"

Don't get me wrong: I worked for 25 years doing exactly that, so I am not necessarily agreeing with Garland Greene's assessment. I do agree, though, that if there is another life that you would rather be living that you are deliberately not choosing out of fear, then you should go out and live it. So if you instead choose the safe way of living your life specifically for financial reasons, then consider this: If you are willing to give up your freedom for security, then you might just end up losing both.

"Working hard for something we don't care about is called stress. Working hard for something we love is called passion."
Simon Sinek

On my last executive assignment, I had 560 people in my structure, lots of stress and a hefty pay cheque every month to compensate for it. Then, at the youthful age of 49, I decided to resign and to chase my career dream – in COVID-19 times, in line with my passion for developing people. This is something that I had wanted to do for at least the last decade.

It's early days and only time will tell whether I made the right financial decision, but I can vouch for the fact that I have never been happier in my working life. Regardless of the outcome, I have no regrets, and to quote my dad, the freedom that this gave me, money can't buy.

"The only way to do great work is to love what you do."

Steve Jobs

You, too, need to choose what you really want to do in life. This needs to be included in your personal goals. Perhaps it's something that you can't realistically achieve within the next year, but my advice to you would be to not postpone it for too long and to attach a realistic, but extended, time frame to it. In saying this I am not suggesting for one second that you need to resign from your current job, because it might just be that your personal goals can be achieved within the organisation for which you are currently working.

"There is no future in any job. The future lies in the person who holds the job."

George Crane

Apply the concept of 'stretch' to your life

"The greater danger for most of us lies not in setting our aim too high and falling short, but in setting our aim too low, and achieving our mark."

Michelangelo

This powerful quote is such an accurate summary of the risks associated with selling ourselves short by not aiming to achieve our full potential. If we don't apply the 'stretch' principle to our personal goals, then we will one day look back with regret when we realise that we could have achieved so much more in life.

> **Stretch principle**: Deliberately expanding your expectations across the various areas in your life in order to achieve or gain more success.

Without fail, Marilé and I physically stretch every night. Well, I call it stretching, Marilé calls it yoga. Before we started this healthy routine, I could feel the effects of half a century's use on my body. I now feel years younger, simply because I am more supple.

When it comes to our personal goals, it is also of benefit to focus on a couple of goals that are 'out there'. These are goals that support dreams that we know might be a stretch, but are certainly achievable. Mark these as stretch goals, as this allows you to pay them special attention, with the added motivation to yield the extra benefits when you achieve them.

I have found that stretching keeps me younger, both physically and psychologically. Not only do I feel years younger physically, but also in my goal-setting. I have started to set goals in my business and on a personal level that not only stretch me, but excite me, as I know that when I reach them, I will grow personally and from a business standpoint.

"In the end we only regret the chances we didn't take."
Lewis Carroll

As we get older, we tend to become more risk averse,[46] which means that we develop a tendency to steer away from taking risks. It is natural to become more cautious with age, as we typically think: "I cannot fail at this, because then I'll have no retirement money left." Well, I tell you what: I would rather sit with Marilé on the porch one day as a poor man at the age of 80 or 90, having a cup of coffee and smiling because of all the opportunities I tried to create for myself, than die rich and safe, but miserable, because of all the opportunities and risks that I regret I never took … We have one life on this Earth, let's live it well.

Don't let the old man in

Clint Eastwood was the inspiration behind singer-songwriter Toby Keith's track, *Don't let the old man in*. The pair had shared a golf cart at Clint's charity tournament in Pebble Beach, California. Toby said he was inspired to write the song by his conversation with the 88-year-old actor-director about his latest movie, *The Mule*, and by his work ethic.[47] The song lyrics send a message that we must not allow ourselves to get old, but that we should keep on putting the effort into living life to the fullest, despite our age.

"How old would you be, if you didn't know how old you were?"
Satchel Paige

Colonel Harland David Sanders did not start out as anyone's idea of a successful businessman. He lost his father at an early age, had extensive disagreements with his stepfather, and was fired from multiple jobs. However, he was determined to never give up. That trait led to his eventual success.

While working at a service station in Corbin, Kentucky, Sanders gained local popularity for his delicious chicken recipe. After the Corbin station was destroyed by a fire, Sanders had the location rebuilt as a motel that included a 140-seater restaurant.

In 1952, at the age of 62, Sanders franchised his Kentucky Fried Chicken for the first time.[48] Sanders only died in 1980 at the ripe old age of 90. Today, KFC has more than 24 000 outlets in 145 different countries and territories around the world.[49]

"You are never too old to set another goal or to dream a new dream."
C.S. Lewis

Colonel Sanders is not the only example of someone who was a late bloomer to success. There are many more like him, although this is not the norm. The point is that we should adopt an approach to life that says: "Don't let the old man or old woman in." This applies to our dreams and goals, too. Live life to the fullest by taking charge of your self-leadership story.

Self-leadership charter and visualising our dreams

When it comes to the personal goal-setting process, some people get carried away. They tend to include the whole suite of dreams, aspirations, purpose, vision, mission, objectives, goals and measures. I prefer to keep things simple and not overcomplicate it.

> **Charter**: From the Latin word *charta*, which means paper, card or map. A formal written document describing the rights, principles or aims of people or of an organisation.[50]

When I refer to a *self-leadership charter*, it is all about exercising your right as an individual to take charge of your life and to document your life principles and what you are aiming to achieve to make the best of the life with which you have been blessed. This charter can also be viewed as a roadmap to not only get us to where we visualise ourselves being, but to also bring what we visualise into our reality.

"Visualising your dreams has its own power to complete your dreams. So, visualise to accomplish."

Diya Raj

> **Visualise**: Form a mental image.[51]

There are many reasons why we can't simply verbalise this important part of our lives: We will forget most of it, and our account of what this picture looks like will differ between days and weeks. We need to put it in writing to help us visualise our dreams. We should not only document it, but also keep it somewhere safe and accessible where we can look at it daily.

The self-leadership charter comprises two parts:
1. Our *own credo*
2. Our *personal goals scorecard*.

My own credo

> **Credo**: A statement of the beliefs or aims that guide someone's actions.[52]

A credo is not only your own statement, but also something that you own. Once you have settled in your ways, become emotionally mature and know what you want from life, and what you want to contribute to the lives of others, your own credo will pretty much remain constant and hold the same content – unless you have experienced a life-changing moment. In short, your own credo reflects what you stand for in life, including your value system and the principles that guide your thoughts, feelings and behaviours. It is the backbone, or core, of your existence.

"True success is reaching our potential without compromising our values."

Muhammad Ali

By documenting and reading your own credo frequently – no less than weekly – you confirm your identity. It might take you days or weeks to write it to a point where you can stand back and say: "This is me, the whole of me."

There is no fixed rule when it gets to scripting our own credo, but the idea is to keep it short enough to remind ourselves of our identity, which I believe we can only find in God and in ourselves. If we find it in anything or anyone else, then we will lose our identity, causing havoc in our lives. Our own credo can even take a bullet-point or paragraph format.

Steve Farrar describes in his book *Finishing Strong* how, for years, his own credo was one simple sentence: "Don't screw up." That meant he must not fail in any key part of his life. He feels so strongly about it that he even suggests that his tombstone inscription should one day read that he didn't screw up. The words that represent our beliefs or aims and that guide our actions are our own credo. They define us as individuals and are an essential part of our personal brand.

The balanced wheel

In the same way that a balanced scorecard allows business leaders to simultaneously view performance in several areas in order to manage the complexity of the organisation,[53] we also need to categorise those areas of our lives that we see as part of our future. We can do this by developing our *balanced wheel*. These areas could be, but are not necessarily, part of our existing lives. We only want to set personal goals in the areas to which we aspire, and not the areas that we are planning to exclude from our future.

"Everything in life … has to have balance."
Donna Karan

For some of you, as for me, the existing and future areas will be the same. The balanced wheel is simply based on a hub-and-spoke principle. The spokes represent all of the important areas of our life, or the different roles that we adopt in our life, like being a spouse, father, son, brother, business owner, and so forth. If we do not perform, or are not strong in all of the areas that we regard as important to our future, then that weak spoke will break, and our life wheel will start to buckle. Put in a different way, if we, for example, only focus on work and family, then our life wheel is unbalanced. This will result in a less efficient wheel. These imbalances mean that we often live sub-optimal lives.

Even though it is important to focus our time and effort on all of the areas that we see as part of our future, it is important to get our priorities straight and to understand those areas that are more important than others in our personal balanced wheel. The priority areas are those areas in which we cannot afford to fail, and where we need to invest special effort to ensure that we are successful.

"Nobody's life is ever all balanced. It's a conscious decision to choose your priorities every day."
Elisabeth Hasselbeck

What follows is a simple version of the balanced wheel, using my life as an example:

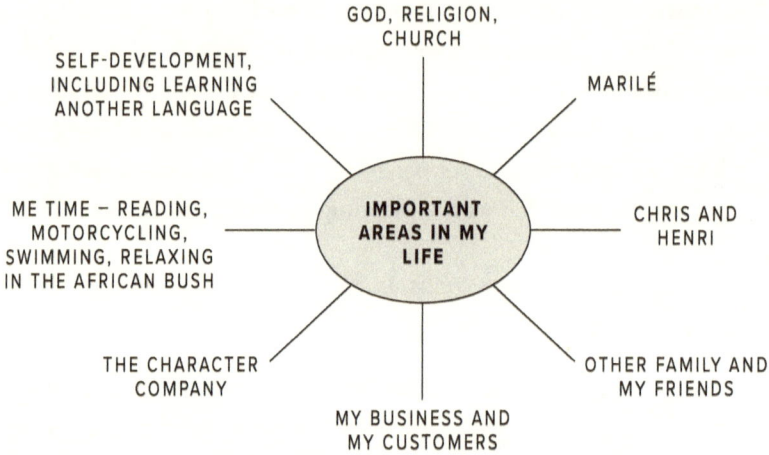

Completing the balanced wheel forms the basis when we set our personal goals to cover the dreams and aspirations we have in all of the important areas of our life.

The personal goals scorecard

The term personal goals scorecard comprises three parts:
1. It is *personal*, as it is unique to making *your dreams* a reality, nobody else's. These are your dreams to improve your life, or the lives of others. Nobody can tell you that they don't make sense.
2. It is a *scorecard*, which is defined as a record used to measure achievement or progress towards a particular goal.[54]
3. *Goals*, in the context of the personal goals scorecard, comprise all of the main and supporting goals we set for ourselves to make our dreams in the different areas of our life a reality. We have the privilege and the right to plan the life that we would like to live.

"I have a dream …"

Martin Luther King Jr

Everything starts with the dreams that we have for our lives, but over time, we need to measure the extent to which we are conforming to the achievement of the goals of which our dreams are made.

If we only have dreams in half of the areas in our balanced wheel, and we are happy to maintain the other areas, because we have achieved in them everything that we want, that's perfectly fine – as long as we are absolutely certain about this. We don't want to regret later in life that we have not achieved our full potential.

If you have no dreams in any of the areas of your balanced wheel, then I would suggest that you are selling yourself short, and I would guarantee that you will end up with regrets at the end of your life. You still have so much runway ahead of you that you are not using to grow, to make a difference and to spice up your life with excitement.

> Now that you have listed all the important areas in your (future) life, it is important to ask yourself:
>
> - "What is my dream for each of these areas?"
> - "What is the best thing I would like to achieve in each area of my life?"
> - "What does success look like in each of these areas within the next year, five years or 10 years?"

These answers then become your main personal goals for these areas of your life.

It is vital that we take enough time to properly think through our main personal goals, and that the words we use to script these goals represent our entire dream in each area. For example, if our dream is to climb Mount Everest, we might want to choose the words: "Successfully summit and descend back to base camp," in our main personal goal description. Otherwise, being fit enough to descend successfully might not form part of our plan, resulting in us becoming yet another name on the long list of those who have died on the descent after successfully summitting Everest. We cannot only goal-set to the point; we need to set our goals through the point.

In addition to our main personal goals, we also then need to decide what the required supporting goals will be to help reach our main personal goals.

"If you can't measure it, you can't manage it."

Peter Drucker

Yes, there are so many routine actions involved in our daily living that almost happen naturally, like making breakfast; getting kids ready and taking them to school; going to work; arriving home; spending time as a family; having supper, and preparing for bed … the list goes on. These mundane tasks cannot be included in our personal goals scorecard, which comprises only the goals that support our dreams, or the personal goals that we really have the desire to achieve as a matter of principle.

By putting pen to paper to prepare our personal goals scorecard, we need to accept the responsibility of committing to the process and to maintaining our motivation to see the process through – whatever it takes. Otherwise, why would we even bother to properly think this through and to prepare such a personal goals scorecard?

In addition to having the continual drive required to succeed in achieving all of our supporting goals to our main goal, we need other ingredients to make our dreams a reality: We need to take charge, plan and execute each of these goals. If we don't work actively day in and day out to achieve these goals, we are, unfortunately, failing ourselves.

If I had used the personal goals scorecard tool to set personal goals to help me make my dream of starting my own business a reality, I have no doubt I would have started the Southern African Leadership Development and Training Institute (SALDaTI™) earlier in my life. A number of factors had to count in my favour by the time that I decided to take this step, but if I had started out using a structured process, like the personal goals scorecard, many years before, it would have definitely helped me to make my dream a reality in a shorter time frame.

Make your goals SMARTER

Whatever our goals are, whether they are main personal or supporting goals, they need to be SMARTER:[55]

- **S**pecific: Our goals should never be vague. They should provide clarity to what we want to achieve.
- **M**easurable: We must be able to use a metric to assess when we have achieved a goal. An example, for instance, would be a timeline.
- **A**chievable: Our goals must be realistic. Be careful not to stretch all your goals too far, or you'll become demotivated before you even start.
- **R**elevant: There must be a reason for our goals. Main personal goals need to represent our dreams or aspirations. The supporting goals break down the main goals into manageable parts.
- **T**imely: This refers to a deadline by which a specific goal should be achieved.
- **E**valuated. It is important to evaluate our progress en route to our goals.
- **R**eadjusted when necessary. This does not necessarily mean changing our goals, but readjusting our approach to achieving them if our current approach is not working. As a last resort, we can decide to add to or change our supporting goals, if they are not providing enough support to the achievement of a main personal goal. We must not readjust our main personal goals though, unless something has fundamentally changed in our lives that caused a well-considered dream to change or disappear.

Affirmations will get you halfway there

The use of affirmations is a good example of how we can take charge of our lives to get to the next level.

> **To affirm something**: To show or express a strong belief in, or a dedication to something, such as an important idea.[56]

Successful people tend to talk about the future in the present tense, as if the future has already been accomplished. Affirmations are, therefore, positive statements that are written as though they are happening right now. They can be used as a way to make our dreams and aspirations a reality. An affirmation is a statement of fact, even though it has not yet happened.

Robin Sharma believes that one of the best ways to rescript limiting beliefs and failure within your mind is through *"the consistent repetition of positive statements about the leader you want to become and the achievements you commit to create ... it will create the mindset of a champion and a winning emotional state for you."*[57]

For each affirmation, we need to visualise that we are already achieving today what we need to achieve on the way to achieving that specific goal ... I call this mindflight – fast-forwarding our thoughts to the point where we have already achieved the success we are describing in our affirmations. By visualising success now, we create a positive mental picture that draws us towards achieving our personal goals.

"Nothing is impossible. The word itself says 'I'm possible!'"
Audrey Hepburn

The power of affirmations lies in repeating them to ourselves regularly.[58] By repeatedly affirming something out loud with conviction and emotion, we secure these thoughts. Through this process, we make them our own. By owning these positive thoughts of achievement, we effectively claim that anything less than the affirmations will not be acceptable to us. We speak of a successful future as though it exists in the present.

We should not only repeat these affirmations as many times as possible, as frequently as possible – preferably daily – but then also visualise what the picture of success will look like to us. I believe that an affirmation should have the conjunction "because" in the middle of it. The reason for this is simple: We need to constantly remind ourselves of the main reason(s) why we are putting all of the focus and hard work into achieving a specific main personal goal.

Affirmations should, however, not only be limited to these goals. They can extend to our supporting goals, and even to events in everyday life that are not part of our personal goals scorecard. For example, affirmations could also be used to assist you to kick a bad habit.

Affirmations are useful in any situation in which we would like to see positive change in our lives. For example, if I have to speak at a conference in two days' time, then I will affirm to myself: "As the expert in the room on my topic, and because I will speak with confidence and be a great success,

I will be able to field all the questions from the audience to everyone's satisfaction." According to research, spending just a few minutes thinking about our best qualities before high-pressure events like these can help to calm our nerves, increase our confidence, reduce stress and improve our chances of a successful outcome.[59]

Bearing in mind that an affirmation is effectively stating and envisioning in the present that a future goal has already been achieved, I would suggest that your affirmations need to at least be specific and timely. Please note the words highlighted in the affirmation in my self-leadership charter excerpt on pages 68 and 69.

You may have too many affirmations to remember all the details off-hand, so I suggest that you write down all of these affirmations on individual cards, or save them as notes on your phone. That is what I do. Whenever you have idle time, while standing in a queue or waiting for someone, you can use your time productively to read your affirmations – even if it is quietly to yourself.

Affirmations are like mind exercises. These positive mental repetitions can reprogram our thinking patterns so that, over time, we begin to think and act differently.[60]

Some might argue that we are simply tricking our own minds by stating and visualising the future in the present already, but by following this process we are actually reinforcing our goals and ensuring that all of our being is aligned with achieving these goals. Affirmations can also be used to effectively dispose of any negative thoughts as soon as they surface in our minds. By countering these negative thoughts with repeated positive affirmations, you are blocking that negativity from causing harm in your life.

In summary, by successfully using affirmations, we are halfway to achieving our personal goals. Affirmations help us to focus on creating the right change inside of us, so that we can grow and live a life of which we can be proud.

Celebrate successes

The last column of the personal goals scorecard refers to celebrating our successes. I believe that it is critical to recognise our goal achievements in this manner. When celebrating these successes, it is important to include our families, because then our successes also become their successes. We are not on a solo mission in life. It could draw us even closer as a family, as they become part of our self-leadership journey. Our celebrations don't need to be expensive or elaborate – they could be as simple as going for a picnic together.

"Never, ever underestimate the importance of having fun."

Randy Pausch

The need for a consolidation page

What works for me is having my own credo and personal goals scorecard content consolidated into the same document. This allows me to structure and organise my personal goal-setting process in one place. It also makes it easier to look at as often as possible. I cannot prescribe how frequently this review should take place, but the more we read it, the more we will feel and be in control of this process. From experience, this review process takes less than 20 minutes. Given its importance, this time is an investment in our future and it is definitely worthwhile.

It is imperative to take note at this point that goal-setting is only an intermediary step towards the second and most important part of the process: Goal-achievement. There is no sense in setting goals if we do not, or cannot achieve or accomplish, the goals that we set ourselves.

Hekkie's personal goals scorecard

At the risk of exposing myself psychologically, I would like to invite you into my world for a while by sharing with you my own credo and a part of my personal goals scorecard that relates to only one of my main personal goals (dreams). My hope is that it will adequately illustrate the points that I have covered in this chapter. I trust that it will help you to better envisage how this process can be used in your personal life to support your success as a self-leader.

One of my dreams is to speak an African language fluently. If I could read and write it someday, that would be a bonus, but for now, I have this burning desire just to be able to speak fluently. Since there are nine official African languages in South Africa, the obvious question was: "Which one do I learn?" I chose Zulu simply because of where I live and where I typically spend my holidays: Johannesburg and the South Coast of KwaZulu-Natal. IsiZulu is the most widely spoken African language in both of these areas. Besides, Zulu is the most widely spoken African language in South Africa.[61] You can view this section of my personal goals scorecard on the following page.

What if you fall behind or fall short?

So what do we do if our timing is out, and we don't achieve what we have set out to achieve in the allocated time frame? The reality is that life happens, and things don't always work out as we planned. We simply can't use this as an excuse to not achieve our dreams and goals. We need to put it behind us, regroup and refocus once again on achieving that which will allow us to reach our full potential. It is also the reason why the personal goals scorecard is not a static document and why we need to regularly update it. These continuous reviews and adjustments form part of the process of achieving our goals.

"If your plan isn't working, change the plan, not the goal."

Darren Hardy

Unlike the content of your balanced wheel and own credo, which will probably remain static, the personal goals scorecard is a dynamic document that needs to be updated, even if it is only to update your progress percentages as you get closer to achieving your supporting goals and ultimately your main personal goals (dreams). At that point where your dream, as contained in a main personal goal, has been achieved, all you need to do is maintain it. Otherwise, you do not achieve through the goal and you start unlearning or undoing your goal achievement. Assuming that you have this part of the goal-setting and -achievement process covered, you can then replace this achieved goal with your next dream in any area of your life that you have captured on your balanced wheel.

HEKKIE'S SELF-LEADERSHIP CHARTER

1. Own credo:

"I will take charge of this one life with which God has blessed me and I will not settle for a life that is less than the one that I am capable of living. I choose to be my own best friend and to do my best to add value to the lives of everyone around me, especially my family. I choose to give back to others and will not only live but will also let live. I will always stand up for what is right and choose to live a life of integrity. I commit to getting out of my comfort zones more and more and to explore opportunities that I was previously too scared to even consider. I will do everything in my power to ensure that I have a healthy body and soul. I will always lead by good example – one that makes me proud. Let this be the legacy that I leave behind one day. Finally, I commit to myself to drive my personal goals hard, as contained in my personal goals scorecard, because only then can I achieve my full potential and not one day feel regret at having lived a sub-optimal life."

2. Personal goals scorecard excerpt:

Area of my life	Main personal goal description	Affirmation for main personal goal	Supporting goals to main personal goal	Planned achievement date	% progress	Celebration activity
Self-development	Learning to be fluent in speaking Zulu before 31 July 2022.	I am already **fluent in Zulu** by 31 July 2022 in such a manner that I am always starting and following a conversation with someone, without feeling uncomfortable, **because** this allows me to build bridges with more people in our country up to the end of my life and is a testimony to the fact that I embrace diversity and inclusion.	See below.	31 July 2022	10%	Visit Shakaland Zulu Cultural Village in Eshowe for a weekend with my family.

Supporting goals to main personal goal	Planned achievement date	% progress
(1) Successfully complete and pass the IsiZulu Elementary course at Wits Language School	22 May-31 Jul 2021	100%
(2) Successfully complete and pass the IsiZulu Pre-intermediate course at Wits Language School	11 Sep to 27 Nov '21	0%
(3) Speak basic Zulu informally to the best of my ability anywhere and whenever I can with anyone that I engage at a shop, restaurant or filling station, to name a few	Continuous	80%
(4) Practise by speaking Zulu with Marilé, as she has the same main personal goal	Continuous	25%
(5) Spend 30 minutes every single day working through the Zulu textbooks and study guides available to me	Continuous	20%
(6) Stay with someone in a Zulu community for a week where I have no other choice than to communicate in Zulu	April 2022	0%

REFLECTION ON THE CONTENT OF THIS CHAPTER – SCRIPTING YOUR SELF-LEADERSHIP CHARTER

Consider the topics that we have covered:

- It's perfectly okay to dream
- The newspaper exercise
- Have vision and translate your dreams into goals
- Living life without goals means not taking charge
- Live a life of significance
- Your fire of burning ambition
- The mistake of playing it safe
- Apply the concept of 'stretch' to your life
- Don't let the old man in
- Self-leadership charter and visualising our dreams
- My own credo
- The balanced wheel
- The personal goals scorecard
- Make your goals SMARTER
- Affirmations will get you halfway there
- Celebrate successes
- The need for a consolidation page
- What if you fall behind or fall short?

Please rate your current overall level of success in Scripting your Self-leadership Charter as a percentage score:

_____%

Chapter 4

Avoiding Time-wasters and Distractors

"Concentrate on your goals. Do not allow other thoughts to enter your mind. If you allow them to, other things could take your concentration away from your ultimate aim."
ARNOLD SCHWARZENEGGER

Although never formally diagnosed, I am convinced that I have mild adult ADHD (attention-deficit/hyperactivity disorder). In 1997, I was appointed as a management accountant for one of the divisions of the largest packaging group in South Africa at the time. Not too long after I started the job, my manager told me that I was like a Bushman (referring to the San people). My immediate thoughts were that he had paid me a compliment. He must have been highlighting the fact that I am friendly, creative and disciplined!

But then he continued to explain: "You get up in the morning, armed with your bow and quiver filled with arrows, and off you go to hunt an antelope for the tribe to enjoy for supper tonight. Just after you leave your camp, you see duiker spoor, which you start to track down. Then, just as the spoor are getting fresh, you see impala spoor crossing the duiker spoor. Thinking that this is a larger animal and that you will be able to offer your tribe more to eat, you decide to rather follow the impala spoor.

"After stalking the impala for a couple of hours, the same thing happens when you see larger spoor from a red hartebeest crossing the impala spoor. Again, you decide to rather follow the larger animal's spoor, and off you go, tracking the red hartebeest.

"The same story then happens with a kudu, and finally, just before dusk, you start to follow the spoor of an eland – thinking to yourself that you would be the hero of the tribe if you could bring that kill home … But then the sun sets just before you track down the eland, and you eventually arrive back at camp with the embarrassment that you have brought nothing back for anyone.

"Hekkie, the moral of the story is that you must stop wasting time being distracted in your work, otherwise you will never achieve or finish anything."

After his story, I had to pick myself off the proverbial floor. It's been 24 years since that day, and the story is still clear in my memory bank. It was a perfect illustration of what my manager had at that point identified as standing between me and achieving my goals at work. Having said this, the same applies to achieving our other personal goals. We allow time-wasters and distractors to be added as toxic ingredients to our self-leadership recipe. These interfere with us achieving our personal goals more quickly and effectively.

> **Time-wasters and distractors**: Anything that does not, directly or indirectly, contribute to us achieving our personal goals.

Some time-wasters and distractors are unfortunately unavoidable, but we need to minimise these as far as possible.

"It isn't the mountain ahead that wears you out. It's the grain of sand in your shoe."

Robert W. Service

The hourglass is running out

I believe that one of the fundamental mistakes that many of us make is living as if we are going to live forever. The reality, though, is that the hourglass

CHAPTER 4: AVOIDING TIME-WASTERS AND DISTRACTORS

is running out, and each one of us has only so much time to achieve the things that we need and want to achieve. I hope that this book is a wake-up call to help you make the best of the rest of the one life you are granted, and that it encourages you to create your legacy and to take charge of scripting your own life story. I see this as a positive challenge, rather than a depressing reality. Let's not waste time. Let's achieve all of our personal goals as best and as quickly as we can.

"I believe every human has a finite number of heartbeats. I don't intend to waste any of mine."

Neil Armstrong

I have spent most of my life in a production environment, where we always had some measure of efficiency. The higher the efficiency number I reported for my division at our weekly exco meeting, the less explaining I had to do and the more smiles I saw around the table. Translating that in terms of our self-leadership process, I would suggest that we work hard each day to improve our personal efficiency. We can only do this by reducing the amount of time that we waste on things that are not aligned to our personal goals.

"Short as life is, we make it still shorter by the careless waste of time."

Victor Hugo

Don't sweat the small stuff

We cannot be successful at achieving the big things (which are included in the personal goals that we have already set ourselves) if we allow ourselves to be distracted by the small things in our lives.

Mom used to say: "Don't sweat the small stuff." This finally makes sense to me, because I now realise that the small stuff are only distractors that take our focus off the important stuff. As a friend of mine would say when referring to someone who is not focused: "You cannot be like a mosquito in a nudist camp." If you are to be successful in your self-leadership story, you need laser-sharp focus to achieve your goals. You cannot allow yourself to be distracted.

When I come across small, menial activities, I ask myself: "What would the consequences be if I left them for later, or just didn't do them?" The answer is usually: "None." So, why worry about them? Perhaps I could delegate those tasks or leave them for later, or not do them at all, while I focus on my main goals in life.

Manage your precious time

"Time is the scarcest resource and unless it is managed nothing else can be managed."

Peter Drucker

If you do a word count, you will find that the word "time" appears almost 200 times in this book, which is an indication of how important this concept is to the context of self-leadership. Time management is a vital part of our self-leadership success, and there are endless benefits to doing this properly. For me, the biggest benefit is that it makes me feel in control of my life and it frees up more time for new opportunities, reduces my stress levels, and ultimately supports the achievement of my personal goals. We only have so many hours in a day, so let's use them wisely and productively.

"If it ain't broke, don't fix it."

Bert Lance

The preceding quote is another beautiful illustration of what we need to prioritise in our lives. It makes sense to prioritise by first focusing on the things that *are* broken. We cannot waste our time focusing on the things that are not broken. To waste time on trying to improve something that is already sufficient, is senseless. However, when we prioritise the things that do require our attention, we need to take the emotion out of the process and prioritise *all* of the things that are enormously important. For example, when I started writing this book, I had so much fun that I did not want to stop writing. However, I am not a full-time writer and I have a business to run, too. I also need to pay attention to other priorities, like addressing client needs to develop their leaders.

Dad used to say: "If you can't do something properly, then don't do it." As a general approach, I absolutely agree, but there is one exception that I think is important to acknowledge and apply: Sometimes, more than one priority requires our attention, and our dilemma is that we don't have enough time to complete all of them properly within the specific time frame in which they are due. In these situations, I find that I have two options: Either I just don't do some of the priority items, which is a mistake, or I rather pick the most important priority item to get absolutely spot-on, and then still complete the other priorities at an average standard. I am convinced that Dad would understand that in exceptional cases, average is acceptable. Especially in those cases where we have limited time available to us. It is also important to not make a meal of something by overcomplicating an issue that would waste even more time that we don't have.

Something else that I find useful in managing my time effectively is picking one priority for each day. I call this my primary focus. For that day, I focus 90% of my time on that one priority. Yes, other issues require my attention, too, but I typically deal with them during the 10% of my day that's left. I call these items my secondary focus for the day. These percentages can obviously vary slightly, but hopefully, you get the gist of the concept.

The point is: Pick the main priority on which you want to spend most of your time each day. The only reason to spend a small portion of your day on the lesser priority stuff is because these niggly items will stay in the back of your mind and divert your attention if you don't deal with them, too.

"Until we can manage time, we can manage nothing else."
Peter Drucker

Automation is another way to create more time to do productive work. It saves time by getting quicker results. For example, I use voice tags to convey messages to people from my phone, rather than typing text messages. Not only is it more personal, but I obviously speak far quicker than I type, and I therefore save a significant amount of time in the process. Just keep your voice tags short enough to not waste the other person's time when listening to them.

Another effective way to manage my time is to use non-productive idle time more effectively. For example, I make a list on my phone of the non-urgent private or business calls that I need to make on a specific day. Instead of using my office time to make these phone calls – which I could rather spend doing more productive work – I make those calls from the hands-free kit in my car while I'm driving somewhere.

Another example is that I do any necessary internet research while I am in a queue at the post office or at the doctor, instead of doing nothing. If we can learn to use our idle time effectively, we can add minutes to our day and, in fact, to our lives, by increasing our productivity.

If we can find ways to 'manufacture' time, then we will not only catch up on the time that we feel we have wasted in our lives up until that point, but we will increase our personal productivity, which will help us reach our personal goals quicker.

I would like to share a final thought on focused time management: It is the value of, when necessary, postponing unimportant things. For example, while I was writing this book, I told all of my friends and family that personal commitments had to be moved until after the main part of this project had been completed. Trust me, they do understand. Even in business, I only focused on priority items that would have harmed my business or customer relationships if they had not been addressed. If I do not adopt this approach when I am involved in important projects or priority assignments, then I simply cannot deliver at the level that I would wish to reach.

Delegate

"Only do what only you can do."

Andy Stanley

The above is an extremely powerful quote because it strikes at the heart of avoiding time-wasters and distractors. It boils down to the fact that we must only focus on the dealmaker or dealbreaker areas in our lives, both privately and professionally. We should then delegate the rest of the tasks on our list to other people.

There are two prerequisites to making this hugely effective concept work:
1. We need to find people to whom we can entrust this responsibility, because ultimately, we are using them as an extension of ourselves to tackle our tasks.
2. We have to be willing to let go. This is something with which I have battled for a long time, but I've realised that if I am not willing to do this, at some point, I will get stuck.

"The best way to find out if you can trust somebody is to trust them."
Ernest Hemingway

One of the great managing directors with whom I have worked, said: "In life, we need to box cleverly." To delegate to someone is part of boxing cleverly, because not only does this allow us to focus solely on the things that only we can do, but it also results in different areas of our responsibility being completed simultaneously. This is a great way to improve productivity. During the process, you are also giving someone else the opportunity to operate on a different level and to learn from the experience. If you are successful in only doing the things that only you can do, it will have an enormous impact on your success as a self-leader.

There is only one time when I wouldn't recommend this approach: When your partner or spouse expects you to do chores in and around the house. It might be harmful to your relationship if you tell them: "I am only doing the things that only I can do!"

Deal with issues quickly and decisively

One of the top time-wasters and distractors has to be dealing with the same issue over and over again. If we don't deal with issues quickly and decisively, we will have to deal with them over and over again as they grow in size. The longer we wait, the more the rotten apple grows rotten. The truth is that we either deal with issues, or they deal with us. So, here is the challenge: Only deal with something once, and do it properly. This includes completing tasks the first time around. Otherwise, issues will just keep lingering.

"Procrastination makes easy things hard, hard things harder."
Mason Cooley

> I was once given a challenge by a friend, which I would like to put forward to you today. Many of us are constantly bombarded and experience 'death by email'. In future, whenever you receive an email, see if you can only deal with it once, by using one of the following actions:
>
> - Forward it on to someone else, like one of your peers – because it's actually their responsibility.
> - Delegate it to someone else.
> - Book a meeting to address the issue.

Falling behind with responsibilities

We all have responsibilities. Personally, I need to do my tax returns for myself and for my business; I need to renew my postbox, the licence for my car, the licence for my motorcycle, and my driver's licence, as well as a number of software renewals related to my business. The list goes on. If I don't renew or submit all of these items by specific deadline dates, there are consequences. I then either have to pay penalties, or I need to pay an external party to help me sort out the issue, or I won't have access to that specific product or service any longer. I think this is time-wasting and distraction in its purest form.

"We never fail when we try to do our duty, we always fail when we neglect to do it."

Robert Baden-Powell

There is another serious consequence of neglecting our responsibilities: The psychological burden, or niggle in the back of our minds that we *still* need to sort out particular issues. It is almost a feeling of guilt. This feeling or burden affects our ability to focus on other things that occupy our time – including the process of chasing our personal goals. I have no doubt that, if you are a 'repeat offender' in this regard, you would dearly like to alleviate this torture going forward.

There is actually quite a simple way to do this: If you don't have the discipline to meet deadlines, then con yourself by moving the deadline in your own mind, or on your own calendar, one month forward. When you then overshoot the deadline, you will still make the real deadline with some weeks or days to spare, without any consequences!

It is acceptable to say: "No!"

I have been told that I am an unselfish person, but I realised at some point that, as part of taking charge of my life, I needed to view my time as my asset – just like my car or my house. In fact, I realised that it is more important than any other asset I own. My time is *my* time, and nobody else has the right to use my time without my consent. If someone wants to use my car or my house, then I need to permit this first. The same principle should apply, too, if someone wants to claim some of my precious time.

If someone asks us to do something, it is absolutely fine to say: "No." Of course, we can do this politely while quoting a reason. Is it selfish to sometimes do this? No. Is it selfish if we do this all of the time? Yes, probably. We also need to understand this concept when we are on the receiving end of someone who cannot give us some of their precious time at a certain juncture. We are ultimately only responsible for ourselves and how we spend our own time in reaching our personal goals.

The definition of insanity

Albert Einstein defined 'insanity' as doing the same thing over and over again and expecting different results. It might sound senseless that we would even entertain something so stupid, but if we analyse our lives, we will see that all of us have done exactly that before, or are still doing it at times. Instead of pausing or analysing why the results of our actions do not conform to the required outcomes, we jump in again and hope that the results will be different the second time around. Talk about wasting time! The only way to stop wasting time in this regard is to adopt a different approach, or to change our actions to get a different outcome, which aligns with what we wanted in the first place. By doing this, we will achieve success and reach our personal goals faster.

Think before committing to something or someone

Sometimes, in the heat or excitement of the moment, we make impulsive decisions that commit us to someone or to some cause. Dad used to say that whenever there's a big decision to make, rather sleep on it before you finalise your decision. If the cause or person that we are about to commit to will consume a significant amount of our precious time, it is definitely worth sleeping on it. Otherwise, you will be obligated to either stick to the impulsive commitment you made, or face the embarrassment of admitting that you can no longer honour your commitment. Either way, this will in all probability, take time and focus off improving your thoughts, feelings and behaviours, to align them to your personal goals.

Stay in the zone

I have found in my life that getting into the zone is not the problem, but staying in the zone is where it gets difficult. It's easy to sign up at our local gym in the first week in January to get into shape again, but to stay in the 'exercise zone' and stick to our resolution of training all year long, is a challenge. I have found the same thing while writing this book and working towards an editor's first draft by a certain date. To get into the zone of writing is actually quite simple, but to stay in the zone and keep on writing until late on a Friday night, and then from 4.30am on a Saturday morning again, is another challenge. The ability to stay in the zone and to keep our heads in the game is crucial, because it allows us to be more productive towards achieving our personal goals.

> The two important questions I believe we need to ask ourselves are:
> - "Can I list or identify what is distracting me from staying in the zone?"
> - "Which mechanism(s) can I use to help me stay in the zone, or get back into it after I have zoned out?"

What is occupying your time?

Check whether you are not busy wasting time or becoming distracted. Ask yourself the question: "Are the things that are occupying my time adding value to my life or supporting my personal goals?" If the answer is: "No," then you probably want to think carefully about continuing with these activities.

The ultimate time-waster and distractor

I have discovered that the ultimate time-waster and distractor is a lack of discipline. Where we lack discipline, we experience constant conflict between the good leader and the stubborn follower within us. This conflict causes us then to 'wheelspin', because until we have sorted out this conflict, our lives cannot move forward towards achieving our goals, and this conflict just slows us down.

REFLECTION ON THE CONTENT OF THIS CHAPTER – AVOIDING TIME-WASTERS AND DISTRACTORS

Consider the topics that we have covered:

- The hourglass is running out
- Don't sweat the small stuff
- Manage your precious time
- Delegate
- Deal with issues quickly and decisively
- Falling behind with responsibilities
- It is acceptable to say: "No!"
- The definition of insanity
- Think before committing to something or someone
- Stay in the zone
- What is occupying your time?
- The ultimate time-waster and distractor

Please rate your current overall level of success in Avoiding Time-wasters and Distractors as a percentage score:

_____%

Chapter 5

Living a Disciplined Life

> *"We must all suffer one of two things: the pain of discipline or the pain of regret ... Discipline is the bridge between goals and accomplishment."*
>
> JIM ROHN

Gary Player is the one person who would qualify for the title of Global Discipline Ambassador, if ever such a title existed. Having won 167 professional golf tournaments worldwide, and as one of only five men to capture golf's coveted career grand slam, he is widely considered to be one of the greatest golfers ever. He won nine Major championships on the PGA Tour and nine Major championships on the Senior Tour, and is the only player in history to complete the career grand slam on both Tours.[62]

Gary has been named Mr Fitness and The World's Most Travelled Athlete™, having covered more than 26 million kilometres. One can't help wondering: How many more Majors would he have won if he had been based in the United States and not needed to travel that much?

Gary Player has also raised more than $62 million for underprivileged children's education globally, and he has designed nearly 400 golf courses worldwide. In recognition of his achievements in golf, as well as his dedication to charity, Gary has received numerous awards, including the Laureus Lifetime Achievement Award and the PGA Tour's Lifetime Achievement Award.

Gary is known for his disciplined lifestyle and rigorous fitness regimen, even now at the age of 85. His tough workouts also include 20-30 minutes of meditation, which he considers vital to keeping the mind strong. He believes that a healthy diet is essential to living a long and prosperous life. He follows the principle of eating breakfast like a king, lunch like a prince and dinner like a pauper. To make sure that he fuels his body with essential vitamins and minerals, Gary created his own liquid potion of sprouts and leafy green vegetables, which gives him a boost of energy to operate at a high level. One of Gary's 10 personal commandments describes what completes the picture of his tenacious commitment to discipline: "*The fox fears not the man who boasts by night, but the man who rises early in the morning.*"[63]

Gary Player understands the power of living a disciplined life. There is no question that if he had not lived such a life, he would not have achieved half of what he has in his lifetime. Nor would he have been half the man he is today.

To become whole and complete

I once had a conversation with Dawie Fourie, the head of the African Leadership Institute in Namibia. He emphasised to me the importance of being whole and complete as an individual. I thought that to be a fitting description of the result of someone having their self-leadership process under control. I then asked myself the question: "What is standing in my way from becoming someone who is 'whole and complete?'" It took me a couple of nanoseconds to get to the simple answer: "Discipline."

If there is one area of my self-leadership journey in which I have battled, it is discipline. Yet, most people around me consider me to be a very disciplined person: I was an army lieutenant during my national service; I did karate as a sport for many years; I have a swimming training programme; I typically get up at 5am or earlier every morning, and I had the discipline to achieve sufficient formal qualifications. Deep down, though, I knew that my self-discipline was probably half of what it could be. That was the one thing that was holding me back from achieving my true potential. Then, one day, not too long ago, I decided that from that day onwards, I would live, until the end of my days, a truly disciplined life. Since then, I have been much more focused on achieving my personal goals, both privately and professionally, and my life is much more of a joy, because I don't go to bed every night feeling some form of disappointment.

That is one of the ironies in my life. I always knew, to a large extent, how I should live my life, but because of a lack of discipline, I held myself back in so many ways. Fortunately, that is now something of the past.

By mastering this area of my life, I found myself much closer to a point of becoming truly and consistently content with my life – and that is a liberating feeling.

Mike Ditka is a former American football player who is now a coach and television commentator, as well as a member of both the College and Pro Football Halls of Fame. Something he said resonated with how I felt after I had conquered the area of discipline in my life: "Success isn't measured by money or power or social rank. Success is measured by your discipline and inner peace."

I trust that my confession will encourage you to live a more disciplined life and to reap the rewards from it.

Tired of living a suboptimal life?

An important question I encountered along my self-leadership journey was: "What has made me fundamentally change, particularly when it comes to self-discipline?" The answer was not a complicated one: I came to realise that I was living a suboptimal life, and I came to the conclusion that that was sad: I was tired of living a suboptimal life.

| **Suboptimal**: Of less than the highest standard or quality.[64]

I do think our approach to life begins to change when we hit middle-age. I fortunately didn't buy the proverbial cabriolet Porsche, but I certainly then started to think about life in a different way. I started to realise that the way I was thinking, feeling and behaving, was of less than the highest standard or quality, and it was not aligned with what I still wanted to achieve in life. I didn't always feel that way, but often enough for it to seriously bother me.

> "The important thing is this: To be ready at any moment to sacrifice what you are for what you could become."
>
> Charles Dickens

When it happened is not that important, but what was critical was that I realised that I had had enough of living a suboptimal life and that I had the power to change that. I have the power to take charge of my self-leadership process, but I can only do this if I capitalise on the power of leading a disciplined life. When I refer to 'discipline', I don't mean a regimented army-type lifestyle. Rather, I mean a disciplined life, as it relates to achieving what is contained in my self-leadership charter: Ensuring that my life conforms to the content of my own credo and achieving the goals set out in my personal goals scorecard.

Doing what is right versus what is easy

Prof Albus Dumbledore is a fictional character in J.K. Rowling's *Harry Potter* series. Throughout most of the series, he is the headmaster at the Hogwarts School of Witchcraft and Wizardry. In *Harry Potter and the Goblet of Fire*[65] he says: "*We must all face the choice between what is right and what is easy.*"

I am very fond of this quote because I have no doubt that this is something with which we all struggle on a daily basis. Abraham Lincoln defines discipline as "choosing between what you want now, and what you want most".

Both of these quotes talk to ensuring that we always choose the things that align with our personal goals versus choosing the alternative, which is typically the things that purely meet our needs for short-term gratification.

Zombie mode

> **Zombie mode**: The moments directly after waking up from sleep, where we cannot speak properly and have an inability to perform simple tasks.[66]

Earlier we discussed the fact that we cannot afford to live our lives on autopilot, because then we don't take charge and we won't achieve our personal goals as part of becoming the best that we can possibly be. There are two exceptions to this 'rule' in my life. I trust that you will find them useful. The first exception is when I am in zombie mode.

At the beginning of 2021, I joined an outdoor pool swimming squad. This was mainly to assist me with freestyle stroke correction. At some point, I eventually converted from swimming open water races using breaststroke to swimming freestyle, because that is the fastest way to swim. I knew I needed help with this new style, and that I could learn a lot to improve my swimming speed. Besides, the last time that I had any swimming coaching was almost 40 years ago, so I thought I owed it to myself.

The only problem is that the one-hour classes are either held at 5.30am or at 7.30am – which is too late for me, from a work perspective. So, every Monday and Wednesday morning, I get up early, get dressed, have a cup of coffee and a light meal before heading out on the 20-minute drive to swimming. I find it hard to get out of bed when my alarm goes off at 4.30am. For a minute or two, I need to go into autopilot mode, which starts with sitting up straight as quickly as possible with my feet next to the bed to avoid falling back to sleep. If I battle to get going before or beyond that point, I then simply fast-forward my life by two hours and ask myself if I would be sorry if I went back to sleep and missed the opportunity to attend my swimming lesson.

Of course, I would regret going back to sleep. That would mean that I could not achieve my personal goal of staying fit and becoming the best possible swimmer that I could be in the shortest possible time. The reality is that I have never been sorry about attending any training session or about doing the right thing, although I have had to sacrifice something small, like a bit of extra sleep. However, I have certainly had remorse every time that I have not gone to train as a result of a lack of discipline. In this instance and to get through zombie mode, autopilot works for me. It forms part of my discipline and acts as a bridge that gets me across to achieving my personal goal.

Ultimate freedom

"Most people equate discipline with an absence of freedom. In fact, the opposite is true – only the disciplined are truly free. The undisciplined are slaves to moods, appetites and passions."

Stephen Covey

These words are absolutely spot-on. I can attest to this. After I mastered self-discipline in my life, I started experiencing freedom, because other forces no longer had control over me, like eating unhealthy food that would harm my body and immune system, having an extra glass of red wine with supper that would affect my sleep or productivity the following day, or rather sleeping in and so depriving myself of the opportunity to build a healthier body and feel great. This is real freedom: I decided to take charge, and now I feel in charge of my life.

The fallacy of intermittent discipline

The thing about discipline is that we cannot selectively choose to be disciplined one day and not disciplined the next, or to be disciplined on certain days when we feel like it. That is not only confusing, but we would be doing ourselves a serious injustice. Discipline has to become part of our DNA, or part of our being, like breathing. Perhaps we weren't that disciplined today, but we need to strive towards becoming disciplined tomorrow, and next week, and next month – in fact, for every single day, week, month or year for the rest of our days on this Earth. We want to have peace of mind and be proud of ourselves for not living a suboptimal life any longer. We want to reap the rewards of being the best that we could possibly be.

REFLECTION ON THE CONTENT OF THIS CHAPTER – LIVING A DISCIPLINED LIFE

Consider the topics that we have covered:

- To become whole and complete
- Tired of living a suboptimal life?
- Doing what is right versus what is easy
- Zombie mode
- Ultimate freedom
- The fallacy of intermittent discipline

Please rate your current overall level of success in Living a Disciplined Life as a percentage score:

_____%

Chapter 6

Refusing to Make Excuses

"Victims make excuses. Leaders deliver results."
ROBIN SHARMA

Jon Morrow is considered one of the most successful bloggers in the world, and he created his wealth through blogging alone. Over the years, he earned the nickname, Mr Blogger.[67] Morrow started, built and then kept or sold multiple blogs worth millions of dollars. He has written some of the most read and shared articles on the web and has generated hundreds of millions of page views.[68] However, Morrow's story is far from the usual one of cyber success ...

Jon Morrow was born with spinal muscular atrophy (SMA). This degenerative neuromuscular disease slowly weakens the body, leading to complete atrophy, and eventually death.[69] As a baby, doctors gave him two years to live, before his body collapsed from weakness and pneumonia. Against all odds, he is still alive today. He has been in a wheelchair for many years and cannot move any other part of his body than his face.

Morrow found himself in a dilemma: He needed $100 000 in medical aid from the US government just to stay alive, but if he earned more than a tiny amount of money, he would no longer be eligible for this aid. He thought to himself: "I can think, and I can talk." With that in mind, he started blogging and working for free. He started writing for an up-and-coming blog free of charge. Instead of being paid, he built up networks, influence and respect. Then, when he started his own blog, he had enough clients to ensure it was a success.

In 2006, disaster struck when he was involved in a near-fatal car accident that put him in hospital for months and left him even more disabled than before. Faced with ever-mounting medical bills, Morrow made the tough decision to leave his life and family. He moved to Mexico where the weather was warmer, and the cost of medical care was far less than in the United States.

At that time, Morrow decided to focus his life on blogging. Since he can only move his face, he writes with speech recognition technology and by controlling a keyboard simulator with his mouth. Morrow built up Kissmetrics into an enormously successful blog, which he then sold for millions of dollars. Subsequently, he started what is now Smartblogger – one of the most popular and respected blogs on blogging in the world.[70]

Jon Morrow has a warrior spirit, and his story of perseverance is inspiring. He is a true example of someone whose self-leadership journey is on track. He refuses to make excuses and keeps his mind on achieving his personal goals. He took charge of his life and delivers results, despite his extremely challenging circumstances.

An excuse is a story

Excuse: A reason put forward to conceal the real reason for an action.[71]

In his book, *No More Excuses*, Sam Silverstein writes: "*An excuse is a story that you tell yourself to sell yourself – and then try to sell to others … The number one reason people succeed in their personal and professional life is that they don't make or accept excuses … Excuses limit our experiences and horizons.*"[72]

Ask yourself:

"Is my story the valid truth, or just an excuse that is derailing my efforts to achieve my goals?"

> In our careers, family and personal lives:
>
> "What are the excuses I am making that are turning me into my own worst enemy?"

The insane thing is, as Sam Altman says: *"Don't let yourself make excuses for not doing the things that you want to do."*[73]

Your personal goals don't care about your excuses

Bruce Nauman is an inventive American artist who is also famous for saying: "If you really want to do it, you do it. There are no excuses."

Jim Rohn says something similar: If you want to, you will find a way; if you don't want to, you will find an excuse.

Writing our own credo and setting our personal goals are signs that we are serious about living a whole and complete life, and that we are taking charge of our self-leadership. We cannot let a lack of discipline or laziness allow us to dream up convenient excuses to not do those things we need to do to support the words we wrote in our self-leadership charter. The content of our self-leadership charter is what we really want in life, and we can make as many excuses and waste as much time in the process as we would like to, but our own credo and personal goals scorecard will not just mysteriously disappear.

"You can have results or excuses ... Not both."
Arnold Schwarzenegger

Making an excuse to someone else is one thing, but betraying yourself by making an excuse to yourself, and undermining your own success in the process, is another matter completely.

Other famous people wrote about the mistake of making excuses. In a letter to his niece, Harriet, George Washington wrote: *"It is better to offer no excuse than a bad one."*[74]

Robin Sharma wrote: *"I stopped making excuses. I assumed total responsibility for the consequences of my actions and stepped into my best."*[75]

Both of these quotes give us healthy impetus when we feel tempted to make excuses. If we stop making excuses, then we are well on our way to becoming the best that we can possibly be. That is when we will start to understand what it means to own up, to be accountable, and to take charge of our lives.

Talking from personal experience

While I was focusing on completing this book, I often caught myself falling back on the excuse: "Let me *just* finish this book, and then I'll get back into my routine of working towards my goals."

I quickly realised that I could not afford that excuse, because if I accepted it, then I would accept the next one, and the next one – and there would always be yet another one. That would lead to a very bumpy self-leadership journey, because then there would be no conscious and focused effort on my part to align my thoughts, feelings and behaviour to achieve my personal goals. What a huge mistake that would be.

"I attribute my success to this – I never gave or took any excuse."
Florence Nightingale

I suspect that I am not alone in feeling this way, and that the issue of making excuses may just resonate with most of us. We need to see self-leadership as the backbone of our existence. Whenever we postpone our commitment to it, we deprive ourselves of a strong foundation on which to live a truly fulfilled life. It is actually as simple as saying to ourselves: "I choose to master self-leadership and live a fulfilled life." Or you could say: "I choose to make excuses, ignore self-leadership and be content with living an emptier life with sub-par results."

REFLECTION ON THE CONTENT OF THIS CHAPTER – REFUSING TO MAKE EXCUSES

Consider the topics that we have covered:

- An excuse is a story
- Your personal goals don't care about your excuses
- Talking from personal experience

Please rate your current overall level of success in Refusing to Make Excuses as a percentage score:

_____%

Chapter 7

Getting through Tough Times

"I have to believe that when things are bad, I can change them."
JIM BRADDOCK

Brett Archibald is an international businessman and entrepreneur who lives in Cape Town, South Africa. He has built a global career that includes directorship positions with worldwide hospitality and travel corporations in Johannesburg, Sydney, Hong Kong and London.[76] Archibald is also a keen surfer and says that the sea is his happy place.

On 17 April 2013, at 2.30am, in the midst of a storm on the Indian Ocean, Brett fell overboard after passing out on the top deck of a hired boat off the coast of Indonesia. It was dark and pouring with rain. As a surfer, and strong swimmer, he knew that he needed to take a deep breath and swim through any oncoming waves, but nothing could have prepared him for the experience that was to follow.

Archibald and nine friends had been on a surfing holiday. He had contracted food poisoning during a 10-hour journey along the Mentawai Strait in Indonesia's West Sumatra province. Archibald had gone to the side of the boat to vomit overboard, but was overcome with dizziness and blacked out. When he awoke, he was in the water and the boat was already

10-15 metres ahead of him. He initially thought that his life was over, but he became more and more determined not to succumb to the elements.[77] For the next 28 hours, Brett Archibald would be alone at sea.

Suffering from exhaustion, his limbs began to cramp, and he started to hallucinate. According to experts, Archibald should have died within eight to 10 hours of being in the water, but a series of events, including a shark encounter and an attack by seagulls, fuelled him with the adrenalin and fight to stay alive. He chose not to die. Instead, he endured the ocean, the elements, the creatures of the deep, and his own inner demons.[78]

Archibald was eventually rescued by the Australian crew of the *Barrenjoey* at 7.15am on 18 April 2013. He had drifted approximately 50 nautical miles – more than 70km – in the open water of the Mentawai Strait. He is fortunate to be alive to tell his tale.

Digging deep

Brett Archibald's story is an extreme example of how tough life can sometimes get. The only way we can then survive is to dig deep – really deep. If I had told Brett Archibald, after being in the ocean water for 10 hours: "When the going gets tough, the tough get going," he would probably have used his remaining strength to strangle me. My point is this: It is not that simple. Sometimes, we really have to dig deep to cope with life. Fortunately, we humans are wired in such a way that when we have to get through tough times, we generally don't want to give up.

"We cannot change the cards we are dealt, just how we play the game."
Randy Pausch

If we want to pride ourselves on being victorious in self-leadership, and to enjoy all of the benefits that come with the hard work of achieving this status, then frankly, we only have one option: To dig really deep and get to the other side of any rough patch in our lives.

We have to believe in ourselves. We can take charge, and when situations get bad, we generally do have the power to change things. Always take comfort from the fact that man-made problems typically have man-made solutions. If it's something more serious, like a critical illness, then we can still decide to take charge and fight it.

"Life is not fair, get used to it."

On the face of it, the words above by Bill Gates are not very comforting, but it is a hard truth and reality check from which no one is exempt – not even the richest or most successful people in the world.

Norman Vincent Peale said that the only people who don't have problems are in a cemetery. Think of the continuous line graph on a heart rate monitor: If there are no ups and downs in our lives, then it means that we have flatlined and we are dead.

"Feeling sorry for yourself, and your present condition, is not only a waste of energy but the worst habit you could possibly have."
Dale Carnegie

We have to face the fact that life sometimes gets tough, but what counts is what we do with our reality. At the end of the film *Angel has Fallen*,[79] President Allan Trumbull (Morgan Freeman) tells Mike Banning (Gerard Butler): "It is our moments of struggle that define us. How we handle them is what matters."

When the proverbial chips are down; when we feel that life is really treating us unfairly, we need to dig deep. The leader and the follower within us must be totally in sync. Then we need to focus on the basic stepping stones of self-leadership and – more than ever – on leading a disciplined life. If we don't, we'll have to be content with staying in our state of rock-bottom, which is something that none of us wants.

The silver linings in tough times

"There is no education like adversity."
Benjamin Disraeli

"When life is sweet, say thank you and celebrate. And when life is bitter, say thank you and grow."

Shauna Niequist

Many of us have had experiences in which adversity has not only taught us something new about life, but we have come out the other side stronger. To me, this is certainly one of the silver linings of going through tough times.

Another silver lining is realising that if we can be successful in tough times, then surely we can be even more successful in better times. I find much comfort in this thought. Rather than letting our circumstances rule us, we must take charge of them and thrive again.

Turning lemons into lemonade

At one stage in my life, I headed up the largest plastic blow-moulding division in South Africa. My point of contact with our second biggest customer – one of the largest fast-moving consumer goods companies in the world – was their strategic sourcing director. Let's call him John for the purpose of this anecdote.

Late one Thursday afternoon, John phoned me, panicked. He said that their company's printed caps had ended up on one of their competitor's bottles. From a brand equity point of view, it was a catastrophe, and he was fuming. My immediate thought was that we had picked and loaded the wrong caps from our warehouse on to the delivery truck to the competitor's business. After hearing him out, and having endured a fair amount of verbal abuse, I could only tell him: "John, my apologies for this mistake, but please give me an hour to investigate the issue before I phone you back."

After an accelerated investigation, in which I deployed everyone at my disposal to get to the bottom of the issue, we discovered that our logistics team was not to blame. Our cap injection moulding division had packed John's company's caps into the competitor's boxes. No one in our logistics department would have been able to spot the mistake. We quickly arranged to not only isolate the affected boxes in our warehousing and distribution system, but to also do the same at the competitor customer's production facility.

In parallel to this side of the investigation, my sales executive spoke to the person in charge of operations at the competitor company. They were surprised that the mistake had slipped through their entire system undetected. Fortunately, by the time we notified them of the error, they had only managed to deliver to specific retail stores and he was able to send staff to uplift the products.

As promised, and within the hour, I phoned John back to explain the root cause of the issue, our plans to address it, and our progress in the matter. When I finished feeding back to him, he was a totally different person from the man I had spoken to an hour before. He was so impressed by what we had managed to achieve in an hour that he actually thanked me for being their plastic packaging partner …

My team and I had been pelted with proverbial lemons, but instead of ducking and allowing them to fly past us, we not only caught them, but we also used them to make lemonade. That incident cemented our good relationship with John for many years to come.

This is an example of turning bad into good in a professional situation, and being able to do this in our private lives is even more important. If we can change our mindset to rather see a potential threat or challenge as an opportunity, then I think we are more than halfway there in making good out of a bad situation.

"You have to make the good out of the bad, because that is all you have got to make it out of."

Robert Penn Warren

It's better to do something than to do nothing

One of the realities in life is that problems or issues that cause us distress never miraculously disappear until we actively do something about them. In fact, from my experience, problems left unattended typically become worse.

Earlier in my working career, the CEO of our group of companies came to visit our region. He walked into one of our project meetings and joined the conversation. We explained to him that we were battling to resolve a manufacturing challenge for a new project for one of our major customers. "It is better to do something, than to do nothing" he told us. I think this phrase is also very much applicable when we are experiencing hardship in life.

"Action is the foundational key to all success."

Pablo Picasso

Rather than doing nothing amidst a feeling of being stuck in the quicksand of life, we have to do something. Otherwise, we are guaranteed to not find a solution or lifeline. What we 'do' does not need to be expensive or time-consuming.

On 7 May 2016, I felt really stuck in my PhD study journey. In the heat of the moment, while thinking how to juggle massive work pressures and feelings of guilt about not spending enough time with my family as a result, I did something to try to help me get unstuck …

Rather than sitting behind my computer and wrestling with myself and my issues, I walked to my garage and got onto my BMW R9T café racer and hit the road to clear my mind. I returned home less than an hour later, having made the decision to not throw in the towel on my studies.

I am not suggesting for a minute that making decisions is always as simple as taking a bike ride, but sometimes we need to break out and do something different to get us out of our 'stuckness' and to stop the spiral down into negativity. Trust me, it works.

"Be strong enough to stand alone, smart enough to know when you need help, and brave enough to ask for it."

Ziad Abdelnour

If we get to a point where we can't get out of a negative spiral, then we need to put our pride in our pocket and ask for help. We cannot allow ourselves to self-destruct. If you are heading for the proverbial cliff and you cannot make a U-turn or put on the brakes, then allow other people to assist you. You would be pleasantly surprised how much it would mean to them to be given the opportunity to support you in resolving your life challenge.

Get to the root cause of a problem

Sometimes, being unsure of the root cause of a problem can present us with a dilemma. If we don't know what is causing a problem, we cannot fix it.

Japanese industrialist and inventor Sakichi Toyoda was the founder of Toyota Industries. He developed the 5 Whys technique in the 1930s, but it only became popular in the 1970s. Toyota still uses it to problem-solve today.[80]

The '5 Whys' is a simple technique that helps me to get to the root cause of problems in both my professional and private life. I now use it automatically within a short space of time, without having to write it down.

"When solving problems, dig at the roots instead of just hacking at the leaves."

Anthony J. D'Angelo

The idea behind the technique is to ask five 'Why?' questions, until you get to the root cause of the problem. It may only take you three, or conversely up to seven questions, to get to your answer.

> Let me illustrate this technique by way of a simple example:
> For too many years I had been running the corporate treadmill too hard. That was a problem.
>
> 1. **Why was I working so hard?**
>   Because I felt obligated to properly provide for my family.
> 2. **Why?**
>   Because I am a proud man and wanted to give them the best possible opportunities and the highest quality of life.
> 3. **Why?**
>   Because I thought that is what they would want.
> 4. **Why?**
>   Because this is my perception.
> 5. **Why?**
>   Because I did not make the time to actually talk to them and ask them if that is what they wanted.

Once we get to the root cause of a problem, we need to ask ourselves if we have the control to fix the root cause. In reality, we normally do have control over a solution. For instance, I know that my family loves me and there is no reason why I cannot have an open discussion with them about it over dinner ... Guess what transpired? My family only wanted me to be happy and to not die of a stress-induced heart attack before I turned 50.

Muddling through

"If you're going through hell, keep going."

Winston Churchill

> **Muddle through**: Cope in a more or less satisfactory way, despite a lack of expertise, planning, or equipment.[81] Pushing through psychologically and just surviving, without thinking too much.

Not giving an issue too much thought does not equate to sticking our head in the sand, doing nothing and hoping that our issues will pass as quickly as possible. Tough patches in our lives are the second exception that allows for the use of autopilot mode as a coping mechanism, while we are doing what we can to resolve the issue.

When we allow ourselves to go into a mode in which we don't let our circumstances rule or dominate us, we are able to operate on top of the problem rather than inside the problem, where it might be drowning us. We keep on doing this until our efforts to find a solution have paid off and our circumstances have normalised again.

Look for the gap

"Obstacles are those frightful things you see when you take your eyes off your goal."

Henry Ford

When riding a motorcycle, I always practise focusing on the gap in the road, rather than on the obstacle. If you focus on the obstacle, you are destined to hit it. That sounds bizarre, but it is the way our minds work: If we keep focusing on an obstacle, we become fixated on it when we drive or ride any vehicle. The net result then, is that, ironically, we hit the very thing that we wanted to avoid – like a pothole.

A similar thing happens when we encounter obstacles in life: We focus so much on the current obstacle or challenge in our lives that we fail to observe the abundance of gaps and opportunities available to us. In tough times, our perception of life unfortunately gets skewed towards the bad thing that is currently taking place, and we end up losing our balanced perspective.

We need to make a conscious effort to always add up, or list, all of the good things that we still have going for us, despite the obstacles that we must face on our life journey. This will restore our perspective and, inevitably, we will develop a much more positive outlook on life and realise how much we still have counting in our favour.

In tough times, be kind to yourself

When things are toughest in our lives, we have to be the kindest to ourselves and focus extra hard on being our own best friend. Maya Angelou wrote: "*I got my own back.*"

The times in our lives when we most need to have our own back is when we face hardships. It takes a brave man or woman to admit their mistakes – but everyone makes them. I have made many, and will continue to make mistakes, even though I try my best to learn from the past and to not make the same mistakes anymore.

"Failure is a bruise, not a tattoo."

Jon Sinclair

If we have one comfort, it is that the greatest lessons in life are typically learned at the worst times and from the gravest mistakes. So, particularly in tough times, let's be gentle with ourselves when we make blunders. Then, we must forgive ourselves. If we have tried everything to make a success of something, or if a negative outcome was outside of our control, then we have to accept that something is simply what it is. We cannot afford to sulk. We have to find the best possible way to move forward in our journey.

Tomorrow is another day

One of the most beautiful blessings in life, especially when things are tough, is the surety that tomorrow there will be a new dawn and a new day for us to experience and celebrate. The healing power of a night's rest is incredible. It is one of life's small miracles that allows us to generate new energy for the following day. Think back to the times when you faced adversity and almost wanted to throw in the towel on life, but then after a good night's rest, you felt rejuvenated again and ready to face your challenges.

"Sleep is an investment in the energy you need to be effective tomorrow."

Tom Roth

I think that we underestimate the power of a night's rest. When we have had a really tough day or face a real challenge in our lives, we just need to hang in there – at least until we can get to bed, fall asleep and start the recovery process for our minds and souls.

You are not alone

I would like to share with you from one of my deepest, darkest moments in life … It might not even be close to the scale of what you have faced, or are currently facing in your life, but for me, it was a seriously tough challenge. I am sharing my story of adversity in the hope that it will bring you some comfort that you are not alone: You don't have to face life's tough challenges on your own; in most, if not all cases, there are people around you whom you can rely on to help you through this rough patch – people who care for you and who would like to see you succeed in your self-leadership quest and life in general.

When my first marriage fell apart and my wife at the time told me that she had lost interest in me, my life fell apart, too. I wasn't overweight at the time, but I lost nine kilograms in six weeks. I couldn't sleep, I couldn't eat, I started developing health problems, and most importantly, I was consumed by the guilt of putting my two young boys through a divorce. I was a wreck, but I had no choice than to put on a poker face. I also had career responsibilities that needed my focus, including a project I was heading up that involved moving 12 complete production lines.

Through that challenging time, I only held on to one thought: God would not have blessed me with life if it weren't worth living. I eventually got through that period, time healed my wounds and my life got back on track again. I was subsequently blessed to have experienced the joys of second chances: A wonderful second marriage to Marilé, and a second chance to build on my strong relationships with Henri and Chris.

"Life is full of second chances. When they come, be more intentional, courageous and appreciative."

Brendon Burchard

Only through my relationships and the grace of God did I persevere through an experience that, for a while, made me feel like an utter failure. As part of my healing, I also needed to rely on time with a psychologist, and the incredible support I received from Dad, Mom and my sister. The fact that I am an 'open book' helped me to vent to my peers at work and to close friends. The thing with rough patches in our lives is that we have to be strong enough to acknowledge that we need help and, more importantly, to ask for it when it is needed.

Remember: We are *never* alone. It doesn't matter who you are and what you are going through, there will always be people there for you. Hitting rough patches is part of life, and with the help of others, we all get through them. Once we get over that 'bump in the road', our self-leadership journey will get back on track and we can actively start to chase our dreams again.

CHAPTER 7: GETTING THROUGH TOUGH TIMES

REFLECTION ON THE CONTENT OF THIS CHAPTER – GETTING THROUGH TOUGH TIMES

Consider the topics that we have covered:

- Digging deep
- "Life is not fair, get used to it"
- The silver linings in tough times
- Turning lemons into lemonade
- It's better to do something than to do nothing
- Get to the root cause of a problem
- Muddling through
- Look for the gap
- In tough times, be kind to yourself
- Tomorrow is another day
- You are not alone

Please rate your current overall level of success in Getting through Tough Times as a percentage score:

_____%

Chapter 8

Becoming more Resilient

"Life doesn't get easier or more forgiving, we get stronger and more resilient."

STEVE MARABOLI

Resilience: Our ability to withstand life's knocks and setbacks.[82] Our capacity to recover quickly from difficulties; our toughness.[83]

Alex Zanardi is an Italian professional racing driver and paracyclist. He raced in Formula One from 1991-1994, and again in 1999. He also raced in the CART championship, where he was the series winner in 1997 and 1998.

When Zanardi returned to CART for the 2001 season, he struggled with his car and experienced a tough year. On 15 September, he started the American Memorial Race, held at Lausitzring, Germany. In that race, it finally seemed that he was getting to grips with his new car.

Zanardi exited the pitlane after his last pitstop, still in the lead, with only 13 laps to go. Then disaster struck. While he was rejoining the race on cold tyres, he spun into the racing lane and a fellow competitor hit him at 310 km/h.

Alex's car was in pieces; its front end obliterated. It soon became apparent that he had lost both of his legs on impact; one at the thigh, and the other at the knee. He was airlifted to a hospital in Berlin while fighting for his life. He had lost so much blood that there was only a litre of blood left in his body. His heart stopped seven times.

Alex Zanardi's team called his survival a miracle. Reflecting later upon his hospital experience, Zanardi said: "When I woke up with no legs, I just noticed the remaining part of myself ... not the lost one."

After his recovery, Zanardi was fitted with prosthetic limbs, which marked the start of a challenging rehabilitation process. However, he was not satisfied with his new pair of legs, so he customed-designed new ones that allowed him both greater flexibility and more stiffness. His main personal goal was to return to car racing.

By 2003, less than 20 months after his horrific crash, with hard work and training, the Italian was back at the Lausitzring. He was not there to wave a flag or to make an emotional speech about his crash; he was there to race again and complete the remaining 13 laps of the race that had changed his life forever ... at close to 300 km/h in a car that had throttle and brake paddles specially fitted to the steering wheel.

Zanardi then partnered with BMW in the World Touring Car Championship for a number of years, where he showcased impressive pace all throughout his touring car career, notching up five race wins and five podiums in his six full seasons.

By then, Zanardi was reaching his mid-40s, and his competitive spirit was itching to find a new venture. "I am out to prove that there are no obstacles for the disabled," he once famously said.

So, Zanardi began his new chapter in life. He took up competitive handcycling, a form of paralympic cycling. In September 2012, he won a silver medal and two gold medals at the London Paralympics. In September 2016, he won both a gold and silver medal at the Paralympics in Rio de Janeiro.

Alex Zanardi is a perfect example of someone who has demonstrated resilience. Everyone would have understood if he had decided to end his career after his crash and see out the remainder of his life in a wheelchair. He had certainly earned enough money to do so. Instead, he decided to live a fuller life and become the best possible version of himself. Remarkably, he bounced back with a positive mindset and statements like: "I'm not more vulnerable than others. Actually, if I break one of my legs, it only takes a 4mm screw to fix it."[84]

Refuse to give up

"Getting knocked down in life is a given, but getting up and moving forward is a choice."

Zig Ziglar

Alex Zanardi chose to get up and move forward, despite the catastrophe in his life. When it comes to giving up on life, our dreams and our goals, we need to be as stubborn as a mule. Never ever give up. We owe it to ourselves to fight our setbacks and difficulties in life and to conquer them. If you entertain thoughts of defeat, then you will probably experience defeat in your life.[85]

"Fall down seven times, stand up eight."

Japanese proverb

It is important that we follow through, even though it's not always on our own terms. The story of Derek Redmond is a great example of doing exactly that.

British runner Derek Redmond was a favourite to win the gold medal in the 400m race at the 1992 Barcelona Olympics, but a hamstring injury forced him to pull up during the semi-final. He decided to not pull out of the race and limped on, before his father, Jim, made his way on to the track to help him continue.

Just before the finish, Jim let go of his son and Redmond completed the course on his own, prompting the crowd of 65 000 people to give him a standing ovation.

He later said: "Someone once asked me: 'How do you become successful?' The easiest, and most relevant answer is to get up just one more time than you've been knocked down."

The story of Derek Redmond has been called one of the purest examples of determination and perseverance in Olympic history.[86]

CHAPTER 8: BECOMING MORE RESILIENT

Learn to be resilient in our VUCA world

VUCA describes general conditions and situations. It is a concept that originated in the US Army War College to describe the **V**olatile, **U**ncertain, **C**omplex and **A**mbiguous world after the Cold War. It is based on the leadership theories of Warren Bennis and Burt Nanus and was first used as a term in 1987.[87] In recent decades, the concept has again gained new relevance to characterise our environment.

We are currently living in one of the worst VUCA periods of the last century – the COVID-19 pandemic. After we get through this storm, we will at some point in the future, unfortunately have to face another such event. We would be naïve to not think that this is a real possibility. The more we have our self-leadership process intact, the more we will be able to weather these storms in life.

From the toughest VUCA times in our lives we learn the most and increase our resilience.

As a 10-year old boy, I started to involuntarily pull my face and other body muscles. I had no control over it. Being a nurse, Mom knew a neurologist who agreed to examine me. Afterwards, Mom and I sat across the desk from the doctor as he told us both that I have a tic, which is an irregular, uncontrollable, unwanted, and repetitive movement of muscles that can occur in any part of the body.[88] At that point, I looked at Mom, very confused. I had no clue what the guy was talking about. Then he dropped the bomb – which I did understand: "… and your son will never recover from it."

Being teased at school because of my weird facial and arm movements was one thing, but the idea of having to live with it for the rest of my life was a real reminder that the world is volatile, uncertain, complex and ambiguous.

Fortunately, my parents sought a second opinion, and I was eventually diagnosed with chorea, which has similar symptoms to a tic, but can be treated. It typically only occurs up to age 15. My symptoms subsided by the time I turned 13. I have no doubt that that VUCA period in my life made me stronger and more resilient. I learned so much during that time, especially about myself. Fortunately, although I lost much self-confidence during those years, I gained it back – and more – over the rest of my life.

Everybody fails at some point

Our ability to deal with disappointment in ourselves is a vital part of our existence as self-leaders. To be successful in this regard, our point of departure needs to be realising that, just as nobody is perfect, everybody fails at some point. Some more than others, but a fact of life is that *everybody* fails.

"*My great concern is not whether you have failed, but whether you are content with your failure,*" wrote Abraham Lincoln. He had lost his job, failed in business, had a nervous breakdown and been defeated in politics on a number of occasions.[89] Despite all of his failures, 'Honest Abe' had many successes and was elected in 1860 as the 16th president of the United States of America.

It is important that we do not stop trying until we have achieved success. We also cannot afford to be afraid of making mistakes, or to be afraid of taking calculated risks. If we can conquer such fears, then we will capitalise on the opportunities we have been given. Now that is an invigorating thought.

"You may have to fight a battle more than once to win it."

Margaret Thatcher

When we experience setbacks and failure, which we all experience at some point, it is important to see them as temporary. The moment we consider them to be permanent, we will lose our courage and motivation to try again.

When I went through the torture of a failed first marriage, I told myself that I had three simple choices: (1) I could give up on life; (2) I could recover and live the same kind of life as before; or (3) I learn from what happened. I could try again and excel from then onwards and live a much happier life than ever before. I chose this last option.

"Our greatest glory is not in never falling, but in rising every time we fall."

Confucius

J.K. Rowling, the author of the bestselling *Harry Potter* book series, delivered her Commencement Address at the annual Harvard Alumni Association in 2008. It was titled "The Fringe Benefits of Failure and the Importance of Imagination". Among other words of wisdom, she shared the following in her speech about her life:

"I had failed on an epic scale. An exceptionally short-lived marriage had imploded, and I was jobless, a lone parent, and as poor as it is possible to be in modern Britain ... without being homeless. I was the biggest failure I knew."[90]

Rowling came out of her failure stronger and more determined, which was the key to her success. She also shared the following profound words during this speech:

"You might never fail on the scale I did, but ... failure ... is inevitable. It is impossible to live without failing at something, unless you live so cautiously that you might as well not have lived at all – in which case, you fail by default."

There are many examples of people from all different walks of life who failed, but who were resilient enough to stand up again and become successful. You and I are no different from them, and there is no reason why we can't follow in their footsteps. If you are successful at self-leadership, then you are resilient and strengthened against difficult experiences.[91]

"Success is the ability to go from one failure to another with no loss of enthusiasm."

Winston Churchill

Agility, speed and responsiveness

"Speed, agility and responsiveness are the keys to future success."

Anita Roddick

I would suggest that these three areas: Speed, agility and responsiveness, are key factors to successful resilience. Those organisations that were innovative and adapted to the new way of working after COVID-19 hit the world, survived. Not only that, but some of these organisations actually thrived despite the pandemic. Why? A key part of becoming more resilient is our ability, as an organisation, team or individual, to adjust quickly to a changing environment – particularly if these changes are causing setbacks. Therefore, the quicker we do something about it and find ways to deal with the changing environment through innovation and determination, the more resilient we become.

Stress and burn-out

"It's not the load that breaks you down, it's the way you carry it."

Lou Holtz

Stress will always exist in some form or other. We can't wish it away; it is a part of our human existence. It does not help if someone tells us not to stress as, unfortunately, there is no stress off-switch. The 'stress monster' will haunt us until the end of our days.

Teaching, or telling ourselves to stress less is not an easy thing to do. I instead prefer to focus on how to deal with it. That, I think, is the trick. The better we control the stress monster, the more we can marginalise its effects in our lives, and the more successful we can be at achieving our personal goals.

The better we are at managing our stress levels, the more resilient we will become when handling life's challenges. If we don't actively work on managing our stress and finding ways to reduce it, then we will never be able to take charge of the stress monster, which will eventually lead to burn-out.

> **Burn-out**: Physical or mental collapse caused by overwork or stress.[92]

Each one of us is unique, and it is therefore important that we find our own, unique ways to manage our stress levels. Apart from the obvious things, like more sleep; eating healthily; taking supplements; trying to laugh more, and spending more time with family and friends, I would like to share with you three other concepts or techniques that I find to be effective:

1. Rolling fortnight planning
2. The zone of proximity
3. Charging our life batteries.

Rolling fortnight planning

Although we discussed planning in some detail in an earlier chapter, I would like to focus here on rolling fortnight planning, which I have personally found to be helpful in reducing my stress levels.

I find that if I go through my plan for the next two weeks on a Sunday evening, then (1) Not only do I have peace of mind that I know what is scheduled when, but (2) I still have enough time to especially influence the events in the second week, and (3) My mind also then starts to work on taking the initiative to ensure that I make a success of the plan.

The following Sunday evening, I will then look at the plan for the new two weeks ahead of me. This implies that week two of the previous week's fortnight plan becomes week one of my new fortnight plan. This is what I mean by the term 'rolling'. Planning our lives better will automatically reduce our stress levels. To live an organised life not only makes living easier and more structured, but it takes away the nagging worry in the back of our minds that says: "There is probably something important that I forgot that might just catch me out tomorrow."

Basic planning starts with using only one calendar. If my calendar tells me that I need to do a presentation on Monday, then I do not spend Saturday with my family and wait until Sunday morning to start my presentation. Otherwise, I will stress the whole weekend about finishing it before Monday. So, unless we have an immoveable family event on the Saturday, I tell my family that I am working on the Saturday, and we'll have good, quality time together on the Sunday. Obviously, it's first prize that I finish my presentation preparation on the Friday afternoon, but life happens, and this is not always possible.

"Always have a plan, and believe in it. Nothing happens by accident."
Chuck Knox

Another important aspect of planning the next two weeks of my life is that it gets my short-term priorities straight. My simple rule around prioritising correctly is to first do the things that I don't like doing, and to then finish with the things that I really would like to do. This assumes, though, that all of these tasks have the same level of urgency and importance. You will typically find that the things you don't like doing are the have-to-do tasks that are more challenging and urgent.

If, after a meeting that took a couple of hours, I listened to three messages that were left on my phone, I would typically first phone back the difficult person to whom I enjoy talking the least. Why? After that, it would be all downhill. However, if I had phoned back the easy or pleasant person first, I would experience an uphill, mini-battle until I had contacted everyone on my list.

Zone of proximity

'Zone of proximity' is an effective stress-reduction technique that I was taught many years ago during the Investment in Excellence programme at The Pacific Institute®. It describes the *real* area in which we can get hurt; the area in which we can experience the thing that we are really stressed about, such as retrenchment, pain, bankruptcy, or even death. It refers to the area in which there is no turning back; where we have no choice but to confront the issue that we are most stressed or scared about.

The example we were given on this course was Muhammed Ali. There was a man who mastered the concept. Ali was someone who only stressed when he got into the zone of proximity – only when he was in harm's way and in danger of being hit by his opponent. Well, unless he was a brilliant actor, that was certainly the way it seemed.

During the months of preparation leading up to an important fight, Ali would appear relaxed and unstressed. He would remain in that state of mind during the weeks, days and even minutes leading up to a fight. As he entered the arena and walked down the aisle to the boxing ring, he would smile and wave at his fans. After climbing into the boxing ring and sitting on his stool before the first round, he would still appear to be relaxed while chatting to some of the important people with ringside seats.

Ali would remain in this relaxed, seemingly stressless, state even after the bell rang for the first round. Getting up from his stool, his arms would still hang next to his body – until he got into the zone of proximity, where someone like Joe Frazier or Larry Holmes could potentially land some blows to his body. Then, and only then, would Ali move into fighting mode in which he was alert and solely focused on his opponent, when he would "float like a butterfly, sting like a bee".

Muhammed Ali understood that he could only get hurt when he entered that zone, which was close to his opponent. He understood where the zone of proximity was located. That was not before a fight; not before the first bell rang; not after it rang, but only when he got into the danger zone. He also understood that this awareness did not take away any of his responsibility to meticulously plan and prepare for each fight.

Do yourself a favour and recall how many times you have been stressed – sometimes seriously, for months, weeks and days before an important event in your life, only to realise afterwards that it was all pointless. I have had countless moments like this, before I started applying, to the best of my ability, the concept of only stressing when I am in the zone of proximity. By mastering this technique, I am able to relax more, which helps me to get more physical and mental rest, which in turn helps me to become even more resilient. Assuming that you plan and prepare well for something, there is no reason why you can't also benefit from this technique.

Charge your life batteries

"Give your stress wings and let it fly away."

Terri Guillemets

The best way that I give my stress wings to fly away is by continuously charging my 'life batteries'. This makes me resilient enough to face the challenges of life and to handle the setbacks that I experience. In turn, it also then allows me to stay more focused on achieving my goals in life. It is critical that we keep every part of our inner being strong. If we understand the value of successful self-leadership, then we also need to understand the importance of keeping our life batteries charged, which only we can do. We simply need to choose the right 'charge activities' that work for us as individuals.

Our charge activities give us the motivational and energy charge to cope with life and its challenges. I have found that it is crucial to frequently slow down, take a break on the highway of life, and to then charge my life batteries by doing charge activities that work for me. These activities revitalise my soul. For me, they include riding my motorcycle, spending time training in the pool or doing open-water swimming events, or by spending time in the bush. Your charge activities would probably be different. It is important, though, that you identify them and ensure that you do these activities as often as you need them – not all of the time, but certainly on a frequent basis.

Charging your life batteries has to be a continuous process. If you don't charge your life batteries, you will become emotionally empty and demotivated. Motivation then, unfortunately, does not just magically appear again. If, at that point, you don't do something about your emotionally empty state, then your life will spiral to a point where you will battle to operate optimally. A car can't operate on an empty fuel tank, and in a similar manner, we can't operate or move forward in life if our emotional tanks are empty and we feel demotivated. Motivation follows action, not the other way around.[93]

Having flat or deflated life batteries not only brings us to a point of demotivation, but also of no longer having any energy.

"If we have positive energy, then we will always attract positive outcomes."

Steve Buckley

Constantly high energy levels make us more resilient, and one of the ways to ensure this is by charging our batteries.

Grow a thick skin when receiving feedback

Can you field criticism without getting defensive? Are you at a point in your self-leadership story where you no longer take criticism personally?

We should view criticism as a form of feedback.

"Feedback is the breakfast of champions."

Ken Blanchard

Champions, or successful self-leaders, understand that they learn from feedback and that they typically improve as a result of it. We have to view feedback as constructive and part of the toolset that we need to use for continuous personal growth. Seeing feedback as positive to our personal growth also helps us to do better next time.

"We all need people who will give us feedback. That's how we improve."
Bill Gates

I have learned in my life that it's extremely important to first give credibility to the feedback we receive based on who gave it to us. If it's from someone who's opinion we value, then we should see the feedback as valuable. If, on the contrary, it's from someone who is known for being controversial or not credible, then use your own discretion and decide, based on its content, if you need to use it or not. Take the feedback or criticism from whence it comes. Regardless, it is important that we not take it personally, even though it might come across as an infliction on our character. This does not in any way mean that we don't value the opinion of others, or that we don't care about what they say; it simply means that we are strong enough self-leaders to handle it in the right manner.

"There is a huge amount of freedom that comes to you when you take nothing personally."
Miguel Ruiz

We can also never assume that what someone else tells us is a reflection of what they think of us: It is a reflection of what they think of something we said, felt or did. Don't make the mistake of misinterpreting other people's feedback and responses and making it personal. Always try to give someone the benefit of the doubt. If you are unsure, assume that their intentions were pure.

> Ask yourself the following question:
>
> "How quickly do I overcome criticism or negative feedback?"
> Your answer will indicate how much crocodile skin you have – how resilient you actually are in this area.

Put your mistakes behind you

In life, we unfortunately don't have the luxury of pressing the rewind button, as we kids used to do on our Walkman cassette players in the 80s. We can't go back and undo our mistakes; we can only learn to accept them and put them behind us as soon as possible. In the context of resilience, we need to learn the ability to step back from failure, and to frame it as a learning experience. If our self-leadership journey is on track, then we'll use life's lessons and experiences – even those that are tough to swallow – to continually build our self-efficacy. We need to be able to learn from our mistakes and to move forward in life. This will make us more resilient and able to achieve even greater things.

The importance of a work-life balance

Maintaining a healthy work-life balance is not only important to health and relationships, but it can also improve our productivity and ultimately, our performance.[94]

When we looked at our balanced wheel, we referred to the different areas of our lives. That formed the foundation for our personal goals scorecard. In this section, we look at this balanced wheel again, assuming that it represents all of the different areas that we would like to see as part of our lives. This time, we will look at it from a different perspective.

True effectiveness requires balance.[95] I have no doubt that to become whole and complete and be successful at self-leadership, we must have balance in our lives. Otherwise, we might end up robbing time from another area that actually requires our attention, or from an area that we actually require in our lives to become whole and complete. If we tell ourselves that we need to adopt a focused approach to life and only focus on one thing, like making money, then we are telling ourselves a lie and we will never become whole and complete.

"The whole point of being alive is to evolve into the complete person you were intended to be."

Oprah Winfrey

We will typically find that living a balanced life includes the areas that charge our life batteries and revitalise our souls again, like spending time with our family, doing community work, or our favourite sport or hobby. Imagine if we, for example, only focus on a career and then lose our job. We then would have lost everything in life. If we are leading a balanced life, there are many other areas in life in which we can succeed, too. Living a balanced life makes us more resilient, because the other areas in our lives will pull us through and assist us in handling a potential setback in one area.

We cannot tell ourselves: "One day, after I have made money and when I retire, *then* I will start living a balanced life." The reality is that we might die before we retire, and then the only thing we will have achieved or lived for was money. We would have died without really living and experiencing so many other exciting aspects of a healthy, balanced life.

Whatever it takes

Part of being resilient is adopting the philosophy and attitude of "whatever it takes". When we think like that, we are impossible to stop. People with this approach to life usually find alternate ways to get to the solution or to the other side of rough patches in their lives. They persevere until they overcome hardship. When they see a problem in front of them, they don't stop and give up; they try to go over it. If that does not work, they try to go underneath it or around it. If all else fails, they go through it. The point is that people who adopt this approach think outside of the box to find a solution to conquer the challenges with which they are faced – whatever it takes.

Cliff Young was one such man. Australia hosts an annual 543.7 mile (875km) endurance race from Sydney to Melbourne. It is widely regarded as one of the world's mostABD gruelling ultra-marathons. The race takes five days to complete and is typically only attempted by world-class athletes who train specifically for the event. These entrants are normally younger than 30 years of age and sponsored by large companies.

In 1983, Cliff Young showed up at the start of the race. Cliff was 61 years old, and he wore overalls and work boots. To everyone's shock, Cliff wasn't a spectator. He fetched his race number and joined the other runners.

The press and other athletes were curious about Cliff. They told him: "You're crazy; there's no way you can finish this race."

He replied: "Yes I can. I grew up on a farm where we couldn't afford horses or tractors, and the whole time I was growing up, whenever the storms would roll in, I'd have to go out and round up the sheep ... Sometimes I would have to run those sheep in for two or three days. It took a long time, but I would always catch them. I believe I can run this race."

When the race started, the professional athletes quickly left Cliff behind. The crowds and television audience were entertained because Cliff couldn't even run properly – he appeared to shuffle instead. Many people even feared for the old farmer's safety.

It was a well-known fact among professional athletes that the race takes about five days to complete. The norm was that one had to run about 18 hours a day and sleep for the remaining six hours. Cliff Young didn't know that. When the morning of the second day came, everyone was surprised: Not only was Cliff still in the race, but he had continued jogging throughout the night. Cliff was asked about his tactics for the rest of the race. To everyone's disbelief, he claimed he would run straight through to the finish, without sleeping.

Cliff honoured his claim and did exactly that. Each night, he grew a little closer to the leading pack of runners. By the final night, he had passed all of the young, world-class athletes. He was the first competitor to cross the finish line – and set a new course record.

When Cliff was awarded the winning prize of AU$10 000, he said he didn't know there was a prize, and he insisted that he had not entered for the money. He gave all of his winnings to several other runners in an act that endeared him to all of Australia.[96]

By always adopting a whatever-it-takes philosophy to life, you will gain a natural level of resilience that will be hard for any challenge to defeat.

REFLECTION ON THE CONTENT OF THIS CHAPTER – BECOMING MORE RESILIENT

Consider the topics that we have covered:

- Refuse to give up
- Learn to be resilient in our VUCA world
- Everybody fails at some point
- Agility, speed and responsiveness
- Stress and burn-out
- Rolling fortnight planning
- Zone of proximity
- Charge your life batteries
- Grow a thick skin when receiving feedback
- Put your mistakes behind you
- The importance of a work-life balance
- Whatever it takes

Please rate your current overall level of success in Becoming more Resilient as a percentage score:

_____%

Chapter 9

Being in Charge of Your Emotions

*"When you react, you let others control you.
When you respond, you are in control."*

BODHI SANDERS

When a duck swims away from danger, it still looks cool, calm and collected above the surface. However, below the surface the duck uses its feet to furiously propel itself away from the source of danger as fast as possible – almost like an outboard motor. When I was part of one particular executive team, we used to say: "Make like a duck." That meant we needed to take charge of our emotions.

"Leadership is the ability to hide our panic from others."

Lao Tzu

Nelson Mandela, or Madiba, as we South Africans fondly called him, was a courageous man known for being in charge of his emotions. He understood the concept of hiding his fears from others.

Richard Stengel, author of the book *Mandela's Way – Lessons on Life*[97] tells the story of how he agreed to meet Madiba at the then-Durban airport in 1994. Mandela had chartered a small twin-prop aeroplane to the very politically-charged Natal province in the run-up to the first democratic elections in South Africa. Madiba was only accompanied by a bodyguard named Mike, and the two pilots. When the plane was 20 minutes from landing, an airport official informed Richard that one of the plane's engines had failed. Fire engines and an ambulance had been deployed to the tarmac.

After a slightly rocky landing, and amidst the presence of all the emergency vehicles, Richard recalled that Madiba had entered the airport lounge with a smile, besieged by a busload of Japanese tourists with whom he graciously agreed to shake hands and take pictures.

While Madiba was posing, Richard went to talk to Mike, who told him that two-thirds of the way through the trip, Madiba had leaned over to him, pointed out of the window, and calmly said that the propeller of that engine did not seem to be working. He then requested that Mike please inform the pilots. Madiba went back to calmly reading his newspaper, which he continued to do until the plane touched down.

Mike, who was not an experienced flier, told Richard that he had trembled with fear. The only thing that had calmed him down was staring at Madiba, who was peacefully reading his newspaper as if he were some suburban commuter on the morning train to the office.

When Madiba and Richard were alone in the backseat of the car on the way to the rally where Madiba was scheduled to speak, Richard asked how the flight had been. Madiba leaned over to Richard, opened his eyes very wide and said in a dramatic voice: "Man, I was terrified up there!"

Rather EQ than IQ

> **Emotional intelligence (EQ)**: Our capacity to be aware of, control and express our emotions, and to handle interpersonal relationships sensibly and empathetically.[98]

Never once in my entire working career did I ever come across anyone with an IQ so low that they could not be effective or add value in some area of the workplace. Yet, I have met numerous people – even senior people in organisations – with low EQ. Wherever they went, they caused controversy and friction. They were grown-ups, but for some reason they acted like children who needed attention and embarrassed both themselves and others.

"It takes something more than intelligence to act intelligently."
Fyodor Dostoevsky

It is important to distinguish between people with a lack of technical knowledge versus people with a lack of EQ. The ideal is obviously to only have in an organisation people without either shortcoming, but in my experience, people typically get dismissed for a lack of EQ rather than a lack of technical skill.

The HR director in one of the companies for which I worked always said that, when someone's nuisance value starts to exceed the value they are adding, it's time for the person to leave the organisation.

Being in charge of our emotions is critical to our self-leadership success. A low EQ and successful self-leadership are like a prawn and custard milkshake – they just don't gel. Not being able to control our emotions is a self-leadership dealbreaker. If we can't keep our feelings under control, we will always battle to build relationships with anyone who could support our efforts to achieve our personal goals. The real test of whether we are in charge of our emotions is if, when we are furious and at the brink of losing control, we can dig so deep emotionally that we always do or say what we *have to*, versus what we *want to*.

As self-leaders, we are human, and certainly not perfect. It is normal to get upset. The difference is that thriving self-leaders can deal with their upset on their own. Their emotions don't boil over into an outburst in which other people can clearly see their upset. The other difference is that they don't stay in an upset state for long. They quickly get through it and return to their usual state of happiness.

Without question, EQ, as a measure of intelligence, outperforms IQ, or any other measure of intelligence for that matter, every day of the week.

Perception versus the facts

In July 2018, Marilé and I enjoyed a two-week visit to parts of France and Italy. On the second-last day of our trip, we drove from Verona to Bologna. I remember asking Marilé how far the airport was from our hotel. As the good co-driver she is, she responded in a flash that it was less than a 20-minute drive away. That put my mind at ease: It meant that we had more time to explore Bologna before our flight to Paris the next afternoon.

After visiting the Ducati factory the following morning, we realised that we were quickly running out of time to buy gifts for people back home. Fortunately, I am married to a seasoned traveller who searched her phone for the right shops, and off we went, bearing in mind that we had a flight to catch that same afternoon … "Only 20 minutes to the airport," I thought to myself.

The shops we visited didn't have what we wanted, so we went elsewhere, and our shopping experience was extended. Fortunately, Marilé was operating her phone's GPS, and we knew where we were going.

When we finally returned to the hotel, a little behind schedule, we quickly checked out and packed the car. As we left the basement parking, I asked her to please activate her GPS to get us to the airport. When I looked in her direction a couple of seconds later, I realised that she had turned almost the same shade of white as our rental car.

"What is it?" I asked.

She turned to me and said: "The GPS says its more than one-and-a-half hours to the airport."

I almost overturned the car in shock. I realised that we'd probably be too late to catch our flight. Just before I exploded, she smiled and said calmly: "Google Maps is still on 'walking mode' on my phone. It's actually only 20 minutes to the airport."

It is so easy to get emotional, even for a short while, about something that is based on *our reality*, but not necessarily the *real reality*. If we don't have all of the facts or truths at our disposal, we shouldn't respond – certainly not emotionally.

"Your opinion is your opinion, your perception is your perception.
Do not confuse them with 'facts' or 'truths'."

John Moore

The importance of consistency

When we are consistent, people around us learn to trust us.[99]

For many years I worked for someone who was inconsistent. That was one of the main reasons why I ultimately left that organisation. One day, he would act like a close friend, but then the next, I would have to deal with a confrontational person who was out to find fault with my work.

People hate it when others are inconsistent. I have found that being consistent is more supportive of achieving the goals we set ourselves. It helps to create a more relaxed environment of trust in which the people around us support us in achieving them.

"Trust is built with consistency."

Lincoln Chafee

Dad used to say that everything is fine and well, up until the point where you add "too" to it – as in "too" emotional or "too" unemotional, as opposed to remaining consistent. When people are emotionally all over the place, they upset the environments in which they operate. Nobody knows from one day to the next whether they are getting Personality A or Personality B. That makes them feel uneasy. People then start avoiding such a person and could typically say: "I am not going into his office, because I don't know in what mood he is in and what version of him I will encounter."

In such a scenario, growing or building relationships, teams and organisations is extremely difficult. The flip side is also true: If people consistently show almost no emotion, then this results in a dull working environment, which is not good, either.

So, sticking to the law of averages, the best environment would be one in which people have enough emotion to create warmth, while remaining emotionally consistent, so that the way they are now is very much the way they will be later today, tomorrow or next week.

Instead of snapping, snap out of it

We are all human and, to a lesser or greater extent, we have all wanted to snap or crack at some point. It is highly likely that we have all been tempted, at least once in our lives, to give our manager or someone else, what we thought would be a legendary speech that we would actually end up regretting for the rest of our lives. The difference between successful and unsuccessful self-leaders is that the former have mastered certain techniques to ensure that they do not step over the cliff and fall into the abyss of low EQ. Successful self-leaders don't allow that one weak moment in their EQ armour to destroy the good reputation they have built over their lifetimes.

In my previous role as a general manager, my procurement executive was a pleasant, middle-aged Italian lady. Let's call her Sofia, for the sake of anonymity. Sofia was extremely good at what she did, with one exception: At times, she would totally lose it and have emotional outbursts that made everyone around her feel uncomfortable.

Since leadership development is my passion, I made it my mission to coach Sofia to master this weakness. Eventually, Sofia started to follow the technique that I taught her. Just before exploding in a meeting as a result of strongly disagreeing with someone, she would say: "Excuse me, I need to go to the ladies' room." She finally found a way to deal with her emotional weakness.

"If you aren't the one who is controlling your own thoughts, feelings and emotions, then you are one who is being controlled."
Clyde Lee Dennis

Sometimes, defusing your emotion and protecting your legacy could take something as simple as getting up, excusing yourself and walking away. It would be better than snapping at someone.

I have fortunately 'grown up' over the years, and I have learned how to control my emotions as part of my self-leadership story. On the odd occasion when I find that I want to allow my emotions to control me, I force myself to pause for a second. I then ask myself: "Would you regret it, or would you be proud of what you are about to say or do next?"

Set your own boundaries

As successful self-leaders, we always need to be aware of the fact that only we are in charge of our emotions, nobody else. When it comes to our emotional state, it is therefore within our power to set the boundaries in our lives. I can't set those boundaries for anyone else, but I can certainly set them for myself. I am in charge of my own life. Years ago, I promised myself that I would never again engage in an emotional outburst with someone in a public forum, like a meeting. Firstly, it reflects low emotional intelligence on my side, and secondly, it is an embarrassment to me and to the other person.

> "The fluidity of thought is based on the flexibility of beliefs and the emotional boundaries surrounding them."
>
> Michael Arndt

When we camp or hike, or just have our weekly mentoring sessions with our boys at The Character Company, we set certain behavioural boundaries. These support the activities that we do with them and the values that we teach them. For instance, we tell the boys that nobody is allowed to be grumpy – not the mentors, and not the boys. By setting these boundaries, we make it clear what behaviour is acceptable, and what is not. In a similar way, it is important that as self-leaders, we define the emotional and behavioural no-go-areas in our lives. By doing this, the follower in you knows and understands that those boundary areas are non-negotiable. This consequently results in the follower and leader in you becoming more aligned.

"Just smile and wave boys, smile and wave ..."

Someone once said: "If the right words can make you, the wrong words can break you." It is critical that we speak or write the correct words, or not say anything at all. Sometimes the right thing to do is to guard our mouths and test to see if we can resist the temptation to say something.

Sarcasm is a perfect example here.

> **Sarcasm**: The use of irony to mock or convey disrespect.[100]

I don't know about you, but I don't want to be associated with such a description.

"Better to remain silent and be thought a fool than to speak out and remove all doubt."

Abraham Lincoln

So, why then are we sarcastic? Probably because we think it is funny, and that we can gain some popularity in the process. However, we do this without thinking what the person on the receiving end goes through. For too long, I have been part of an executive team in which no boundaries were set for issues like sarcasm. It is toxic, and sarcasm only gets worse. Our short-term need for emotional gratification should never influence the way that we interact with people. We need to understand that and be an example of: We are what we speak.

Not only should we sometimes be putting a guard in front of our mouths, but also in front of our pens or computer keyboards. I always advised the managers in my work team that when they received an emotionally charged email, or one that charged them emotionally, they should rather wait a day before responding – despite that burning desire in them to respond with vengeance and tell that person where to get off.

If you, too, follow this approach, the next morning, both you and the other person would have cooled off and had a night to think about the right thing to do. It is highly likely that the sender of the email would have experienced some remorse, which would put you in a better position to resolve the issues at hand.

As an African, one of my favourite computer-animated films is *Madagascar*.[101] At some point in the movie, Skipper, the penguin, says to his fellow penguins: "Just smile and wave boys, smile and wave." Sometimes, if we as self-leaders don't have anything good to say or write about or to someone, then it is best not to say anything.

Choose the counterintuitive response

> **Counterintuitive**: Contrary to intuition or to common-sense expectation.[102]

Walking away in the heat of the moment without saying anything is a last resort, and it might not always be appropriate to do so. As a result, I have taught myself and developed a counterintuitive response. This initially went against my whole being, and it takes a massive amount of focused discipline, but it is the right thing to do – and it works to defuse situations.

For example, if while I am driving, a taxi pulls out right in front of me and makes a U-turn in my lane, I now give the driver a smile. If that had happened 10 years ago, I would have hooted at him in frustration. Choosing the counterintuitive response is not easy, but every time I succeed at it, I smile to myself with a sense of pride. I am living up to the challenge I set myself.

Identify and work on your own limitations

I have a confession to make: I have a constant feeling of restlessness. Specifically, I am restless and anxious about not achieving my personal goals faster. I guess this is a form of impatience, but I am mostly impatient with myself. This can be a good thing, because it means that I am not content with the status quo, which then pulls me towards my goals. It helps me to 'get the job done'. There is a flipside to this, though: It is the experience of never being content with where I am in life. It is a problem, and every time I sit and analyse this feeling, I realise that I am not only not being fair to myself, but also to my Creator, as it may seem that I am not thankful for what I have.

So, I am working on this area of my life. Although I am making progress, I am still a work in progress. I constantly remind myself that I need to be patient with myself. I also remind myself that life is not perfect, and that neither are we. Life happens in different shapes and forms, which means that I need to be more patient, and to be realistic and fair. To identify, and even share, our glaring developmental areas is important – particularly if it involves habitual, emotional ways of showing up in a negative manner. It is right that we, as self-leaders, continue to work on and improve ourselves – particularly when it comes to taking charge of our emotions.

Avoid impulsivity

"It is the mark of an educated mind to be able to entertain a thought without accepting it."

Aristotle

Letsitele, where I grew up, is 33km away from the closest decent-sized town, Tzaneen. That was where we did most of our grocery shopping. One fine Saturday morning, during my high school years, Mom asked Dad to please drive to Tzaneen to buy cheese and polony that she needed for the week and for our lunch that day.

Upon arriving in Tzaneen, Dad parked his car next to the supermarket, as usual, but since it was Saturday, he had plenty of time. He noticed that his mate, Eddy, who owned a second-hand car dealership next door to the supermarket, was working that day.

So, off Dad went to have a cup of coffee with Eddy before doing his shopping. On his way to Eddy's office, his eye caught a Toyota Cressida standing on the dealership floor. He asked Eddy about the car, finished his cup of coffee and then took the car for a test drive.

When Dad eventually arrived home, he told Mom that he had bought a car. There was only one problem, though – he had forgotten to do the shopping. He was so excited about buying another car that he had totally forgotten about the cheese and polony – which was the only reason he had gone to town in the first place. That didn't surprise me, though … What did surprise me was that Dad had broken one of his own rules: "When you have to make a big decision in life, always sleep on it first."

> **To be impulsive**: To act or do something, or to make a decision without proper forethought.[103]

That day, my father had been impulsive. When he made the decision to buy that car, he was not in charge of his emotions. We should be avoiding impulsive decisions like the plague. Not only are they a sign of a low EQ, but they can also get us into trouble – as many couples who have married on the spur of the moment can testify. Fortunately, it worked out for Dad, and the car he bought gave our family great service and joy, but it could easily have ended in regret the following morning.

It is great to feel passion for something, but we shouldn't allow our passion to clutter our judgement when it comes to making the right decisions.

Let go of bitterness and grudges

The saying goes that bitterness, like a burning match, only burns the one who holds on to it.[104]

"As I walked out the door towards the gate that would lead to my freedom, I knew if I didn't leave my bitterness and hatred behind, I'd still be in prison."

Nelson Mandela

After 27 years in jail, Nelson Mandela is the best example of how to leave our bitterness behind us. Holding grudges does not help anyone, and it especially does not help you. The person or organisation against whom you hold your grudge has probably moved on long ago, yet by holding on, you are still allowing yourself to experience pain.

"People say that forgiving is my flaw, but I really believe that holding grudges and anger is a waste of energy."

Mayte Garcia

Bitterness and grudges are the balls and chains that, if not cut loose, will hold us back and slow us down in pursuit of our personal goals. There is no place for either of them on a successful self-leadership journey.

Being on the receiving end of a lack of EQ

Being on the receiving end of someone else who is not in charge of their emotions will quickly remind us how important this aspect is to self-leadership.

"Sticks and stones may break my bones, but words shall never hurt me," is an old children's saying, but the reality is that words can sometimes hurt more than physical pain. The trick, though, is that words can only hurt us if we give them the power to hurt us. Although it's not always easy, we need to refuse to let another's words hurt us. We cannot just accept the hurt that they are trying to inflict by using verbal cruelty.

"No one can hurt you without your consent."

Eleanor Roosevelt

Inner peace and being in charge of your emotions

"Your inner peace is your outer foundation."

Allan Rufus

If you had to ask me what I wish for, especially for those people close to me and for myself, it would be peace, continuous inner peace … That would be my choice if I were able to pick something that money couldn't buy.

Anything that costs us our peace is too expensive. I have found that when my emotions control me, I lose my inner peace. If, on the other hand, I have control over my emotions, I find it much easier to reach a state of contentment and inner peace. Not being in charge of our emotions costs us much more in life than we could ever imagine: We hurt ourselves and we hurt others. If this is not enough of an incentive to continuously work on building a higher EQ, then nothing is.

REFLECTION ON THE CONTENT OF THIS CHAPTER – BEING IN CHARGE OF YOUR EMOTIONS

Consider the topics we have covered:

- Rather EQ than IQ
- Perception versus the facts
- The importance of consistency
- Instead of snapping, snap out of it
- Set your own boundaries
- "Just smile and wave boys, smile and wave …"
- Choose the counterintuitive response
- Identify and work on your own limitations
- Avoid impulsivity
- Let go of bitterness and grudges
- Being on the receiving end of a lack of EQ
- Inner peace and being in charge of your emotions

Please rate your current overall level of success in Being in Charge of your Emotions as a percentage score:

_____%

Chapter 10

Living in the Present Moment

> *"Living in the present and finding what's good about it, is how I want to live."*
>
> ALI MCGRAW

The movie *Click*[105] was released in 2006. Adam Sandler plays the lead role of Michael Newman, an architect, married to Donna. The pair have two children, Samantha and Ben. Michael has a bullying and overbearing boss named John Ammer, who is the main reason why Michael often chooses work over his family.

One day Michael visits a retail store called Bed, Bath and Beyond to buy a universal remote control. He stumbles around the various departments before deciding to lie down on one of the beds, where he falls asleep. When he awakes, a man named Morty gives him a free remote control. Morty warns Michael that the remote can never be returned.

While trying to learn how to use the remote, Michael realises that it can control reality – very much like a television. He decides to use it to his advantage at work, causing some light-hearted mischief at times. He then starts to use it to fast-forward past uncomfortable and bad moments, like illness. Morty told Michael that during these times, his body would be on autopilot and go through the motions of everyday life while his mind skipped ahead.

At some point, Michael cannot afford to buy bicycles for his children, but he knows that his boss plans to promote him to a partnership, so he uses the remote to skip ahead to the promotion. Using the fast-forward button, he is shocked to find how quickly a year passes by. During this time, he and Donna have entered marriage counselling, his children have grown out of their desire for bicycles, and the family dog has died. Things then get worse when Michael realises that the remote control has learned his preferences. It starts time-skipping in response to casual wishes that Michael expresses about not wanting to experience certain moments in his life.

Michael attempts in vain to destroy the remote control, and Morty refuses to take it back. His life quickly spins out of control, but he makes the biggest discovery ever: It was a massive mistake to skip certain moments of his life.

Pilgrim or tourist?

About a decade after I watched *Click*, I heard a sermon that challenged me with the question: "Are you a pilgrim or a tourist?" That sermon made a massive impact on my life and gave me significant perspective. The reverend used the imagery to explain to us how to live our lives: A tourist only wants to experience the highlights package, while moving from the one high point to the next – similar to what Michael Newman did. A tourist typically travels by plane, bus or taxi to their destination. They are seldom content in the present moment and always plan ahead to be at another point in the future.

"Be happy in the moment, that's enough. Each moment is all we need, not more."

Mother Teresa

On the contrary, a pilgrim is someone who literally experiences all parts of life, including the highs and lows. They live a more complete life, realising that it is important to experience, cherish and appreciate every single moment – the good and the bad. A pilgrim typically travels by foot, so they see and experience the here and the now – the fresh air; the rain on their skin; the light breeze against their cheeks; the song of the birds; and the insects in the grass next to the path. A pilgrim learns from difficult times, which equips them to better face the same challenge the next time it arises.

So, again I ask the question: "Are you a pilgrim or a tourist?" Michael Newman was undoubtedly a tourist, but you and I, who want to be successful self-leaders, cannot afford to choose the route of tourism.

ATGATT

I grew up in an era in which lead-based paint, asbestos panel heaters and car backseats without seatbelts were the norm. I would ride my off-road motorcycle every afternoon after school on farm roads wearing flip-flops, shorts and a T-shirt – but no helmet. Things have changed since then, and I suppose my bones have become more brittle. For this reason, I now believe in ATGATT, which is an acronym for the motorcycling term: All the gear, all the time. This basically means that I don't ride anywhere without wearing my full motorcycle safety kit. This is a pain, though, because it takes time, so it often stops me from taking shorter trips.

Then one day, I shifted my mind, after realising that gearing up and down before and after a trip is part of the riding experience. My riding experience does not only begin when I turn the throttle of my motorbike. It is actually much longer, and it incorporates all aspects on either side of the ride.

This is an important principle, and if we don't make this mindshift in all of our experiences, we won't appreciate every moment of life. Then, like Michael Newman in *Click*, or the tourist in the sermon, we will only live for life's highlights. The sad net result will then be that when we are 80 years old one day, we will have actually only lived for 60 years. We will not have experienced 25% of our lives, because we wished to bypass certain parts of it as quickly as possible …

Live in the present moment

Dad used to tell me that if I work, I need to work hard and if I play, then I need to play hard. He warned me against trying to combine or confuse the two. By implication, he was saying that if we work, we shouldn't pollute our minds with thoughts of play, and if we play, we must enjoy it and not deprive ourselves of those happy moments. We need to be focused in the moment on what is required of us. All we have is now, not the next minute, hour, day, or week – only now. As self-leaders, we certainly have vision, and we have to plan for the future, but we can only live in the now.

"Yesterday's the past, tomorrow's the future, but today is a gift. That's why it's called the present."

Bil Keane

Only the now is guaranteed, and that is where our focus should be. If we daydream about tomorrow or focus our attention on something else, as opposed to really paying attention to what someone tells us at that point in time, then we are not living in the present moment.

Lao Tzu said that if we are depressed, then we are living in the past. If we are anxious, then we are living in the future. If we are at peace, though, then we are living in the present moment. We cannot afford to rob the only certain moment that we have by focusing on a future that is not guaranteed, or a past that we cannot change. Don't let your past or future be the thief of your present.

Practise mindfulness

One way to really use the present moment to our advantage is by practising mindfulness.

> **Mindfulness**: A mental state achieved by focusing one's awareness on the present moment, while calmly acknowledging and accepting one's feelings, thoughts and bodily sensations.[106] Mindfulness is a wisdom tradition of individual practice in which one studies their thoughts and feelings as they occur.[107] Underpinning mindfulness is self-observation, the foundation of self-awareness,[108] and self-leadership starts with self-observation.[109]

> **Self-observation**: The process of observing and recording the targeted behaviours that we experience, and using this information to observe our own actions.[110]

Mindfulness and self-observation allow me to do introspection, giving me an almost out-of-body experience from which I look at myself from the outside. This is particularly useful whenever I realise that my thoughts, feelings and behaviour are out of line, or when the follower in me does not follow the leader in me.

Fortunately, we do not just think about things, but we are also aware of what we are thinking.[111] Mindfulness helped me to become more aware of my habitual, and sometimes damaging, thought patterns and feelings, as well as typical actions that I might demonstrate in response to what others say. Having this awareness has helped me to change some of these critical aspects of my life and to modify some of my behaviours. Being in control of my life, and choosing to take charge as a self-leader, made me realise that I have the power to change these thoughts, feelings and (re)actions, to ensure that they are aligned with achieving my personal goals ...

"The great benefit of practicing mindfulness ... is presence of mind within a storm of emotions."

Phillip Moffitt

The practice of mindfulness has helped me to become aware of negative feelings, or feelings of anxiety. I am now able to let them come and go as quickly as possible without getting stuck. It's almost as if I talk to those unwelcome feelings. I acknowledge that they are there, but I do not allow them to control me, my emotions or my reactions. I then release them and let them disappear while waving them goodbye.

We can't let toxic emotions or thoughts hold us hostage, and the quicker we release them, the quicker we get out of the emotional quicksand[112] and back on track to living a life that aligns with the goals that we have set for ourselves.

I am certainly not claiming to be an expert on mindfulness, and the idea here is not to convey the full body of knowledge around the subject. It is simply to share with you that this is a powerful concept. In my experience, it can definitely assist anyone in becoming a better self-leader. Mindfulness is about waking up to the thought that the present moment is all we will ever have. It has also been found to significantly boost our personal resilience.[113]

The benefits of meditation

I was initially sceptical about the idea of meditation, until I started reading up about and practising it.

> **To meditate**: To focus one's mind for a period of time, in silence or with the aid of humming, for religious or spiritual purposes, or as a method of relaxation.[114] It is extended reflection in order to achieve focused attention to gain insight into oneself and the world.[115]

Meditation can be as simple as doing breathing exercises for a short while. I find that it allows me to centre my thoughts, stabilise my emotions and to just *be* in the present. It can take as little as one minute, but the reality is that regular meditators are happier and more satisfied in life than the average person.[116] I only practise basic meditation, but when I do, I always feel revitalised and more content afterwards.

> "One does not practise meditation to become a great meditator. We meditate to wake up and live, to become skilled at the art of living."
> Elizabeth Lesser

REFLECTION ON THE CONTENT OF THIS CHAPTER – LIVING IN THE PRESENT MOMENT

Consider the topics that we have covered:

- Are you a pilgrim or a tourist?
- ATGATT
- Live in the present moment
- Practise mindfulness
- The benefits of meditation

Please rate your current overall level of success for Living in the Present Moment as a percentage score:

_____%

Chapter 11

Improving Self-confidence

"Have faith in your abilities. Without a humble but reasonable confidence in your own powers you cannot be successful or happy. But with sound self-confidence you can succeed."

NORMAN VINCENT PEALE

In 2001, Andrew Bryant, a motivational speaker, leadership coach and proponent of self-leadership, lost his business, money, properties and cars because of circumstances beyond his control and bad decisions he had made. He found himself in debt without any assets, job or business.

Bryant confesses that for weeks, his inner critic ran wild within him.[117] Then, after feeling sad and sorry for himself for long enough, he started to coach himself back on to the road to recovery. He told himself that he had the necessary knowledge, experience and skills, and he convinced himself that he would be in demand for those, which he could then sell.

Bryant started calling numerous organisations to offer his services. Although initially met by much rejection, he persevered and kept using self-talk to tell himself that he would soon find an opportunity. He eventually found a company that was prepared to pay him for some consulting work, and then he found another. Bryant then started to capitalise on the references from those initial companies and began to build a business that allowed him to coach and speak around the world.

Time went by, but then Bryant was faced with a new challenge – one that he didn't expect. The love of his life told him that there were things about him that she didn't like, and she questioned whether they should remain in a relationship. That took Bryant by complete surprise. He was angry and shocked.

In considerable pain and feeling out of control, his inner voice screamed how unfair everything was and how his needs were not being met. Although he fully understood what was going on, he was unable to stop the negative critic within him, nor the inclination to play the blame game. At that point, he realised that he needed professional help. After a couple of sessions, his leader inner voice began to take control again, and he was able to marginalise his inner, toxic, follower voice. He then started to successfully rebuild the most important relationship in his life.

The power of self-talk

"Self-leadership is grounded in self-confidence ... Self-motivation is another intrinsic component of self-leadership ..."

Andrew Bryant

Self-motivation is probably the most important component of self-confidence. I have found that other people, or other external factors, can only motivate me for a short time. They can only take me to a certain point, which is certainly not far enough. Self-motivation generates personal energy that helps us to take action. We need to realise how important it is to motivate ourselves each day to grow in confidence. It is only up to me to motivate myself on a continuous basis to achieve my personal goals.

If we lack motivation, we are 'up the creek without a paddle', so to speak, and we will never achieve what we set ourselves to achieve in life. The secret to self-motivation that can unlock *all* of our potential, lies in our effective use of self-talk. The story of Andrew Bryant is a good example of someone who understood this. He used self-talk to successfully get his self-leadership journey back on track – even though it didn't happen immediately, and he needed professional help to get through adversity.

> "The only thing standing between you and your goal is the bullshit story you keep telling yourself as to why you can't achieve it."
>
> Jordan Belfort

The above quote summarises the impact of self-talk in the context of achieving our goals. The reality is that: As I think, I am. As I talk to myself, I will be. If our self-talk is not constructive, powerful and uplifting, then we are in trouble. Our self-talk then becomes a lethal time-bomb, and we start to convince ourselves of negative things – like the future is bleak or that we are not good enough to achieve our goals. Talk about self-destruction! Destroying ourselves, rather than building ourselves up to become better, more content, successful, and therefore able to contribute more to our family and to society, is, in my book, the definition of insanity!

If we ever realise that our self-talk is starting to spiral into negativity, then we need to do a quick reality check and ask ourselves if the negative thing that we are telling ourselves is the *real truth* or just *our truth*.

Our truth is our version of how things are, which is not always an accurate account of reality. Our truth is our perception, which is often a lie that we tell ourselves. Why do we do this? I can't give you the answer, but I can tell you that each one of us requires constant, positive attention to keep us on track and sufficiently robust to face the challenges that life throws at us. We are planted on Earth for a specific reason, but without being watered, nourished and fed, we die, also psychologically.

> "Positive self-talk is the key to any successful person. If you can change the voice in your mind, you can do anything!"
>
> Jaanu Dhingreja

If we make the mistake of using self-talk in a negative, destructive manner, then our psychological termination will be accelerated. In essence, we become guilty of psychological suicide. If we realise that we are even starting with negative self-talk, we need to tell ourselves immediately to stop, make a U-turn and get our self-talk back on track. We usually know when our inner voice talks sense versus when it is toxic; we just need to make the distinction and apply the necessary self-discipline to either listen to it or ignore it.

Negative self-talk is like bullying: If we pay attention to it, it will grow bigger and get worse. If we ignore it, it will eventually disappear. If we learn to consistently use self-talk in a positive manner, then we will give ourselves the edge in becoming successful self-leaders, and offer ourselves the best possible chance to successfully live, thrive and achieve our goals.

"If we can change the way we think, we can change the way we act."
Lou Tice

Our present thoughts determine our future – as does our ability to successfully use self-talk to our advantage. In every single moment in life, we have a permanent mentor with us, called "Self". Let's mentor ourselves to think of success, to apply profitable self-talk, and to reap the rewards from achieving our personal goals.

Do not sell yourself short

I recently used the above phrase to respond to a comment made by a friend. I thought that he was not portraying himself in a way that was doing him any justice. In my view, it sold him short and did not mirror his past and potential future accomplishments. His comment revealed to me that he didn't believe in himself. Or at least, that's how it seemed. The challenge that we all face is managing and dealing with negative or toxic thoughts in such a way that by the time we are about to verbalise disempowering thoughts, we should have replaced them with empowering thoughts. We need to do this before we convey to the world that we don't believe in ourselves, that we view the world negatively, or that we are not happy individuals.

"Your self-worth is more important than your net worth."
Raju Ghosh

You owe it to yourself to be your own best marketing manager – obviously without overdoing it and coming across as arrogant. If you don't feel comfortable talking with confidence about your abilities or potential, that's perfectly acceptable, but *don't* make the crucial mistake of talking yourself down in conversation with someone. Obviously, if we see a pattern developing in which we keep selling ourselves short by uttering words that are damaging to our self-confidence and we can't seem to break this pattern, then we need to seek help and talk to someone.

Only you can improve your self-confidence

"If you wouldn't say it to a friend, don't say it to yourself."

Jane Travis

I have experienced enough in my life to know that when all is said and done, you only have *you*. If we are not our own best friend when it comes to boosting our self-confidence by what we tell ourselves, then we have a problem – a serious problem. Building a healthy self-esteem is the foundation of successful self-leadership.[118] Since self-motivation and self-esteem go together, we need to believe that, when necessary, we can rely on ourselves. Our success in life is made easier with the help of others, but ultimately it is *us* who make the decisions and commit to not giving up on our dreams and goals.[119]

"No amount of self-improvement can make up for any lack of self-acceptance."

Robert Holden

We can't grow our self-confidence if we don't accept who we are, and if we can't love ourselves. We all make mistakes and have weaknesses, but I can't love and accept myself if I don't accept my faults as they are now, with the view that I am working with and on myself every day to improve these areas. If we love ourselves and accept the fact that we are all works in progress, then we have created the launchpad to further improve our self-confidence.

"I am good enough"

"Too many people overvalue what they are 'not' and undervalue what they 'are'."

Malcolm Forbes

For many years, before I got serious about making a success of my self-leadership story, I entertained feelings of not being good enough. I had this persistent need for recognition from others, and for them to tell me that I had done well. I can speculate about the root cause(s) of this, but I can't really put my finger on it. That is how I felt ... Period. If this resonates with you, find peace in the fact that you are not alone when you experience these toxic negative feelings – but what you do with these emotions is most important. If you don't deal with them, they will keep on dealing with you, until they eventually start to control or rule you. Nobody should tolerate these type of feelings. We all are worthy.

"Respect yourself and others will respect you."

Confucius

For me, the game-changer came when I took a hard look at my life and asked myself the question: "How much more do I still have to achieve in my life to prove to myself that I am actually doing well and that I am certainly good enough?" I couldn't answer that question, and that was when the penny dropped ... I realised that what I was feeling, was rubbish. I just couldn't entertain thoughts like that anymore. By using mindfulness, I was also able to rid myself of those thoughts if and when they occurred. Over time, and as a result, those thoughts occurred less and less ...

"The most important day is the day you decide you're good enough for you. It's the day you set yourself free."

Brittany Josephina

When we experience contaminated thoughts and feelings of inadequacy, we often think that we are unique in this regard, but we are not. I am a bit of a petrol-head, and earlier in my life I would literally watch every single lap of every Formula 1 race, season after season. Like so many, I was a devoted fan of Michael Schumacher. Having won seven World Championships, five of them back-to-back, he is widely regarded as one of the best to have ever graced the sport.

I recently came across an article that revealed, to my surprise, that Schumacher was plagued by self-doubt throughout his career.[120] That confession was made just two months before his tragic, life-changing skiing accident in 2013. He admitted that he felt he was not good enough, although that ultimately helped him to become so successful.

When I read that article about a living legend whom I admire, I realised that I was not alone and there must be many people out there who also feel: "I am not good enough."

There is a question that flows from this: Why, at some point in our lives, do people like Michael Schumacher and I entertain such venomous thoughts? The unfortunate reality is that every single person on this Earth, at some moment in their life, has had a similar feeling of not being good enough. Let's just acknowledge that it is part of our human nature. However, if this is a persistent feeling that you can't rid yourself of quickly, or if it lingers for long enough to adversely affect your self-confidence, then it is a problem, and something needs to be done about it. A good place to start would be: As soon as the thought of not being good enough enters your mind, affirm to yourself that you *are* good enough.

"An affirmation opens the door. It's a beginning point on the path to change."

Louise Hay

I read a quote early in my life: "I am good enough because God doesn't make junk." Although it stuck in the back of my mind, for a long time I never listened to it. However, now that I finally have, I am grateful to be able to share it with you.

As part of my daily affirmations, I tell myself: "I do have what it takes. I am worthy, I am certainly good enough, and I won't allow anyone, ever, to tell me anything different." By repeating this affirmation daily, I keep this feeling of insufficiency right where it belongs – in my life's 'Deleted' file. You can also do this with any other negative feeling or story that you tell yourself.

Only *you* can determine your worth and value. You are in control, you are the master of your fate, and you are the captain of your soul.

The acid test of self-confidence

The Dalai Lama wrote that with the realisation of our own potential, and self-confidence in our ability, we can build a better world. This aligns with the way I feel. Still, I have always asked myself: "What is the acid test of having enough self-confidence? When will I know that I am confident enough in myself and in my own abilities?"

I don't think that there is a simple answer here, but I do think that part of the answer includes: When you are comfortable to speak in front of people you don't know; when you are no longer intimidated by what people say about you; when you can handle criticism without dwelling on it for too long; when you are willing to take calculated risks and back yourself; when you can stand up for injustice, and when people laugh at you for making a mistake and you are able to laugh at yourself even louder than they do. If you can do all of these things, you have probably reached a point where your self-confidence has become one of your biggest assets that will bring you ample returns in your life.

REFLECTION ON THE CONTENT OF THIS CHAPTER – IMPROVING SELF-CONFIDENCE

Consider the topics that we have covered:

- The power of self-talk
- Do not sell yourself short
- Only you can improve your self-confidence
- "I am good enough"
- The acid test of self-confidence

Please rate your current overall level of success in Improving Self-confidence as a percentage score:

_____%

Chapter 12

Choosing to be Positive

"A negative thinker gives up when confronted with difficulty, but an optimist rises to the occasion when the going gets tough."

NORMAN VINCENT PEALE

Henry Flescher was born in Vienna, Austria, on 14 March 1924 into a Jewish family. As a young boy, his ambition was to become a doctor, but his education ended abruptly at age 14 when Nazi forces occupied Austria. Henry and his family were forced to leave Austria and flee to Belgium. In 1942, after receiving a letter from Germany, ordering him to report to a work camp, his parents hid money in one of his shoes and paid a stranger to smuggle him into France. He never saw his parents again.[121]

Henry was arrested in Lyon, France, and sent to Drancy, the major detention and transit camp for the deportation of Jews from the country. From there, Henry was transported by cattle car to Auschwitz, where 300 people were selected as workers for the camp. Henry was number 298. Those who were not chosen to work were sent to the gas chamber.

Enduring much pain and suffering, Henry was transferred from one camp to another. He was first taken to Ottmuth, a forced labour camp, where he worked to make shoes for the German army. After four weeks, he was transferred to Peiskretscham, a forced labour camp in Poland, where he worked 12 hours a day, carrying cement to build and repair bridges.

From Peiskretscham, he was transported to Blechammer, a satellite camp of Auschwitz, where he was tattooed with the number "177153". He spent two years at Blechammer. During that time, the Nazis broke his jaw with a rock and repeatedly lashed him with dog whips. He described his experience at Blechammer as: "Hell."[122]

While the Allied Forces were approaching Germany, Henry was marched from Blechammer to Gross-Rosen. From there, he was transported to Buchenwald, from which he endured a death march to Altenberg. On his third death march, Henry escaped and hid in a hen house until he saw American soldiers, whom he approached. They saved him.

After the war, Henry returned to Belgium, where he lived until moving to the United States in 1950. He had two daughters, three grandchildren, and two great-grandchildren.[123]

When asked about his Holocaust experiences, Henry Flescher responded that he did not dwell in the past, he always looked to the future. During his time in the Nazi camps, he had always stayed positive and lived for tomorrow. Henry was a happy, content person who loved every moment of his life. Even though he had endured the unthinkable, he said: "Most people are never happy and complain too much … Life is beautiful. No need to complain so much … We have one life to live, and you have to enjoy it. There is no room for hate in this world."[124]

Henry Flescher passed away on 29 August 2018 at the ripe old age of 94 years.[125]

Optimism is a choice

I do count my blessings, but probably not often enough. One of those blessings is being married to a wife who is never negative about anything. She always has an almost superhumanly positive outlook on life, which I have never really understood.

One fine morning over breakfast a couple of years ago, in a weak moment, I made a comment to Marilé. I can't even remember what that comment was, but I clearly remember her response to my pessimism. She said in a firm voice: "You know, to be positive in life is a choice …"

In that moment, I realised that she was right. I also realised that I had never before thought about the fact that it really is that simple. We are in charge, and we, therefore, can choose to be positive. In the same way, we have the option to choose to be negative. Before choosing either of these two options, we can also decide whether to let our circumstances determine our choice, or whether we will make the decision, regardless of the situation in which we find ourselves.

> **Realistic optimism**: When we accept that both good and bad things do happen, but we can make 'good' in either of these circumstances.[126]

Henry Flescher understood the concept of realistic optimism, and his whole approach to life was aligned to it.

"We can complain because rose bushes have thorns or rejoice because thorn bushes have roses."

Abraham Lincoln

I try my best to actively reject pessimism, because I came to the conclusion that if I entertain it, I cannot benefit in any way. The reality is that I, like everyone around me, only hurt as a result of my negativity. I choose to be optimistic, and linked to optimism is happiness; and happiness, just like unhappiness, is also a proactive choice.[127]

Successful self-leaders believe that, generally speaking, the world in which we live is a good place, and they are happy with life. Chances are that if you are optimistic and happy, you are also content and have a considerable amount of inner peace. That, I think, is something for which we are all striving.

"Optimism doesn't wait on facts. It deals with prospects."

Norman Cousins

The important role of constructive friendships

John Maxwell observes that having people around you with negative attitudes is like running a race with a ball and chain on your ankle.[128] I refuse to surround myself with negative people because they either pull me down or irritate me. They don't live by a value about which I feel strongly. I choose to only have friends who are optimistic about the present and future, and who believe in living life to the fullest ...

"Anything is possible when you have the right people there to support you."

Misty Copeland

I pick friends with a likeminded approach to life because, as the saying goes: "Iron sharpens iron." I choose friends I can talk to, who listen to me, and who keep me accountable if they see me stray off the path of successful self-leadership. I want friends who want the best for me, are there for me in bad times, and who will celebrate with me in good times. Very importantly, I try my utmost to be the same kind of friend to them ... I can recommend this approach to friendship, as it contributes to constructive, lasting relationships, which also support us in maintaining a positive approach to life. Besides, we are not meant to journey through life on our own.

Find your passion and then live with passion

Life is too short to be mediocre, especially when it comes to those things that we really enjoy.[129] When we are passionate about something, it's contagious, and very often we impart in other people an electrical charge to feel that same amount of passion. People admire those who are passionate about something, or about a cause that is pure and just. It is, therefore, important that we find our passion in life and identify those areas that makes us tick. When it comes to our career, or making a living, Mark Twain said that if we find a job that we enjoy doing, then we will never have to work a day in our lives. If we choose to live a positive life, then passion for what we do, while choosing to be around people with passion, supports such a life.

"A life without passion is not living, it's merely existing."

Leo Buscaglia

At the age of 50, I have finally found my passion in my career. I can honestly say that for the first time ever, I truly enjoy what I am doing. I trust that it does not take you as long. I sincerely hope that you are also feeling the same amount of passion for your career. I would suggest, though, that, if you can no longer do your work with passion, then you need to find out why and do something about it – for your sake, the sake of those people around you and for the sake of the organisation for which you work.

First and foremost, you need to make sure that the problem does not lie with you though, before you decide to make a career move. The reality is that we take ourselves to wherever we go – if you are the reason for the lack of passion that you experience in your current career, then you will in all probability also experience the same lack of passion in another career. It all starts with Self. Whatever the reason might be for the lack of passion that you might be experiencing – trust me, it's not worth doing something that doesn't get you up every morning with a spring in your step and a smile on your dial.

Privilege

When my son, who was 17 at the time, shared his wisdom with me about making an impact in this world a priority in life, it made me reflect on being an African. It confirmed in my own mind that I will see out my last days, whenever that might be, on this continent. There is no other place on Earth where I would rather be. I guess that's why the saying goes: "There is no place like home."

The fact that each one of us calls somewhere else home is great, because otherwise we all would live in the same place, which is obviously not possible. Whenever I travel overseas and land back at OR Tambo Airport in Johannesburg, I always jokingly tell the immigration officer: "I am back!" When she or he responds by saying: "Welcome back," then I know I am right back where I belong – at home.

"The secret of happiness is to count your blessings while others are adding up their troubles."

William Penn

There is another reason why I choose to be an optimist, and I can probably ascribe this to privilege, which I suppose is linked to obligation. People in

CHAPTER 12: CHOOSING TO BE POSITIVE

sub-Saharan Africa are more than twice as likely to live in poverty than those in South Asia, which is the next poorest region globally. Sub-Saharan Africa also accounted for roughly 60% of the global population living in poverty in 2020. About 40% of people in Africa (550 million people) live on less than US$1.90 a day.[130] These are just a couple of the shocking poverty statistics of this continent. So, I came to the conclusion that I cannot dare moan or be negative, because I am privileged when compared to all of those people. I am not better than they are, but I am more privileged. I have no reason to complain – ever. It is also my privilege to be and stay positive, and Africa is where I would like to make a positive impact on the lives of others. Right here.

The power of thought

Marcus Aurelius was the great philosopher who ruled the Roman Empire from 161–180 CE. He was the last of the rulers known as the Five Good Emperors. He was famous for saying: "Our life is what our thoughts make it."

We need to learn to fill our minds with good, positive and constructive thoughts, because we are what we think, and we become what we continue to think.[131]

I was an active karateka for many years, until I sustained a labrum tear in my left hip – probably as a result of too much kicking and not enough suppleness. I enjoyed this sport not necessarily because I enjoyed the physical confrontation, but because I was really attracted to the combination of art and discipline, which kept me fit, too.

As a boy, one of my heroes was Bruce Lee – and I still think he is an icon. He said that what we habitually think largely determines what we will ultimately become. These words are a great summary of the power of our thoughts. If we fill our minds with good thoughts, then good will come from that. If we fill our minds with garbage, though, the results could be devastating to our success as self-leaders.

A vocabulary of positivity

A negative word is symbolic of failure, and it is important that we remove these potentially harmful words from our vocabularies.[132] It is also important to our self-preservation that we adopt a positive approach when choosing our words – not only sometimes, but always. I used to say: "I have to go to work." Then at some point, I realised that if I "have to" go to work every day, then frankly I have the wrong job and I need to rather choose another career in which I "want to" go to work.

It helps that I am now running my own business, which focuses on something that I love doing. I now specifically focus on including "I want to" phrases in my vocabulary, instead of "I have to". For example, I choose to say: "I want to go to gym," as opposed to "I have to go to gym." It's actually disempowering to give someone else, or the organisation for which we work, power over us. Effectively, we are making a statement that we have no power or authority over our own lives if we say: "I have to," which is not true. Remember, as self-leaders, we have decided to take charge of our lives. We are in charge. Therefore, we don't "have to" do anything that we don't "want to" do.

"Words can inspire, and words can destroy. Choose yours well."
Robin Sharma

Another example in my life in which I made a conscious decision to eliminate a specific word from my vocabulary is to never use the word "suffer", or "suffering", when referring to myself. This is not the kind of word that we use when we have decided to take charge of our lives. It portrays us as a victim. As self-leaders, we are not victims, we are leaders. Instead of "suffer", I would use the word "experience". "I have experienced something that was not ideal, and I have learned a great deal from it …"

Attitude determines altitude

The above words are part of a well-known quote by Edwin Louis Cole that I had stuck on my office wall for many years. I kept it to not only remind myself of its power, but also to remind every single person who entered my office, especially the members of my team.

In his book, *The Spirit of Leadership*, Myles Munroe writes: "*Attitude dictates your response to the present and determines the quality of your future ... It is the servant that can open the doors of life or close the gates of possibility ... The distinguishing factor between a winner or a loser is attitude.*"[133]

I think this is an exceptionally good description of the power or influence that the right or wrong attitude can have in our lives.

"Two things define you: your patience when you have nothing and your attitude when you have everything."

Morgan Freeman

Attitude is so important in our lives that it is critical we pick a positive one. An attitude of: "It can be done," becomes a self-fulfilling prophecy.[134] An attitude of: "I can," motivates and builds our self-confidence. Unfortunately, the opposite is also true.

"Being positive won't guarantee you'll succeed. But being negative will guarantee you won't."

Jon Gordon

If we have an attitude of "I can't," then we have a guarantee that we won't succeed. Theodore Roosevelt wrote that if we believe we can, then we are halfway there. In my mind, it's quite simple: We need to make an "I can" attitude part of the way that we think, feel and act. That way, we will make our self-leadership story a successful one in which we achieve our personal goals, and more.

I grew up with the old question that everyone always asks to determine attitude: "Is the glass half-full or half-empty?" I realised early in life that our attitude is simply the way that we choose to see things. When we have to leave for work and it's rainy and miserable outside, we can greet the day, thinking: "What a miserable, gloomy day." Or we can adopt the attitude: "Great! We need to fill our dams for winter. What a miracle! What an amazing day this is to experience nature at its best." I don't know about you, but I choose the latter attitude towards life and all of its challenges.

Sometimes, life will change without permission, but our attitude will determine the success of our journey … I am far from perfect, and there are obviously some days when my attitude is not absolutely aligned with my good intentions. From personal experience, though, I can recommend that we all adopt an attitude that allows us to choose to become a better person by the time we get out the other side of the dark times in our lives. It is simply the best possible option we can choose. Any other would be suboptimal, and it wouldn't give us the life we deserve or are capable of living.

REFLECTION ON THE CONTENT OF THIS CHAPTER – CHOOSING TO BE POSITIVE

Consider the topics that we have covered:

- Optimism is a choice
- The important role of constructive friendships
- Find your passion and then live with passion
- Privilege
- The power of thought
- A vocabulary of positivity
- Attitude determines altitude

Please rate your current overall level of success in Choosing to be Positive as a percentage score:

_____%

Chapter 13

Stepping out of Your Comfort Zones

"Life begins at the end of your comfort zone."
NEALE DONALD WALSCH

Businessman Patrice Motsepe was South Africa's first black billionaire. Despite growing up during the apartheid era, Motsepe fared better than most other people. His father, once banished for voicing opposition to apartheid, became a successful liquor distributor through an affiliation with South African Breweries. Throughout his youth, Motsepe worked at his father's store and in his beer hall. These jobs taught him crucial lessons in business management and exposed him to the lives of the mine workers who frequented the store.

Largely because of his father's opposition to South Africa's segregated schooling system, Motsepe and his six siblings attended a Roman Catholic boarding school in the Eastern Cape province. He then went on to complete his tertiary studies and graduated as a lawyer before joining the law firm of Bowman Gilfillan in 1988. He became a partner in 1993. When Bowman Gilfillan reorganised in the post-apartheid era, Motsepe made a big career move and left the firm to apply his business acumen to the mining trade. He believed that he could use management techniques, such as low base pay coupled with production incentives, to transform less productive shafts into money-making operations.[135]

In 1994, Motsepe founded mine services company Future Mining. In his new venture, he utilised all of his life experience, knowledge of the mining trade and its workers, his entrepreneurship, school connections, and an understanding of political and legal structures. In 1997, he launched African Rainbow Minerals (ARM), which merged with Harmony Gold in 2003, and then acquired Anglovaal Mining. Motsepe was named Chairman of the newly reorganised ARM in 2004. By 2006, the company had expanded beyond gold and other metals into coal mining.

Motsepe is not only someone who made his fortune through mining interests, but he is also an important role model in our country. In 2013, he donated half of his wealth to charity. That money is managed by the Motsepe Foundation, which was created to give back to his fellow South Africans. It supports, educates and helps people in need, with the ultimate goal of rendering them self-sustaining and independent.[136]

Patrice Motsepe understands the significance of getting out of one's comfort zone, especially when it comes to one's career. As a partner at Bowman Gilfillan and at the dawn of a new South Africa, he must have been poised to benefit from a bright future when black law partners would have been in high demand and as scarce as hen's teeth. Yet he made the bold move to choose a new, different career, which ultimately not only benefited him, but also many needy South Africans with whom he was willing to share his wealth. If he hadn't stepped out of his comfort zone to venture into something different, none of these achievements would have been possible ...

Your past can strengthen your future

I grew up in a loving, yet conservative environment, and because I was raised in a small town, I was shielded in many ways from the outside world. I lived in my own 'bubble', without an awareness of all the challenges and negative forces out in the real world. All of this changed when I went to the University of Pretoria to study BSc Agriculture, almost 400km away.

At university, I got involved with the Day Student First Year Committee even before classes started. In so doing, I set myself up for failure before I had even begun. Instead of taking my studies seriously, I seriously partied. Instead of supporting Van Schaik (bookstore) as a brand, I quickly became a loyal supporter of the Castle Lager (beer) brand. The introvert in me died a rapid death and I transformed into a socialite. I certainly got out of my comfort zone, but in the wrong way.

"Don't be fooled by the calendar. There are only as many days in the year as you make use of."

Charles Richards

Socialising was one escape from the responsibility, and perceived burden, of attending classes. The other escape was watching movies. I would never miss a new movie release. One of those was *Dead Poets Society*,[137] which opened in June 1989, mid-way through my first year of university.

That phenomenal movie generated worldwide box office revenue of almost $240 million.[138] In the film, Todd Anderson (Ethan Hawke) starts high school at Welton Academy, an elite, all-male institution, in 1959. He is taught by John Keating (Robin Williams), the new English teacher and a Welton alumnus himself, who inspires his students through his teaching of poetry.

John Keating fascinates his students with his unorthodox teaching methods, and encourages them to make their lives extraordinary. He summarises this with the Latin term: *"Carpe Diem"*. Keating actively inspires his students to break the mould and to be more than they ever dreamed that they could be. As part of this process, he takes them on a journey to question the status quo, and to do things that are totally out of their comfort zones.

When I first watched *Dead Poets Society*, I didn't take particular note of the message of *"Carpe Diem"*. I am confident, though, that in some way, it contributed to me living my life on my terms, and that it helped me to get out of my own comfort zones.

I share this experience with you because sometimes in life, we regret that we have spent time on wasted activities, but then later realise that it was actually part of the process that helped mould us and make us better self-leaders.

Criteria for stepping out of our comfort zones

Jack Steyn is one of the local legends of the tissue paper industry, and as a young manager, I had the privilege of working with him for many years. He used to say to me: "Most people dream, but only a few actually wake up to make their dreams a reality." That always stuck with me, and his wisdom was top of mind when I decided to step out of my comfort zone and leave the corporate world to start my own business. What Jack meant was that only a few people have the courage to move out of their comfort zones and actively chase their dreams. I decided to make the move and to chase my dreams because I realised that if I didn't do it at that time, then I never would. That would have been a sad mistake.

"Two roads diverged in a wood, and I –
I took the one less travelled by,
And that has made all the difference."

The road not taken – Robert Frost

Sometimes we need to conquer our fears and take the road less travelled in order to realise that that decision made all of the difference to our lives. Unfortunately, this is something that too many people are too scared to do. But we don't just wake up one day, decide that we are going to make our dreams a reality, and pick the road that most people are not willing to journey on. A couple of things first need to be put in place before we can make such a bold move. I can assure you that someone like Patrice Motsepe also had these two things in place before he ventured down the road of entrepreneurship to chase his dreams:

Trust and belief. This includes trust in God's plan for our lives and/or in our own abilities. Trusting and believing in our own abilities relies partly on having the right skills to confidently move out of our comfort zones into a new environment. We might want to acquire these skills before we make this move.

"You must either modify your dreams or magnify your skills."

Jim Rohn

Courage, lots of courage. Being able to face and conquer our fears. I shall elaborate upon this further in the next section.

A third potential prerequisite to making a move, which I think can be classified as 'optional', is including in our own credo something that embodies our personal commitment to stepping out of our comfort zones.

Every January I watch as much of the Dakar Rally as I possibly can, bearing in mind that our local television coverage is limited to about 30 minutes per race stage. The Dakar slogan is "Dream. Dare. Live it". I think this is a great way to summarise this point.

Courage – to face our fears and conquer them

Courage is one of the five core values that we, as mentors, teach our boys at The Character Company.[139] If we want to be successful at achieving our personal goals, especially the stretch goals that make us slightly nervous, then we need to be courageous. On top of this, we need to have faith in our own abilities, as well as the self-confidence to go for it.

As a little boy, I used to watch cowboy movies. John Wayne defined courage as being scared to death but saddling up anyway. Still, it is important that we don't confuse courage with recklessness. In my mind, courage means that we acknowledge that very few things are guaranteed in life, but we are not scared to take calculated risks that make us feel slightly uncomfortable. We do this because we believe they will add value to our lives. If we don't have courage, then we won't be willing to step out of our comfort zones, especially when it comes to the big steps of making our life dreams a reality.

"Life will only change when you become more committed to your dreams than you are to your comfort zone."

Billy Cox

Many years ago, while preparing for a conference presentation, I came across two meanings of F-E-A-R, which typically describe our fight-or-flight response to the feeling:

Forget Everything And Run
or
Face Everything And Rise!

I once read that the fear through which we move when we go to the edge of our limits actually causes our limits to expand.[140]

> When you are too scared to do something that you suspect you would learn from, and you know would add value to your life, ask yourself two questions:
>
> - "What is the worst that could happen?"
> - "Am I the first person ever to attempt this?"

Are you facing a "one-small-step-for-man-but-one-giant-leap-for-mankind" moment, like Neil Armstrong did when he became the first man to ever set foot on the moon? Or are you simply one of many others who have successfully attempted what you are too scared to try?

If you are attempting something that has never been done before, then obviously, before you take the giant leap, consider all of the risks and how they can possibly be mitigated. Chances are, 99% of the things that you are too scared to try have been done many times before, so you can actually ditch your fears and go for it.

"Do the thing you fear to do and keep on doing it ... That is the quickest and surest way ever yet discovered to conquer fear."
Dale Carnegie

John Maxwell wrote that the greatest mistake we make is living in constant fear that we will make one. When I was looking for my first real job after graduating with a B.Com degree in Finance, I encountered the conundrum that everyone was looking for people with experience, yet nobody was willing to give a guy like me the opportunity to gain the experience in the first place. The same goes for mistakes: We can't be scared of making mistakes if we are not willing to run the risk of making them in the first place. Nobody deliberately makes mistakes, but the reality is that our fear of making them robs us of the opportunity to grow and move closer to achieving our personal goals.

If you are too scared to potentially make a big mistake, rather start by potentially making a small one, because then you don't really have much to lose in the process.

Baby steps are necessary for us adults, too. Since you have strong faith in yourself and in your abilities, your chance of achieving success in something that is not really a stretch, is high. This will give you the confidence to attempt a bigger challenge, which will probably also be a success, allowing you to experience all of the benefits of that, including personal growth.

If, in the unlikely event that you get your risk calculations wrong and you do make a mistake, then you can simply rely on the self-leadership stepping stones that we have already discussed to carry you through, such as getting through tough times and becoming more resilient. Practice makes perfect, though, and the more I practise getting out of my comfort zones and the less fear I have in this regard, the more I develop as a person and the more confidence I gain.

"Thinking will not overcome fear but action will."

W. Clement Stone

The extreme alternative to conquering our fears, which allows us to escape our comfort zones, is depriving ourselves of the wonderful opportunity to dare. In that case, we only exist; we do not truly live. Or, we can go out into this world and really live, which will make us smile at the end of our journey and leave us with a feeling of: "What a ride this has been!" I have no doubt that you would choose the right option and focus on ridding yourself of your fears.

Give yourself permission to experience discomfort

I realised early enough in my life that when it comes to achieving my personal goals, I should see discomfort as my friend. Once we view discomfort in this context, as part of personal growth and gain, then we can allow ourselves to go to places where we have never been able, or willing, to go before. The results in our lives can be quite surprising.

> If the thought or the fear of discomfort is too daunting, then ask yourself the following question:
>
> "If I am old one day, would I tell myself that I should have taken fewer chances in life?"

In my case, I would not even consider such a question. I would always wonder how those chances could have worked out, had I been willing to take them. The saying goes: "Nothing ventured, nothing gained." Give yourself permission to step out of your comfort zone and to explore the good things in life. You owe it to yourself, and you'll be amazed at what the results can be.

"Discomfort is the sign you are on the right track."
Jeff Goins

I believe that one of the differences between successful and unsuccessful people is that successful people are willing to endure the discomfort for long enough, and to push through to eventually benefit from it in some form of success.

Where the learning and growing takes place

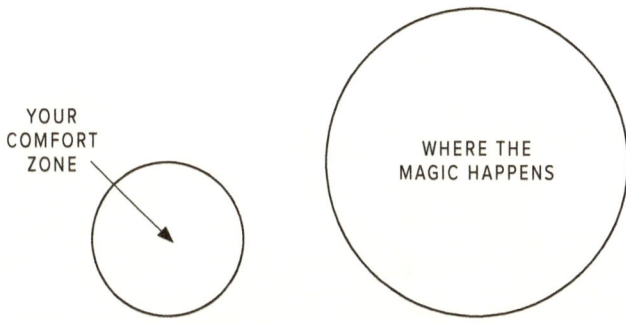

The above illustration very simply shows that the magic and the learning happens outside of our comfort zones.

"If we are growing, we are always going to be outside our comfort zone."
John Maxwell

This growth is going to happen both professionally and privately. However, you cannot force yourself out of your comfort zone, because you won't allow yourself to go far away from what is familiar to you. You first need to learn to visualise and practise in your mind's eye what it will be like to be in the new situation.

This alone is not enough, though. You then need to combine visualisation with affirmations of already being in the future environment – albeit in the present tense. If you visualise and affirm enough times to already place yourself in the new situation that represents your personal goal, then you will find ways of getting there, and you will be drawn towards this goal, which is typically out of your current comfort zone.

Diversity and inclusion

We as humans are social creatures – up to a point. That point is where most people begin to feel a little uncomfortable, as they need to engage with people who are different from them. It is fascinating to see how so many people are scared to cross these boundaries.

> "We may have different religions, different languages, different coloured skin, but we all belong to one human race."
>
> Kofi Annan

Kofi Annan's words highlight the fact that there is no reason why we should not be willing to actively get out of our comfort zones to connect with people of different cultures, languages, skin colours, religions and social status – especially on our continent and in our country, with its richness in diversity. Removing ourselves from this comfort zone has to be a personal goal that we set ourselves. We must embrace diversity and inclusion as a way of learning more from one another.

> "Africa is one continent, one people and one nation."
>
> Kwame Nkrumah

There have been many times in my life when I felt too scared to start connecting with people who were different from me, but when I actually stepped out of my comfort zone and made the effort, I was always glad I had. Through this process and these experiences, I learned so much and became richer for it.

On one such occasion, I took Marilé to the local Soweto soccer derby at the FNB Stadium in Johannesburg to watch Orlando Pirates, her team, and Kaizer Chiefs, my team, face off on 27 October 2018. I am fortunate to have had many stadium experiences in my life, including games at the Emirates Cup in London in 2015, but I have never experienced anything close to that day. We experienced such a warm embrace from fellow supporters in our own backyard – despite the fact that our skin colour probably made up less than 0,5% of those in attendance. One way that we will fix our world is if we make more of an effort to cross the bridges between us to meet those people whom we deem to be 'different'. Only then will we reap the real rewards of being one world and one global nation.

A life-long commitment to growth

> "Work harder on yourself than you do on your job."
>
> Jim Rohn

True leaders possess a passion for personal development.[141] We must never become so busy with sawing that we don't take time to sharpen our saw.[142] What will carry us through to a good finish is our desire and determination to keep growing.[143] To me, a life-long commitment to learning and self-development, as part of continuous growth, represents the essence of self-leadership.

Self-leaders focus on improving themselves on a continuous basis. They also keep in check with what is current and ensure that they don't fall behind others. Growth and self-development have a positive psychological effect, as every time we learn something new, we feel like we have achieved something, also as a result of being brave enough to step out of our comfort zones.

"Great leaders encourage leadership development. By openly developing themselves."

Marshall Goldsmith

A willingness to have crucial conversations

> **A crucial conversation**: A discussion between two or more people where (1) stakes are high, (2) opinions vary, and (3) emotions run strong."[144]

Part of being willing to step out of our comfort zones is having the courage to face conflict and engage in crucial conversations. If we are too scared to have these adult conversations in which we tackle the issue and not the person, as part of getting to a solution, then we will bounce around in life like a ball in a pinball machine.

"When there is trust, conflict becomes nothing but the pursuit of truth, an attempt to find the best possible answer."

Patrick Lencioni

We have to be willing to face conflict because we learn from these crucial conversations. We need to understand, though, that although crucial conversations are acceptable, it is aggression in these conversations that is not acceptable. The only win-win is to take the emotion out of abrasive conversations or interactions, and stick to the facts.

We need to take charge of our conversations. There can be no verbal war if I am not willing to enter into verbal war. By encouraging meaningful debate, our lives and the life of the person on the other side of the debate become richer.

Embracing change and new ideas

"The measure of intelligence is the ability to change."

Albert Einstein

By this standard set by Einstein, I had a relatively low intellect for many decades. My ability and willingness to change was poor. As in many things in life, I am a late bloomer in this regard. Part of stepping out of our comfort zone is embracing change and new ideas.

Over the past couple of years, I have learned to embrace change and how important this can be. My biggest fear, but dream, was to start a business in something in which I really have an interest. Why would I fear this, you might ask? The answer is quite simple: I have been raised to follow the path with the lowest financial risk. However, this can only be an excuse up to a point.

Despite all the great things that my dad taught me, and the positive influence he had on my life, he constantly reminded me that starting one's own business is a bad idea: Chances are it will fail and I will go bankrupt. However, I realised at some point that I needed to break out of that mould …

"If you want something you've never had, you must be willing to do something you've never done."

Thomas Jefferson

REFLECTION ON THE CONTENT OF THIS CHAPTER – STEPPING OUT OF YOUR COMFORT ZONES

Consider the topics that we have covered:

- Your past can strengthen your future
- Criteria for stepping out of our comfort zones
- Courage – to face our fears and conquer them
- Give yourself permission to experience discomfort
- Where the learning and growing takes place
- Diversity and inclusion
- A life-long commitment to growth
- A willingness to have crucial conversations
- Embracing change and new ideas

Please rate your current overall level of success in Stepping out of Your Comfort Zones as a percentage score:

_____%

Chapter 14

Learning and Living Good Habits

"In a nutshell, your health, wealth, happiness, fitness, and success depend on your habits."

JOANNA JAST

Habit: A settled or regular tendency or practice, especially one that is hard to give up.[145]

To learn and live good habits is another cornerstone of successful self-leadership. It also defines who we are. In my view, good habits support healthy thoughts, positive feelings and emotionally intelligent behaviour.

At the beginning of 2020, the world's 2 153 billionaires had more wealth than the 4,6 billion people who made up 60% of our planet's population.[146] I would submit that one of the main reasons for their wealth would be that they learned, and are living, good habits.

"Successful people are simply those with successful habits."

Brian Tracy

According to Harvard Health Publishing,[147] the top habits to support heart, artery and lung health are:
1. Stopping smoking cigarettes, cigars and pipes.
2. Becoming active by ideally exercising at least 30 minutes a day.
3. Aiming for a healthy weight, especially by shedding excess weight around our waists.
4. Brightening up our diet with fruits, vegetables, whole grains, unsaturated fats and good protein, and avoiding processed foods, rapidly digested carbs and sugar.
5. Drinking alcohol in moderation.

Some of the bad habits that can negatively affect our mental health are:[148]
1. Perfectionism. This could result in our dissatisfaction with anything less than perfection, a preoccupation with failure or disapproval, and seeing mistakes as evidence of unworthiness.
2. Guilt. This could magnify our problems, as we claim responsibility for creating or resolving problems that had little or nothing to do with us. It could also result in us refusing to forgive ourselves.
3. A failure mindset. This could potentially lead to anxiety and depression, as these negative thoughts discourage us from setting goals, thus diminishing the value of our natural talents and magnifying our missteps.
4. The overuse of social media. This promotes feelings of inadequacy, jealousy and loneliness.
5. A lack of sleep. This adversely affects our ability to build physical and emotional resilience.

I deliberately chose these 10 habits that are obviously important to our physical and mental health. Even though they are basic habits that we ought to have mastered already, it would be interesting to give yourself a percentage score and gauge the extent to which you are actually living these good habits, or steering away from bad habits.

Poor physical and psychological health habits could be pulling us down and standing between us and being the best that we can possibly be. The irony is that we almost always know what our bad habits are, but we don't ditch them owing to a lack of discipline or willpower. Some people even have a fatalistic approach to learning and living good habits. They try to argue, for example, that they know someone who is 80 years old who smokes like a chimney and drinks like a fish. People like this lose the argument on a couple of fronts, and frankly miss the point. We cannot try to justify unhealthy habits by comparing ourselves with the exception to the rule. It's all about one's quality of living.

> "We first make our habits, and then our habits make us."
>
> John Dryden

If you are 70 years old, have tar-filled lungs and a liver the size of a football, you cannot come close to having the same quality of life as Gary Player at age 85. The same goes for adopting bad psychological habits. Aristotle claimed that we are what we repeatedly do, and that excellence is then not an act, but a habit. It is, therefore, important that what we repeatedly choose to do is aligned to our personal goals as self-leaders, to be able to live our lives to our full potential. It is simple: Good habits support a whole and complete life, but bad habits don't.

Focus on habits that make a meaningful contribution

At this stage of our self-leadership journey together, I need to add a disclaimer: I am not underestimating my 'audience', and I won't insult you by covering the no-brainer habits, like brushing your teeth, dressing properly, watching less television and drinking more water. Although I do think these are all good habits, I am only choosing to share with you those habits that I have, over the years, realised make a meaningful contribution to keeping my self-leadership journey on track.

Start by releasing bad habits

I have learned from experience that before we can focus on identifying and learning good habits to live by, we first need to focus on releasing or unlearning our bad habits. The reality, though, is that breaking bad habits takes time, hard work, practice and lots of determination. There is no reason why, if we've learned them, that we cannot unlearn them. We are in control, remember?

It all starts with motivation, and the first step is to convince ourselves that we need to get rid of a habit that is bad for us, or bad for the people around us. Other people can convince us up to a point, but if we are not 100% convinced ourselves, the change will never be sustainable.

As a young man at university and in the army, I used to smoke. Looking back, it seems silly that I ever did it. So many people told me that it was a mistake because it was unhealthy, expensive and made me smell. For a long time, all of their arguments fell on deaf ears, until one day I decided that I wanted to stop smoking. However, I could only do it with the right motivation …

> "It always seems impossible until it's done."
>
> Nelson Mandela

To prove that you have the right motivation and are serious enough to part ways with a bad habit, you need to say to yourself: "The last time that I performed the bad habit, was the last time." If you tell yourself: "The next time will be the last time," then you are definitely not at a point yet where you have the right motivation to rid yourself of the bad habit.

Everyone speculates about the amount of time it takes to unlearn an old habit, or to form a new one, but the reality is that there is no hard and fast rule, and no one-size-fits-all time frame. Some habits are easier to form than others, and some people may find it easier to develop certain behaviours. There is no right or wrong timeline. The only timeline that matters is the one that works best for you.[149]

What is important is that we constantly do our own assessment and take into account the feedback from others as to which habit is causing a problem in our lives. Just as my swimming coach advises me to only focus on one aspect of my freestyle correction at a time, it also doesn't make sense to try to focus on more than one habit correction at a time.

Start by addressing your most damaging bad habit first. Identifying and being mindful of our weak habits and managing them form part of our continuous improvement process. It is not a once-off habit review; we need to constantly review what our bad habits are in order to actively work on releasing them.

Once we have released the number one-priority habit, then we need to do another review to identify the next one that needs to exit our lives. There is no reason why we cannot get rid of all of our bad habits – especially if we use the tools that I have been sharing with you thus far, including self-talk, visualisation and affirmations.

"The best way to break a bad habit is to drop it."

Leo Aikman

By focusing on addressing our worst habit, we can, with enough effort, discipline and willpower, conquer it. We need to be wary, though, of the fact that we cannot stop working on eliminating this habit, even when it has seemingly disappeared. Old habits do indeed die hard. Yes, we can spend less effort on eliminating them from our lives, because we might have broken the proverbial camel's back, but the seed of the bad habit will always be present in our lives, waiting to be watered again in order to start growing back. I quit smoking almost 30 years ago and, to this day, when someone lights a cigarette next to me and I smell the nicotine, it awakens something in me that tries to draw me back into the habit.

"The only proper way to eliminate bad habits is to replace them with good ones."

Jerome Hines

When we scrap a bad habit from our lives, it's important that we don't replace it with a new bad habit. When I quit smoking, I replaced it with eating more, which is typically what happens. This is not necessarily a bad thing, but it was in my case, because I ate everything I came across, including junk food, like chocolates and sweets. Even though I was in the army at the time, I gained 8kg over a period of three months.

If I had only focused on eating healthy foods, like more fruit, nuts and vegetables, and drinking more water, then I would not have gained nearly as much weight. Replacing a bad habit with a good habit is a highly effective strategy, but we can't make the mistake of replacing a bad habit with another bad habit, because then all of the effort and frustration that we have experienced will have been pointless.

Being neat is more than just being neat

At this point I wouldn't blame you if you thought: "But hang on, Hekkie, you promised me earlier that you wouldn't share any no-brainer habits …" You are absolutely right. Being neat ought to be a no-brainer habit that we learn and live, but it's a topic worth talking about, as it overlaps with so many other good habits and areas of our lives. Being neat and organised adds to your value as a person. It shows that we respect ourselves, our belongings and also other people. In my mind, it is a way of showing what we think of ourselves. Unfortunately, we cannot only be neat in one area of our lives. Like most habits, it needs to transcend all areas.

"It does not require money, to live neat, clean and dignified."

Mahatma Gandhi

Stay current and up-to-date

Staying current and up-to-date with local and international news and events is one of the best habits you can ever teach yourself. Not only will you be aware of what is happening in the world, but you will also be able to benefit from the opportunities out there. The cherry on the top is that in conversations with other people, you will also come across as informed, which most people respect. For a very long time, I ignored the news, because at some point I had just grown tired of all the negativity in the media. I then realised that I could not keep ignoring the facts. Slowly but surely, I learned the habit of making it my business to know, on a daily basis, what is happening out there.

Why routine matters

From personal experience, I can tell you that routine helps us to reinforce good habits. It makes us more efficient and provides us with structure to our daily activities, which supports our personal planning process. There are also many more benefits, like saving time; reducing procrastination; getting to complete priority tasks; building and keeping momentum; building self-confidence, and ultimately assisting us in achieving our personal goals.[150] It is, therefore, in our own interests to create a routine that includes all of the important things that we would like to cover in our lives, especially in stressful times.[151] Furthermore, having a good routine forms part of a healthy lifestyle.[152]

"The secret of your future is hidden in your daily routine."
Mike Murdock

I have found that what works extremely well in my life is taking all of the important things that I sometimes battle to perform and making them part of my routine, without accepting the excuses that the follower in me would like to dish up to not include them in a healthy lifestyle. For example, exercising now forms part of my daily routine, and I no longer wonder if I should take the dog for a run on one day, or train in the pool the next. It is part of my routine, and my routine includes all of those important things that I *want to* do. Moving these types of activities into my daily or weekly routine allows me to do them automatically without making them an issue. Even more critically, it allows me to focus my real efforts and energy on all of the activities that I do to achieve my personal goals and, ultimately, my dreams.

Put your pride in your pocket

We all struggle with issues of pride and ego – every single one of us. In its worst form, this sometimes surfaces as arrogance, or an aversion to accountability. Steve Farrar describes pride as a degenerative eye disease that gradually blinds us, although its progress is so slow that we don't even realise we're losing our spiritual vision, until it's too late.[153] What we must realise early in our lives is that if we manage to put our pride in our pocket, that does not mean that we are losers.

> "With pride, there are many curses. With humility, there come many blessings."
>
> Ezra Taft Benson

If we don't get into the habit of managing pride in our lives, it can be toxic. I think a great reality check on whether you have a handle on this aspect of your life is to see whether you are too proud to take advice from people who are much younger than you. I am fortunate to have sons who have figured out life to a much greater degree than I had at their age. Chris, as a 16-year-old young man, will every so often add a valid and wise comment or two to our conversations, and even correct what I have said or done. Who am I to not listen to what he says, and to not use his wisdom the next time around?

"Yes, but ..." and "Pause ... engage"

Don't you just hate it when you tell someone something and they reply with a quick: "Yes, but ..." without even considering what you have just told them? For a long time, I used to be a "Yes, but ..." guy. I used to be that person who thought my view of most things was the only correct one. What a bad habit and big mistake that was. What I did not realise was that every time I responded that way, I was not only being disrespectful, but I was also immediately discrediting or disqualifying what the other person had said without even first considering her or his statement.

> "Most people do not listen with the intent to understand; they listen with the intent to reply."
>
> Stephen Convey

That brings me to my next point – "Pause ... engage" are the last two words of the phrase that the referee used to call out to set the scrum in rugby. I have found them extremely useful in helping to eliminate "Yes, but ..." from my vocabulary. By repeating these two words quietly in my mind, I teach myself to first process and think before I react after someone has spoken to me. Before we criticise someone's idea, first think it through properly and then ask yourself whether it could actually work. If we adopt this approach, then we not only convey respect, but we also do ourselves a favour by really considering the other person's opinion as a feasible alternative or solution to a problem.

The importance of active listening

Taking note and processing what other people say, before we respond to it, is only a small part of learning and living the habit of listening effectively. Richard Branson said that we need to lead by listening, because to be good leaders, we have to be great listeners.

Most of us know the story of the *RMS Titanic* that hit an iceberg and sank to the bottom of the Atlantic Ocean on the night of 14 April 1912, killing more than 1 500 people. What most of us don't know is that this tragedy might have been averted if the right people had applied the most basic communication skill – listening.

The first-hand, real-time record of what happened that night reveals several wireless messages from a collection of ships, including the *Titanic*, giving each other safety information via morse code. It is a telegraphic narrative that reveals that other ships in the same area as the *Titanic* had given her detailed advice and warnings about the location of icebergs. Why this collection of messages was ignored could never be satisfactorily verified during investigations after the sinking.[154]

Pride and ego would most certainly have been one of the reasons why these messages were ignored. So many people thought that the *Titanic* could never sink. We can continue to speculate about this, but the reality is that the messages were ignored. People didn't listen.

The story of the *Titanic* is just one example of the kind of colossal tragedy that can occur if people don't listen. I would suggest that the collective consequence of people not listening to electronic messages or words from other people results in even bigger tragedies across the globe on a daily basis. Fair enough, we live in an era of information overload, but our inability to teach ourselves to filter messages according to priorities, and then react to the most important ones, cannot be used as an excuse.

"When you talk, you are only repeating what you already know. But if you listen, you may learn something new."

Dalai Lama

In the book, *Leadership Embodiment*, Wendy Palmer and Janet Crawford refer to the concept of *"Centred listening as listening for the whole, without taking it personally."*[155]

I think the challenge for most of us is to successfully practise centred listening. Imagine how much value this could add to our lives and to the lives of the people around us. You see, when we listen with empathy to someone, we give that person psychological air.[156] The habit of active or centred listening will not only support us in achieving our personal goals by knowing as much as possible about what is going on around us, but it will also help us to build lasting relationships with people who will feel and know that we care and that we respect them. They will in turn support us in achieving our aspirations in life.

Other basics of communication

"Developing our communication skills, whether through listening, speaking or asking questions, is perhaps the single most important skill we can develop to improve the quality of our lives."

Andrew Bryant

I would like to share with you what I consider to be the most important aspect of effective communication: Being approachable. Don't be that person who everyone is too scared to talk to or approach. The acid test for me here is simply whether the person in the lowest position in any setting or organisation is scared or intimidated to approach the most senior person.

Apart from having confidence, the other quality correlated with success is the ability to communicate effectively. It is important that we communicate assertively, rather than aggressively or passively.

> **Assertive communication**: An honest, direct and confident expression of needs, wants, feelings or opinions.[157]

We should possess or learn the ability to speak our truth with clarity and precision, without speaking with aggression, or conversely in a weak manner. We need to stand behind what we believe and state our ideas.[158]

> "Don't raise your voice, improve your argument."
>
> Desmond Tutu

By raising our voices, we not only come across as aggressive, but it can also be a sign that we are not keeping our emotions in check. I am 6,2 ft tall and have a loud voice. I am often reminded that I need to quieten it down a bit, especially when talking to people who are smaller than me, like children. I have realised that it's not fair to communicate with someone if I do it in such a way that they feel intimidated or threatened.

> "It's not what you say, but how you say it!"
>
> Mae West

I'd like to add to Mae West's words that it's not only what you verbally convey to someone, but also how you convey it through your non-verbal communication. This can be attributed to as much as 93% of all communication.[159]

Something else that's important: If you've made your point, stop talking. Although it's something on which I consciously focus, I still sometimes find myself in a position in which I need to remind myself: "Don't make a meal of it."

My need to sometimes cover all of the bases and to share all of the detail not only gets me to a point where I am bombarding the other person with irrelevant information, but I also lose the main thread of the conversation by even interrupting myself at times. In the process, I waste my time by not focusing on the real issue at hand, and I also waste the other person's time: A luxury none of us have to waste.

> "We only get one life. Wasting someone's time is the subtlest form of murder."
>
> Lindy West

A casual conversation over a cup of coffee is obviously different, but when it's business, or it involves wasting time that I could rather have used productively elsewhere to achieve my personal goals, then I need to ask myself: "Would I have rambled this much if I were part of the rescue team onboard the *Titanic*?"

When communicating, it is also important that we are able to ask the right questions. This comes with experience. Asking the single right question avoids time-wasting and gets to the bottom of an issue as quickly as possible. It is an art ...

"If I had an hour to solve a problem and my life depended on it, I would use the first 55 minutes determining the proper questions to ask."

Albert Einstein

All of the points discussed so far apply to both verbal and written communication. Consider, for example, how we use email to communicate. People lose interest in emails that are too long; they take offence to emails that comes across as aggressive or loaded with emotion, and they certainly get annoyed if you have not listened to what they originally conveyed to you in a previous email. By communicating effectively, both verbally and in writing, we get the best out of ourselves, out of others and out of situations. Practising these communication skills is the only way that we will be able to perfect them. The fortunate thing that counts in our favour is that we get so many opportunities every day to practise and get them right.

Are you part of the solution or part of the problem?

The Achilles heel of any team is the person who does not support the ambitions or aspirations of the rest of the team – that one person whom everyone on the team hopes will take leave on that day that everyone needs to pull together to address a serious business challenge.

One of the key questions I ask myself in any situation involving other people is: "Am I being part of the solution or part of the problem?" Quite frankly, if I can't learn and live the habit, by default being part of the solution, then I have to step out of the situation and not be part of it any longer.

"Whatever the problem – be part of the solution."

Tina Fey

If people always see us as part of the solution, then they will look up to us for guidance and positive influence. That way, we not only become the people that other people like to have around, but we also learn the good habit of not letting any problem defeat us. We do this by using our initiative and spontaneously finding ways to circumvent any challenge facing us or our team. This is a valuable skill that will help us to achieve our goals.

Be on time

Are you always early, or always late? People are typically and habitually one of the two, not both. I sincerely hope that you are the former. Dad always taught me that I must rather be an hour early than a minute too late. In the army, we used to say that a good officer is always seven minutes early. Don't ask me why that time frame, though.

"Wasting someone else's time may be the highest form of disrespect."
Mark Bouris

By being late, we assume that our time is more important than somebody else's, which is neither fair nor respectful. You might disagree, and say that by aiming for too early, we waste time by having to wait for our appointments. I'd still rather make sure that I am early and lift the stress by avoiding the risk of running late – especially for an important appointment.

If, for example, I am 30 minutes early for an appointment, I use the time productively by sitting and working in my car. If, however, you miss an appointment time, the person that you would have met may never want to meet with you again. In their eyes, your tardiness might be a reflection of your work ethic. This could potentially be a hard blow to your self-leadership success.

Avoid "just-in-time"

For most of my life I was a "just-in-time" person. Then I asked myself the question: "Why am I doing this to myself?" I used to wait until the last minute to start with a task ahead of a deadline. The root cause of this was that I loved the adrenaline rush and excitement associated with finishing something just before a deadline. This might sound ridiculous, but it was true.

One-and-a-half years before my MBA dissertation deadline of 4pm on Monday, 28 February 2005, we all knew our deadline. I handed in my dissertation at 2.30pm that afternoon – exactly one-and-a-half hours before the deadline, having averaged less than four hours' sleep a night over the previous two weeks. In hindsight, that was not clever.

"Productivity is never an accident. It is always the result of a commitment to excellence, intelligent planning and focused effort."
Paul J. Meyer

Although "just-in-time" (JIT) is a great concept in a production or supply chain environment that increases efficiency and reduces inventory costs, it is a bad habit to have in our personal lives. At some point, it will catch you out. All of a sudden, you'll have a couple of other unplanned priorities, which then make it impossible to meet your deadline. Then JIT becomes JTL ("just-too-late"), and you have to scramble, or eventually ask for an extension to your deadline. Don't do this to yourself. It's a bad habit and not worth it. Ask me: I have plenty of experience in this regard. Nowadays, I plan ahead and make my deadlines every time, all the time, with much less stress.

Can you be alone ... frequently?

Before my final matric exam, everyone was talking about their planned post-matric holiday destinations with friends. I remember receiving a couple of stares when I said that I would be content to drive through the Kruger National Park and stay there all on my own for a week. This might sound weird to you, too, but I realised soon enough in my life that I was perfectly okay being alone. Besides, could there be any better place than the African bush?

It might sound less weird if I told you that my need to be alone after matric was mainly to figure myself out. Years later, I realised that part of that need related to me not being sure about studying the right course at the time. That turned into two years of expensive 'school fees' that I needed to fork out after not listening to my leader inner voice.

> "Being alone has a power that very few people can handle."
>
> Steven Aitchison

I have discovered that by being alone, with only my Creator present, especially in times of hardship or when I am dealing with important questions in my life, I am able to reflect and figure things out. Being alone, now and again, is a good habit to develop. It is something that makes us stronger.

Become streetwise by always being curious

> **Streetwise/street-smart**: Having the experience and knowledge necessary to deal with the potential difficulties or dangers of life in an urban environment.[160] Continuously and actively gaining the knowledge and practical know-how to operate effectively, efficiently and optimally across all aspects of the unique context or environment in which we find ourselves.

I took the route of formal education because I love to lecture and be involved in business schools. I have four university degrees, but in my mind, that does not count for much if I am not also streetwise. Yes, formal education is important, but only to a point.

> "The best university is the university of life."
>
> Henrique Capriles Radonski

In my mind and experience, being streetwise is as important as any other qualification – if not more important. One of the reasons why college dropout billionaires are so prolific is because they are streetwise. An important aspect of being streetwise is understanding the value of reading a lot of non-fiction, facts, statistics and news. Another is learning the habit of being curious about the important things in life and about your environment.

Adopting a curious mindset, like a toddler, is critical to forming the right foundation in any area in which we operate. I know it's an age-old saying, but there is no, and will never be, a stupid question – assuming that you genuinely don't know the answer. The only stupid question is the one that you were too scared to ever ask, which leaves you feeling empty afterwards and regretting that you never asked it. The skills that you learn from a streetwise approach are something that money can't buy.

Invest in yourself

During the secondary and primary phases of my PhD research, it was again highlighted that participants in a leadership development programme must have a long-term commitment to self-development.

"Live as if you were to die tomorrow. Learn as if you were to live forever."
Mahatma Gandhi

The irony is that so many of us choose to make significant investments in material things, even though investing in ourselves is the best investment we could ever make: By learning; attending conferences on things that interest us; reading; sharing; having conversations; lecturing and by being influencers in our areas of expertise. Sometimes, we learn the most by sharing and giving to others in our field of interest. This leads to conversations, which leads to new ideas, which results in more learning and stronger relationships.

"The best investment you can make is in yourself."
Warren Buffet

By learning and living the habit of investing in yourself, you will generate the biggest returns that any investment could ever give you.

Laziness – possibly our worst enemy

While I was writing this book, my sensei for many years turned 90. He is a great man, a great sensei and a great example of how to live life. When we used to train in his dojo, he would sometimes shout: "As humans you are lazy by your very nature, but I will train this laziness out of you."

The reality is that we cannot rely on someone else to help us triumph over our laziness, and we cannot use our 'lazy nature' as an excuse. We have to conquer it ourselves by learning and living the habit of not being a lazy person. I have been around for long enough and have seen enough to be able to testify to the fact that lazy people battle to get anywhere in life. Other people don't like to have lazy people around them, either.

"Laziness is nothing more than the habit of resting before you get tired."
Jules Renard

To master my laziness, I ask myself every time I realise I am experiencing a little laziness whether I would feel better after doing something or not. The answer to this question is simple, and I know it every time. I have *never* felt sorry that I made a special effort to do something that required discipline, and that I knew I had to do for my own good. Instead of asking ourselves: "Should I?", we should rather ask ourselves: "How soon can I?" do the thing that I very well know will be good for me and for the people around me.

Get over the advantage line

Trying to 'get over the advantage line' is important, both in terms of short- and long-term goals. This is a sport analogy, but it is definitely also applicable to personal goal achievement. I used to wash my motorbike ahead of my next ride, and my golf clubs ahead of my next game. Now I do it after a bike ride, as soon as it has cooled off, or after playing golf. Then I know it is done. Besides, I get a much warmer feeling each time I walk past my clean motorcycle and golf clubs. These are simple examples, but they illustrate what I mean by getting over the advantage line.

Another example would be that I used to leave old emails in my Inbox or Sent folders, and then archive them once a month. Now I archive each email after I read or send it. Then it's done and I don't have to worry about spending time doing it later. You might argue that overall, it takes the same amount of time to do the task, so why bother? But it won't. I am immediately familiar with the detail of the mail, so I can transfer it to the right archive folder quicker, rather than trying to figure out later where it belongs.

What I also do these days to get over the advantage line, which I never got right in the past, is that I rather work on a Friday evening and Saturday so that I can enjoy a restful Sunday with my family. I used to leave important things for the new week until a Sunday afternoon. I then had to live through the first part of the weekend with the feeling of not doing the stuff that I actually should have done first. Now, the satisfying feeling of contentment I experience when I wake up on a Sunday morning is precious.

"The fundamental level of success is doing the hard things first – if you go for the feared thing first, then the rest of the day is easy."
Robert G. Allen

By approaching my tasks differently, I have one thing less to worry about. By learning these small habits, I address my responsibilities as soon as possible and they are no longer a niggle in the back of my mind. This removes the clutter from my life, allowing me to focus on the really important issues – achieving my main personal goals.

Take shorter, but frequent breaks

Early in my career, one of my colleagues told me: "We work to live, not live to work." Initially I thought that was quite a selfish and laid-back statement to make. However, the older I get, the more I see his comment in a different light. We need to learn to relax more. Not only does this allow us, as individuals, more time to reflect, charge our life batteries and get our creative juices flowing again, but it does wonders for our marriage and family life. Taking shorter breaks, more frequently, does not have to be costly, but I find that time away from our normal environment helps. It also allows us to experience new adventures and typically meet new people in the process.

Find the right type of exercise

We all know the virtues of exercise, and I am not going to delve into that detail. I train for both the psychological and physical benefits, and it is hard to distinguish between these aspects since they are so interlinked. The simple reason why I train is because it makes me feel good and I am better able to handle the pressures of life. Each one of us needs to choose the best form of training for us. This might change over our lifetimes. I used to do a bit of running, but I soon discovered that my build, weight and physical frame do not support that type of exercise. I then switched to karate, and after my hip injury, I started to swim. That will, hopefully, be something that I can do for the rest of my life. Cardiovascular exercise, meditation, yoga, Pilates, or any other form of frequent physical or mental release that you choose, will be of help. The one that makes you feel good is the one for you.

Finish what you start

After school, I studied a BSc degree for two years. If I am brutally honest with myself, I did not think that decision through properly and I never should have studied that course. Part of my failure to complete the course can be attributed to this, and the rest purely relates to laziness, poor discipline and a lack of motivation. Assuming, though, that we have spent enough time thinking about something beforehand, and that it is aligned to the content of our self-leadership charter, it would be a mistake to start something and not finish it.

"If you're brave enough to start, you're strong enough to finish."

Gary Blair

If we start something that we know we really want and that it would benefit us – maybe not immediately, but sometime in the future – then we need to push through, whatever it takes. That was the approach I adopted when I finished my PhD. In the heat of the moment, we sometimes feel that we want to throw in the towel, but then we need to think about it carefully – like I did on 7 May 2016, when I wanted to stop my PhD research for 'good' reasons. We can then carefully reflect, gain new perspective, and realise why we chose that particular worthwhile, yet challenging, path in the first place, before we continue the journey.

Stopping something that we have started in good faith might be the easy way out and seem like the right thing now, but the psychological impact of having failed at something can haunt us for an exceedingly long time. This is exactly what I experienced when I didn't finish my BSc degree, even though I realised that I should never have enrolled for it in the first place.

On the flip side, to have completed something significant that we have thought through properly gives us a satisfied and victorious feeling that we are one step closer to achieving the goals that we have set ourselves in life.

Indecision and delaying tactics as unhealthy habits

"Indecision and delays are the parents of failure."
George Canning

Whenever we make a decision that influences the lives of others, it is important that we think it through properly before we commit and get others involved. To make a habit of taking decisions and then changing them again, is not only messing your life around, but the lives of other people, too. Rather take longer to make the right decision before you commit, than have to change things again later.

Also, falling into the habit of moving meetings or appointments to whenever it suits us, or shifting them whenever we don't feel like it, is not only a bad habit, but also a sign of inconsideration towards the other people involved. The saying goes: "From delay comes cancellation." This is a problem, particularly when it involves something important. Again, don't commit to an appointment if you are not absolutely sure that you can honour it.

Never assume ... follow up

"Follow up and follow through until the task is completed, the prize won."
Brian Tracy

I have been bitten many times in my life by assuming that what's important to me is also important to someone else. So, I realised that I needed to do something different to ensure that others take responsibility and play their part in supporting the achievement of my goals. I realised the importance of getting into the habit of following up, because to assume that others will play their part is not always realistic. I don't look over someone's shoulder and become a pain every day, I merely follow up at regular intervals to ensure their progress is in line with my plan to achieve my goals, professionally and personally.

You only have one body

If there is one thing with which we cannot mess around, or neglect, it is our bodies. One of the most important habits that we could ever learn and live, is to look after it. Without this body, we can't do anything. It's not a car that we can trade in for another one after we have badly bumped, bruised and abused it. We only have one body, yet so many people don't care about it. Some people are young and obese, not because of an underlying disease, but purely as a result of eating too much, eating unhealthily and just simply lacking the discipline to look after the biggest asset that they have ever received … This is really sad. I have also been at a point in my life where I smoked and overindulged in different ways, but somewhere along our life journey, sooner rather than later, we need to realise the value of our bodies and start looking after them.

"Take care of your body. It's the only place you have to live."

Jim Rohn

For too many years I committed deferred suicide by not following a healthy diet and not exercising enough. I simply expected my body to cope with what I threw at it, despite the fact that I had much healthier options available to me. What I also failed to realise was the positive connection between a healthy body and my mental health.

"I believe that when the body is strong, the mind thinks strong thoughts."

Henry Rollins

One day, I decided: "No more." Part of my resolution to start addressing these issues has been that I will rather go hungry and only drink water until I can eat healthy food. Otherwise, it is just too easy to, for example, eat junk food and make the excuse that there is no healthy food around. Since then, I have experienced first-hand that there is a direct link between healthy living and feeling better. Another link, proved by research, is that there is a direct correlation between self-leadership and physical wellbeing.[161] The more we improve as self-leaders, the more we will experience physical wellbeing.

Get enough sleep

One of my post-COVID-19 symptoms was that for quite a while, I would get serious headaches from alcohol – even from half a glass of wine at the supper table. I now battle to stomach alcohol. My more social friends accuse me of using this as an excuse, but I have since made the decision to limit my alcohol intake. The fact that I still don't have any sense of smell, or most of my sense of taste back, made this decision quite easy. To no longer be able to enjoy the taste of craft beer or red wine in moderation, but to then still drink it for its effects, sounds too alcoholic for my liking. This change in habit, combined with my evening stretches, makes me sleep like a baby. The net result is that I feel fresh and recharged in the morning, in a way I haven't felt for a long time …

"Each night, when I go to sleep, I die. And the next morning, when I wake up, I am reborn."

Mahatma Gandhi

Another habit I ditched years ago was my afternoon nap on weekends. What used to sound like a relaxing idea on a Saturday or Sunday afternoon very quickly turned into a decision I regretted that same night, when I found myself staring at the ceiling, unable to fall asleep. Instead, I now spend quality time with my family or friends, go for a walk, or watch live sport on television. Enough scientific research has been conducted on the physical, psychological and social benefits of getting seven to eight hours' sleep a night. By getting enough sleep, we will feel revitalised every morning and ready to work hard on achieving our personal goals. Whatever we do has to be aligned to, or in support of, this good habit.

Consciously learn to worry less

My mom used to repeatedly say: "If you worry you die, if you don't worry you also die, so why worry?" And then just to make the point, she would add to this that "85% of everything that we worry about never happens". Mom was right.

"My life has been filled with terrible misfortune; most of which never happened."

Michel de Montaigne

Stress is a bad habit, but it is something that we can learn to control. In his book, *How to Stop Worrying and Start Living*, Dale Carnegie writes about Herbert Hawkes, Dean of Columbia College, Columbia University for 22 years, who said the following: "Half the worry in the world is caused by people trying to make decisions before they have sufficient knowledge on which to base a decision."[162]

It is important that we first get our facts straight before we even think to start worrying. Otherwise, I can almost guarantee you that up to 100% of the things you are worrying about will not happen.

> When we have all the facts about the situation that we are worrying about, then it is important to ask ourselves the question:
>
> "According to the law of averages, what are the chances that this event I am worrying about will actually ever occur?"[163]

Based on the assumption that we (a) have our facts straight, and that (b) we are convinced that the situation we are worrying about will actually occur, Carnegie also describes a simple technique that was developed by Willis Carrier, an engineer best known for inventing modern air-conditioning and launching the air-conditioning industry.[164]

> It comprises three steps:
>
> *Step 1:* Honestly and fearlessly analyse the situation you are worried about. Figure out the worst thing that could happen if it materialises.
>
> *Step 2:* Work on reconciling yourself to accepting it, if necessary, as a worst-case scenario.

> *Step 3:* Calmly devote your time, effort and energy to trying to improve upon the worst-case scenario, which you have already accepted mentally.

If we have accepted the worst, we have nothing more to lose. Then we can work from there to improve the potential loss to a negligible loss, a zero loss, or preferably a positive gain. I think this is a great technique, but it might not work for you. Regardless, find out what does work for you because worry reduces our energy levels. If we allow it to consume our lives, it will ultimately make us sick. We need to take action and take charge to free ourselves from the shackles of worry, which are depriving us of a life filled with peace and contentment.

"Our main business is not to see what lies dimly at a distance, but to do what lies clearly at hand."

Thomas Carlyle

It is human nature to stress, and if we don't stress at all, then we are not human – or we are dead. If we stress too much, though, to the point where we are conscious of the fact that it is starting to rule our world, then we need to deal with it. Factors like enough sleep, a healthy diet and exercise help us to experience less stress.

A good place to start unlearning the bad habit of stressing too much, is to apply the zone of proximity principle, which we discussed earlier. It is insane to stress about the things that we cannot be certain of, so let's immediately reduce our stress levels by teaching ourselves to focus only on the things that we can control in a stressful situation, that we are absolutely certain are, or will become a reality.

Appreciate what you do have

We can sometimes be so focused on what we don't have, and on chasing our personal goals, that we forget what we already have and what we have already achieved in life. It is important to create the habit of taking a couple of moments every day to acknowledge what we have and to be grateful.

"Acknowledging the good that you already have in your life is the foundation for all abundance."

Eckhart Tolle

When we realise that what we have is actually enough, we will automatically show this gratitude by smiling more, which is another great habit to learn and live.

Find inspiration, when necessary

"To succeed, you need to find something to hold on to, something to motivate you, something to inspire you."

Tony Dorsett

If we can't inspire ourselves, or achieve this by living a life that includes reading books; doing what we love; listening to sermons; charging our life batteries; getting enough sleep; leading a healthy lifestyle and engaging with other people on a daily basis, then we owe it to ourselves to find inspiration elsewhere. We then need to try something different, or arrange to see someone who can offer us inspiration. We cannot ever afford to lose our flame and passion for life. Finding inspiration from someone else might only be temporary, but it is critical that we keep on being inspired if we are to chase our personal goals – the goals that will keep us growing and will make us stronger and better.

Sample habits rather than no habits

"If you can't do great things, do small things in a great way."

Napoleon Hill

We can never allow ourselves to get too busy to maintain our good habits. Even though we might sometimes get distracted by work pressures or projects, we shouldn't fall into the trap of stopping good habits. These habits will also carry us through the stressful times when we don't think that we have time for them.

With or without riding partners, I have a habit of going for an outride on my motorcycle to charge my motorcycle's battery and my life batteries. Now, while I am busy finishing this book project, I don't just put a good habit like this on hold for a couple of months. I know that this would be a mistake. Instead, I only do a 30-minute outride on my own after a quick breakfast at home, rather than a three-hour outride with friends, which includes a breakfast with them in Hartbeespoort.

The same principle applies to my swimming routine. Instead of spending an hour in the pool at the gym, in crunch times, I only spend 30 minutes in the pool, or even just take a brisk walk through our neighbourhood with Marilé. Not only do I then get some exercise, but I also get to enjoy nature, a good dose of oxygen and vitamin D, and most importantly, I get to spend quality time with my best friend.

The same goes for family time: I cannot totally neglect my family, but I spend shorter stints with them, which they know is only temporary. I call these short stints of good habits *sample habits*, which are much more helpful than not doing them at all. By adopting this approach, I keep the balance in my life, even though for now, I spend more time on my book project work than on anything else. If I don't practise these sample habits, then I know that I will become more stressed, less productive and even run the risk of completely losing that specific habit, which would be a mistake.

The link to personal goal achievement

Learning and living good habits, combined with living a disciplined life, accelerate personal goal achievement in more than one way. Not only does such a lifestyle or way of living create absolute focus, but it also eliminates doubt, which wastes time and distracts us from achieving our goals. This ties into our discussion on having a good routine. The doubt to which I refer includes internal conversations like: "Should I eat junk food and lie on the couch, or go to training?" I no longer even waste energy on these time-consuming thoughts. I simply don't tolerate them. I know that I eat healthily and that I exercise when I need to. The net result is that I not only achieve my personal goals, but that I exceed them in a quicker time frame than I had originally set for myself.

REFLECTION ON THE CONTENT OF THIS CHAPTER – LEARNING AND LIVING GOOD HABITS

Consider the topics that we have covered:

- Focus on habits that make a meaningful contribution
- Start by releasing bad habits
- Being neat is more than just being neat
- Stay current and up-to-date
- Why routine matters
- Put your pride in your pocket
- "Yes, but ..." and "Pause ... engage"
- The importance of active listening
- Other basics of communication
- Are you part of the solution or part of the problem?
- Be on time
- Avoid "just-in-time"
- Can you be alone ... frequently?
- Become streetwise by always being curious
- Invest in yourself
- Laziness – possibly our worst enemy
- Get over the advantage line
- Take shorter, but frequent breaks
- Find the right type of exercise
- Finish what you start
- Indecision and delaying tactics as unhealthy habits
- Never assume ... follow up
- You only have one body
- Get enough sleep
- Consciously learn to worry less
- Appreciate what you do have
- Find inspiration, when necessary

- Sample habits rather than no habits
- The link to personal goal achievement

Please rate your current overall level of success in Learning and Living Good Habits as a percentage score:

_____%

Chapter 15

Controlling Personal Finances

"Working because you want to, not because you have to, is financial freedom."

TONY ROBBINS

I was brought up in a middle-class home where we had enough. We were happy, and finances never needed to be a topic of discussion. I received my pocket money every month and my parents took care of the rest. At no point did I make it my business to find out how to make more money, and neither of my parents ever had a discussion with me along those lines while I was at school.

I never chased money and I never had this burning desire to, for example, become a millionaire by a certain age, or to accumulate wealth that would last for generations. I am content with what I have, and as far as I am concerned, I have enough …

I am definitely not a financial guru, but I have a couple of 'war stories' that I would like to share, which I trust will be of benefit to you. When I got married at the age of 26, I, ironically, held a Financial Management degree and had a job as a financial accountant that commanded a good salary. My-wife-to-be was a law student and had a couple of years to go before she finished her studies. At that time, I had to make the normal buy-or-rent decision around our first property. At that point in my life, that was the first and only major financial decision I had ever had to make.

I was quite verbal about the fact that I did not want to pay off someone else's bond, so a rental property was not an option. The only problem was that I could only afford a one-and-a-half-bedroom flat in an area that was deteriorating. Still, I convinced myself that it was a good idea, because we were buying in one of the best blocks of flats in the best part of that neighbourhood. Needless to say, the neighbourhood declined further and property in the area showed negative growth. It wasn't a seller's market at the time, and almost four years later we sold our little flat for a 10% loss.

> **Shared investment learning: Number 1**
>
> Rather buy a modest property in a great area that is growing in reputation and value, than a stunning property in an area that is in decline from an image or value point of view. It's all about the location, location, location of your property. When making a substantial buying decision, think with logic and facts, not emotion.

"If you cannot control your emotions, you cannot control your money."
Warren Buffet

We then moved to Johannesburg and rented a house for a while so that we could get to know the property market before we bought again. That time around, I followed my own advice: We bought property directly from the owner, in a great area, and at the right time. As a result, we sold it after three years for almost double our original purchase price. Then we went all out and bought a piece of land on a golf estate to start building a house for our growing family. We rented another small house close by. We knew from the start that we were overextending ourselves financially, but we were building our dream house, and we had the courage to take that giant leap …

Our house should have taken a year to complete, but disaster struck. Our building company went bankrupt, and I needed to take over the building project – before we had even completed the brickwork. I had considerable responsibility at work and obviously needed help with the project, so I employed a part-time site manager, who also oversaw a couple of other projects. More than two years after we started the building project, we eventually moved into our home. Little did we know the next disaster was about to strike …

The prime interest rate increased from 11,0% to 15,5% within a period of two years. This amounted to a massive difference in our bond repayments on our home loan. By the end of the first week of each month, we had no disposable income left, which put a massive strain on our family in more ways than one.

> **Shared investment learning: Number 2**
>
> Invest prudently and don't financially over-extend yourself. You will need enough of a financial buffer for the unforeseen events in life.

"A big part of financial freedom is having your heart and mind free from worry about the what-ifs of life."

Suze Orman

Through our divorce, I was fortunate to have kept the house, and everything worked out fine, but things could easily have gone south. I was living on the financial edge. If anything else had gone wrong, like I had lost my job, I could have been forced to declare bankruptcy. The stress and other impacts it had on my life were not worth it.

To fast-forward to a decade later, by the age of 47, I was debt free, and I have no intention of ever owing anybody or any institution any money again. I am thankful for this, and also for the psychological freedom and relief that comes with it.

You might be wondering why I have included a chapter on finance in a self-leadership book. There is a simple answer to this: Money is a strange thing – if you have it, it's not an issue, but if you don't have it, then life can very quickly become miserable. A couple of times during and after building our dream house, the thought crossed my mind that I was going to enter bankruptcy. While I was experiencing that period of severe financial stress, I simply could not focus on my self-leadership process, or at least not nearly as much as I ought to have done.

That kind of serious financial stress was different from any other stress that I have ever experienced. I realised that it affected my wife and kids, too. I was not alone, but I was the man of the house and I needed to fix it. I eventually did, but it came at a price.

I would like to share with you more financial advice, most of it from past experience of things with which I have battled at some point, in the hope that you do not make the same financial mistakes that I have made in my life. If you follow this advice, I have no doubt that it will help you to avoid becoming bogged down by your financial situation, and so allow you to stay focused on making a success of your self-leadership story.

The right approach to debt

I have a wealthy friend in Stellenbosch, who we'll call Peter for the sake of the story. Peter understands money, although you wouldn't say that he is this wealthy. He and his family live in a nice home, but it is certainly not extravagant. He drives good, quality cars, but they are more than five years old and have high mileage. I recently stayed with him while on a short visit to the area. One day, while Peter and I were driving through town, we passed an extremely expensive SUV. He made an interesting comment: He said that people with flashy cars typically have debt and more stress, compared to those people with a lot of equity and investments, who have no debt and sleep peacefully at night …

"Every time you borrow money, you're robbing your future self."
Nathan W. Morris

It is important that we verbalise our approach to debt and then stick to it – assuming that your approach is a sensible one. Most people don't have the luxury of using cash from savings to buy a house, or even a car. If we had to do that, we might only have been able to afford a car by the time we were 30, or a house by the age of 40. For most of my life, I have had both of these types of debt, but I think that Marilé, who is a chartered accountant, has the right approach to debt. She approves of having a home loan, but she pays that off as quickly as possible (and I'll explain to you why shortly). My wife also understands how to work with money, which is part of the reason why we paid off our bond in less than five years.

Marilé does not believe in any other type of debt, including car debt. She will continue to drive her old, well-maintained, good-quality car until she has saved enough money to buy a new one. I think Marilé's approach to debt is the ideal one. It is something to which we should all strive. I am finally in a position to do the same, and there are very few things that can compare to the relief of not having any debt.

Compound interest – the 8th wonder of the world

"Compound interest is the eighth wonder of the world. He who understands it, earns it ... he who doesn't ... pays it."

Albert Einstein

There is no better way to explain the power of compound interest than with a house bond calculation. People who understand this concept do anything and everything in their power to pay off their home loan as fast as possible, because this is the one area where we can save a massive amount of money. Unfortunately, there are many people out there, like most of our parents, who didn't understand or know about the impact of compound interest. As a result, it took them the full 20 years of their bond term to pay it off. In a country like ours, where the interest rates are far higher than in first-world economies, this is a cardinal financial sin.

> I would like to illustrate this by way of an example:
> If you buy a house and take out a bond of R1 million at a prime interest rate of 7% over a standard 20-year term, assuming that you couldn't negotiate an interest rate better than prime, and that the prime interest rate stays the same over your bond repayment period, your monthly repayment amount would be R7 753 (rounded). This implies that if you decide to pay off this bond over the full term of 240 months, the total repayment amount would be R1 860 720. You, therefore, paid a staggering R860 720 in interest and R1 million in capital.

If you decided to eat out a little bit less, or to save elsewhere and to earn a bit of extra part-time income, then you might be able to add R2 000 per month to your required repayment amount. This would then increase your bond repayment amount to R9 753. Assuming that you can pay this amount until your last instalment, then your term will reduce from 240 months to 157 months (rounded).

I might need to repeat this in a different manner for you to fully grasp this financial impact: By increasing your bond amount by only 26% (rounded), your new repayment period is only 65% (rounded) of your original term.

If we keep on paying this increased monthly bond repayment amount, then the net result would be a total repayment of R1 531 221, which is a saving of R329 500 (rounded), versus the original total repayment amount. That could be used to buy a very good car 'cash'. In addition to this, you would have the peace of mind that your bond has been paid off in 13 years, rather than 20 years. That will give you a period of seven years without house debt.

If you can afford to further increase your repayment amount, or if you keep it at this inflated amount of R9 753 per month if the interest rate reduces even further, then you would obviously benefit even more from the exponential effect of compound interest. I don't know about you, but in my mind, that makes absolute sense …

Avoiding credit card debt

When you let their debt carry over, credit cards are evil. If you cannot settle your credit card debt with your next salary, you run the risk of starting to pay super-interest. This means that you are effectively paying a much higher price for the item that you bought, but you unfortunately still get the same value from it as if you had paid cash. We need to ask ourselves: "Do I want it, or do I really need it?" Successful self-leaders understand the difference, because we take charge, and when it comes to purchasing decisions, we don't let our emotions dominate our sound judgement.

> "If you buy the things you don't need, you will soon be selling the things that you need."
>
> Warren Buffet

In my view, if someone has low levels of self-discipline and low emotional intelligence, they should, frankly, not own any form of credit until they have addressed those issues. Fortunately, we as self-leaders have the discipline and the EQ to manage our credit card debt and, at worst, settle it at month-end.

Trying to keep up with the Joneses

Our insecurities and a lack of self-confidence often get us into trouble. This also happens when we buy the wrong thing, or the right thing at a too high price, just to keep up with friends and family. Right now, I might have everything together financially, but this was not always the case. At the time I was building our dream house, I had maxed out my credit cards and I was paying the price for stretching too far. In some ways, I was also trying to keep up with the proverbial Joneses. I did this without having enough of a financial buffer to weather the storms that we were experiencing at the time.

As self-leaders, we have to align our behaviour, feelings and thoughts to our personal goals, but we must always be realistic. This is where the fine line of calculated risk runs, capitalising financially on opportunities that come our way.

Save steadily, invest wisely

Saving and investing go hand in hand. As a rule, we will only invest what we have saved, or we reinvest what we have already invested. We often ignore the necessity of saving for the future, because we are so busy living in the present moment. I think it would be wise to have at least the equivalent of six months' net monthly income saved or invested, which could be converted into cash quickly, should you encounter financial difficulties. Your retirement funds and long-term investments should not be used for this purpose.

If we have the discipline to save money every month – without having to be stingy – then we are already halfway down the road to financial freedom.

"Do not save what is left after spending, but spend what is left after saving."

Warren Buffet

The above quote offers wise advice from someone who really understands money. If we only allocate savings after our expenditure, then we will typically have no money left to save. If we have a personal or household budget – which is something that we will cover in the next section – then we know how much our expenses should be. With this in mind, and by then first allocating our savings amount to a separate bank account, as an example, we will force ourselves to spend according to our budget. This is the disciplined way to accumulate savings.

This savings buffer can, at some point, be invested to potentially generate bigger returns that far outweigh inflation, compared to the relatively low interest we receive from leaving it in a savings account. Alternatively, and depending on the other return options available to you, the wise thing would be to pay your savings amount into your bond account to pay your house off sooner.

Budget and track your expenses

"It's not your salary that makes you rich; it's your spending habits."

Charles A. Jaffe

The only way to effectively track our spending habits is to do it against a personal budget, which is effectively a short-term financial plan. Even if we have small expenses, we must account for these, because they all add up.

"Beware of little expenses. A small leak will sink a great ship."

Benjamin Franklin

The post-COVID financial mindset has changed the way that we work with our money, and there is a bigger need than ever for proper financial planning. So many people were caught off guard, and although none of us could have planned sufficiently for such a pandemic, better financial planning and more savings would have benefited most of us.

I read an online article, dated 20 May 2019, which stated that millions of Americans were just one pay cheque away from financial disaster.[165] I am convinced that America is not unique in this regard, and it would be scary to know what this statistic would look like worldwide today, taking into account the financial impact that COVID had on most of us.

The power of negotiating and alternative quotes

"In business as in life, you don't get what you deserve, you get what you negotiate."

Chester Karras

At some point I had to refinance my house, and my bank's initial interest rate offer to keep me as a valued client was prime interest less 0,25%. I was obviously not satisfied with that response and I started to consult other banks to try to get a better quote – which I did. In fact, all of the competitor banks offered me a better interest rate than the bank of which I have been a client for more than 25 years.

I wasn't too keen to move banks or to have my home loan at another bank, because that in itself had its own implications. With the alternative quotes in hand, I eventually settled with my bank on the same interest rate that one of the alternative banks would have offered me, which was 1,75% below prime.

By negotiating with my bank and by sourcing alternative quotes, I was able to benefit significantly. I potentially saved R 581 520 over the total bond repayment period. We managed to pay off our bond much quicker, but if we had paid it off over the full term of 20 years, that would have been the total amount I would have saved Marilé and I – the price of a very nice new SUV vehicle.

> "Let us never negotiate out of fear. But let us never fear to negotiate."
>
> John F. Kennedy

On a professional or personal level, it makes absolute sense to get alternative quotes and to negotiate a better price – assuming that we also take the quality of the service or product into consideration. It is simple: If you don't ask, you don't get, and if you don't ask, you would never know if you could have negotiated a better price. Do yourself a favour and ask your local paint shop for a discount next time you have to repaint your house. See what their response is. I did exactly that and was offered a 5% discount without hesitation.

Negotiating or getting alternative quotes is not limited only to large expenses. It could be as simple as learning what to buy from which retailer. That could make a massive difference to your grocery bill. Again, it all adds up, and in the long run, we could save a small fortune by applying sound financial principles.

The blessing of financial peace

By successfully controlling our personal finances, we not only achieve our financial goals, but we also set a foundation that will help us achieve all of our other personal goals. Although I have only covered some basic personal finance concepts in this chapter, they are principles that worked for me, and I trust that they will also assist you in gaining more financial peace. In my experience, financial peace is a vital component of successful self-leadership.

> "I believe that through knowledge and discipline, financial peace is possible for all of us."
>
> Dave Ramsey

REFLECTION ON THE CONTENT OF THIS CHAPTER – CONTROLLING PERSONAL FINANCES

Consider the topics that we have covered:

- The right approach to debt
- Compound interest – the 8th wonder of the world
- Avoiding credit card debt
- Trying to keep up with the Joneses
- Save steadily, invest wisely
- Budget and track your expenses
- The power of negotiating and alternative quotes
- The blessing of financial peace

Please rate your current overall level of success in Controlling Personal Finances as a percentage score:

_____%

Chapter 16

Valuing Personal Brand Equity

> *"We'll lead not merely by the example of our power,
> but by the power of our example."*
> JOE BIDEN

To understand the meaning of personal brand equity, it is important to look at its separate parts.

> **Personal brand**: Similar to a corporate brand, it is who we are, what we stand for, the values we embrace, and the way in which we express those values. Just as a company's brand helps to communicate its value to customers and expresses what differentiates it from the competition, a personal brand does the same for us as individuals. It helps us to communicate our unique identity and clear value to everyone and anyone that we interact with.[166]

> **Equity**: Refers to value. Therefore, personal brand equity simply implies the value of your personal brand.

It can be argued that personal brand equity is perceived value, and different people might value my personal brand differently. There is some truth to this, but only a little. If I ask you to consider the following names and to rate them according to their personal brand equity, I think the ranking around the world (assuming that you know who these people are or were) would be the same 99,9% of the time: Nelson Mandela, Tarzan, Adolf Hitler …

The following words all relate to our personal brand in some way or another. Please read them carefully and, before you continue, try to figure out how they apply to your personal brand equity.

"You too are a brand. Whether you know it or not. Whether you like it or not."

Marc Ecko

In the previous names listed as examples of personal brand equity, I deliberately added the fictional character of Tarzan into the mix, because someone's personal brand equity gets formed by our perception of them. Furthermore, our perception of someone is our reality, which implies that even a fictional character has a specific personal brand. When it comes to each of us, as individuals, over time people will get to know our real personal brand and the equity of our brand.

However, if we aspire to become the brand that we think people would find appealing, then: (1) we won't be able to maintain it or be happy to live this brand, because it is not really who we are – it is not authentic, and (2) not all people will like this brand, because people have different preferences. This will then disappoint us, because our intentions of pleasing others, as opposed to being true to ourselves, will fail.

People can only fool others for so long. This applies to our real, personal brand, too, because it reflects who we really are and the way that we show up wherever we go. If we cannot live our personal brand, then our personal brand equity will be zero.

The collage of words presented on the previous page, are all attributes that can be included into someone's personal brand. The seven words in bold have been identified as attributes that can make or break our personal brand. We need to decide the way in which we would like to approach these attributes.[167] For example, when it comes to our appearance, do we want to look professional and neat, or do we want to portray sloppiness in the way that we dress, our hairstyle, and in the way that we approach our personal health?

The 13 words written in regular text are all attributes that form part of a winning personal brand.[168] The final category of words, which are underlined, represents attributes that will damage our personal brand.[169] We ultimately need to decide which attributes will form our personal brand, and contribute to the equity of that brand …

"Everyone has a personal brand – by design or by default."

Lida Citroën

Whatever our personal brand looks like, it has a direct link to our behaviours, thoughts and feelings. It also aligns with our personal goals. If we want to transform into a better version of ourselves, then it needs to be part of our goal-setting, affirmation and reflection process. If we don't actively work on changing or maintaining the brand that we have designed for ourselves, then we will lose this personal brand identity. That would be a mistake, as we would then lose all of the equity that we have thus far invested in our brand.

Our personal brand needs to be strong enough to support our self-leadership story, in such a way that we achieve our personal goals in time and in full. I am not suggesting that people with weak or bad personal brands cannot achieve their personal goals, but it would take them far longer, or forever, to achieve goals that are sound, ethical, good for society and in fact, sustainably good for them.

In this chapter I highlight those areas that I have discovered can break or build one's personal brand equity. It is therefore important to consider these areas as part of becoming more successful self-leaders …

Choose core personal values early in life

"What defines me?" This is an important question that we all need to ask ourselves. Depending on who you ask, you will get different answers to this question. Some people might answer: Our experiences, upbringing, relationships, or even our DNA. If you ask me, it is primarily my values or value system.

> **Values**: The beliefs for which a person has an enduring preference.[170]

It is important that we choose our core personal values early in life because they form a key part of who we are and what we stand for. Other people also instinctively trust those whose personality is founded upon correct principles.[171]

We need to list all of the core values that represent us as a brand and ask ourselves if we are happy with these values, or if we need to change some of these beliefs to align to a new personal brand by which we would like to live. Our core values are the ones that we live by, whatever it takes – the values on which we *never* comprise. These values are typically included in the *own credo* section of our self-leadership charter that we covered in Chapter 3.

"It's not hard to make decisions when you know what your values are."
Roy E. Disney

Your core values might include integrity, humility, loyalty, passion and reliability. At The Character Company, we discuss our core values on a weekly basis with the boys we mentor. These are: Honesty, courage, respect, self-discipline and kindness. We acknowledge that there are many other good values, but these are the five values on which we don't compromise, and we teach them to the boys from four years of age.

The three boys that I mentor every Saturday afternoon will very quickly tell me that we must not only talk about these values and live by them, but that we also have to teach other people about them. Coming from 10- and 11-year-old boys, this gives me so much hope for our youth, our country and for humanity.

"Patience is a virtue, and I'm learning patience. It's a tough lesson."
Elon Musk

Design your own personal brand

We need to become the brand that we consistently want, and can sustainably be. Perhaps while reading this chapter you are thinking that you are happy with your personal brand and its equity. You are fortunate. You might also think that you are mainly happy with this aspect of your life, but that you could make some tweaks. The last possible place where you might find yourself is entirely unhappy with your personal brand equity and wanting to do a total makeover of your brand. Some people might tell you that this is impossible, because of your personality, engrained values or your circumstances. As someone who believes in leadership and people development, and who practises it as a full-time profession, I would beg to differ. I have experienced it first-hand. People can change, and people do change.

"If you don't build a personal brand, someone else will brand you with the wrong label."
Richie Norton

If I look back to when I was a university drop-out in 1990, my personal brand included the following attributes: Recklessness; irresponsibility; negligence; laziness; ill-discipline and a lack of focus. In that era of my life, my self-leadership journey derailed. Through my own negligence, my personal brand equity eroded to a point where I came to the biggest crossroads in my life and I needed to make a life-changing choice, which

I will share with you in more detail at a later stage. Since that time, I have been working on increasing the value of my personal brand equity, which is a critical part of my self-leadership success. I certainly don't have the same value system, personal brand or personality that I had in 1990. I am living proof that we can change and totally transform our individual personal brand.

"To be in business today, our most important job is to be head marketer for the brand called You."

Tom Peters

If you have any trouble designing your personal brand, then simply think of the corporate product or service brands that resonate with you, and what you aspire to. Gain a clear understanding of what they represent and what they stand for. Based on this, you then need to choose whether your personal brand must portray you as being 'exclusive', or 'value-for-money', or 'rugged' or 'fast', just to name a few examples.

You are in charge and you need to decide what your brand must look like and what the value of your brand will be. Like so many corporate brands that have reinvented themselves, there is no reason why you, too, can't reinvent yourself – especially if it will be better for you and those around you.

Lead by example

"Setting an example is not the main means of influencing another, it is the only means."

Albert Schweitzer

Are you a role model for others? I once read that we should live our lives in such a way that the preacher won't have to lie at our funeral one day. Leading by example is a big part of this. But the question is: Who's example should we be following?

If you are a religious person, you probably aspire to live by the example that your God has set for you. Normal Earthlings who set great examples for us to live by include Nelson Mandela, Mother Teresa and Mahatma

Gandhi. It does not matter who we are, though, we should be leading by the power of our own example. Leading by example is one of the most powerful tools available to us to positively influence change in other people.[172]

"My life is my message."

Mahatma Gandhi

If we have strong personal brand equity, then we will act in a way that not only shows others how to act, but typically inspires others to look up to us and try to follow our – hopefully, good – example.

By working on creating our unique personal brand, we not only have a responsibility towards ourselves, but to others, too, to ensure that the equity of our personal brand is of such high value that those around us would like to follow our example. We should do this not only because it is the right thing to do, but because they will see the benefits that are generated in terms of achieving our personal dreams and goals as part of our successful self-leadership journey.

"The most important thing is to try and inspire people so that they can be great in whatever they want to do."

Kobe Bryant

What is your influence on others?

"I don't do drugs. I am drugs."

Salvador Dali

I first saw the above quote painted on a panel and showcased on a wooden tripod in Covent Garden Market in London, in July 2015. It really intrigued me, and during our trip to Paris in 2018, Marilé and I visited Dali Paris, which is located in the heart of the artist village at Montmartre. The museum exhibits more than 300 artworks by Salvador Dali from a private collection. The meaning of his quote is that we can live to be someone else's drug. It got me thinking about the influence we have on others.

"Aspire to inspire before you expire."

Eugene Bell, Jr

What do we project towards those people around us when we talk, think, feel and act? Is it positivity, confidence, empathy, energy, discipline and passion, or are we projecting the opposite? Think of those people who look up to us, like our children. We can never underestimate the influence and impact on them of what we project through our behaviour.

Beating, or at least keeping your promises

"Formula for success: under promise and over deliver."

Tom Peters

The content of the above quote is a key part of increasing the equity of our personal brand. As we get older, we grow wiser. In my first marriage, I used to make a promise to my then-wife to get home after, for example, a work function, at a specific time that was maybe a little bit difficult to make. Why would I do that? I am not sure. I probably wanted to please her by saying that I would be home earlier, rather than later. Then I would sometimes miss my own deadline by a small margin, which would make me feel guilty, and she would question why I had arrived home later than promised. It was all my own doing.

In my second marriage, when I communicate my timings to my wife, I typically add 15 minutes to the actual time that I expect to be home. That way, I am the hero every time without the associated feelings of guilt.

I have shared this story simply to illustrate that, again, you are in charge. If I had initially moved my promised arrival time by 15 minutes, it would not have affected my first wife in any way, but the fact remains that I over-promised and under-delivered. People with strong brand equity under-promise and over-deliver every time.

"Undertake not what you cannot perform, but be careful to keep your promise."

George Washington

By the way, we should never use the word 'promise' unless we are prepared to pay the necessary price to keep it.[173]

I worked with a supply chain director named Wayne Griffiths just before the turn of the century. I was his management accountant and he had promised to provide me with feedback on a large budget exercise that I needed him to check by the end of a specific week. Wayne then fell extremely ill with the flu, and later that week, his circumstances changed and he needed to move to a new house earlier than planned. I totally understood his circumstances, and I no longer awaited his feedback before finalising the exercise.

About an hour before the end of the workday that Friday afternoon, I got a call from a guy with a really fluey, husky voice that I barely recognised. "Hi Hekkie, it's Wayne. I've just mailed you my feedback …"

He went on to give me a brief rundown of the key points, and just before we ended the call, I had to ask him: "Wayne, given your circumstances, why did you even bother checking my work and sending me the feedback?"

"Because I promised you that I would," was his reply. Wayne is a man of integrity, and he understood what it meant to under-promise and over-deliver, despite the fact that he could easily have used his circumstances as an excuse. He understood what it meant to be a man of his word, every time, whatever it took.

> "People with integrity do what they say they are going to do. Others have excuses."
>
> Laura Schlessinger

I know a couple of people who promise things just in passing, to try to look like a hero in that moment, but they never honour their promises. They don't realise the harm it does to their personal brand and that, over time, it projects a message of: "Don't believe what I promise you." Talk is cheap. If we say something, then we need to do it, because then people will learn to trust and respect us. As successful self-leaders, we need to own what we say. To us, over-promising and under-delivering is not an option. If we do this, we not only disappoint others, but ourselves, too.

Live a life of integrity

Keeping our promises is just one example of living a life of integrity.

> **Integrity**: The quality of being honest and having strong moral principles.[174]

If I had to choose one single word that everyone should use as the point of departure when building their personal brand equity, it would be 'integrity'. If you use strong moral principles as the foundation for your personal brand, then you probably have the best guarantee that you will not end up miserable, unsuccessful or in trouble at some point in your life.

"In the end, your integrity is all you've got."

Jack Welch

Making promises to yourself

Whenever I made a promise to myself in the past, it was always about something that I felt serious about. The thing is, whenever we make such a promise, we need to be committed enough to follow through on it – not only temporarily, but as long as is necessary to keep our promise. In line with our quest, as self-leaders, to be our own best friend, we cannot afford to disappoint ourselves by not committing to ourselves. Previous studies have shown that roughly 80% of all New Year's resolutions fail,[175] which implies that four out of every five times people make promises to themselves, they don't keep them.

My view on this is simple: If you are not sure that you have the dedication and discipline to follow through on your promise, then don't make that promise to yourself. You will always remain accountable to yourself, and there is no more important aspect to personal brand equity than being true to yourself by keeping those promises. Otherwise, you'll start to doubt if you can trust yourself – and that is the most important trust relationship that exists. If you can't trust yourself, then your personal brand starts to lose serious value, which will lead to many other issues, like a lack of confidence.

Working hard as a core value

"Hard work does not necessarily guarantee success, but no success is possible without hard work."

T.P. Chia

Most of the time, life is actually quite simple. It is us humans who tend to complicate it. For example, think of lazy people who expect to be successful, but are then disappointed when they don't achieve what they wanted to achieve. I am a firm believer in causality, which is simply the relationship between cause and effect.[176]

"For every action, there is an equal and opposite reaction."

Isaac Newton

Here is one of the ironies in life: A lazy person goes to bed at night, just as the conscientious person does, but there is one big difference. The hardworking person has a good night's sleep because of psychological fulfilment. They are also tired as a result of exertion during the day. The languid don't sleep as well because they don't feel tired enough. They might also worry about not having enough to provide for themselves or their families.

"Successful people are not gifted. They just work hard, then succeed on purpose."

G.K. Nielson

We can't expect to get a different result in our lives if we are not willing to put in the required effort and hard work to achieve our personal goals. This is one of the core values of successful self-leaders and it is at the heart of a personal brand with high equity. There is no substitute for hard work. Some people might argue that the substitute is smart work, to which I would respond that in working hard, we should in any case be working smart, too, because that way, you get optimal results.

Nothing comes from nothing. I have always told myself that, and it is something that I have taught my boys. We get out of life what we put into it.[177] My dad always told me that the only people who start from the top are gravediggers. The rest of us have to work hard, start from the bottom and work our way to the top.

"Nothing in life that's worth anything is easy."

Barack Obama

Other personal brand equity boosters

In addition to what we have discussed so far in this chapter, I would like to summarise and share with you further areas of personal brand equity that I have encountered in my life:

- *Standing up for what is right.* Most of us hate what is wrong, but only a small group of people are willing to stand up and publicly voice their objections.
- *Respecting others.* This increases the value of our personal brands by, for example, respecting others' time by being on time. We discussed this as a habit, but it applies to our personal brand equity, too.
- *Being a pleasure to be around.* These kind of people attract others to them like a magnet.
- *Honouring others.* Whenever I hear somebody publicly honouring or acknowledging others, I just think so much more of that person who did the honouring.
- *Simply smile.* Do this even more when you interact with others or just simply walk past a stranger. People with smiles light up our world.

"Peace begins with a smile."

Mother Teresa

Do not underestimate the difference you can make

"If you think you're too small to make a difference ... try sleeping with a mosquito in the room."

Dalai Lama

We should never underestimate the difference that we can make in this world. People with high-value personal brands typically make, or have the potential to make, a bigger impact on this world. But people who realise they can make a lasting difference in this world can make an even bigger impact. The ultimate impact is created when these two types are fused into someone with high personal brand equity, who also realises that they can have a positive impact – and then continues to do exactly that. Those are the people who truly make a mark on this world; they are the people behind great legacies that last for many generations. One thing they all have in common is that they are willing to give something of themselves back to others, either in the form of time or money, or both. If we become part of this group of people, others will follow our example. This in turn makes our world a much better place.

The importance of marketing your own brand

In 2020, Apple was ranked as the most valuable brand in the world, followed by Google, Microsoft, Amazon, with Facebook as the brand with the fifth highest equity.[178] Ten years earlier, Apple was also the most valuable brand, followed by Microsoft, Coca-Cola, IBM and finally Google, to complete the top five.[179]

Apple hit many headlines in 2015, exactly mid-way between these brand value surveys, when it considerably increased its global advertising budget by 50% to a record $1.8 billion. The explanation from the people at Apple was that they believed ongoing investment in marketing and advertising was the key to the development and sale of their innovative products and technologies. That year, they reported record profits of $53.4 billion on turnover of $233.7 billion.[180]

> "The only personal branding consultant who can ever hope to have a clear understanding of you and your value can be found in the mirror."
>
> Ryan Lilly

We all know that marketing works, otherwise companies like Apple would not spend billions of dollars on it. Although we are fortunate that we don't need to spend large amounts of money to market our own personal brand, we must recognise the fact that we do need to market our personal brand to generate the maximum profit, or return, from it. The other reality is that the best person to effectively market your brand is you.

In the digital age, be careful with personal branding

In today's digital age, we are encouraged to do things, like define our audience. Following the advice of experts, we prepare elevator pitches on who we are, we grow our online presence, and perhaps even start a blog.[181] Yes, this is part of the 'new' way of doing things, but we need to be careful that we don't allow external forces and our desire to satisfy the needs of others, to influence who we are. Our personal brand is much more than our online persona. How we show up at home, at work, in the way we speak and how we interact with others ultimately defines our personal brand.[182]

> "Your brand is what other people say about you when you're not in the room."
>
> Jeff Bezos

REFLECTION ON THE CONTENT OF THIS CHAPTER – VALUING PERSONAL BRAND EQUITY

Consider the topics that we have covered:

- Choose core personal values early in life
- Design your own personal brand
- Lead by example
- What is your influence on others?
- Beating, or at least keeping your promises
- Live a life of integrity
- Making promises to yourself
- Working hard as a core value
- Other personal brand equity boosters
- Do not underestimate the difference you can make
- The importance of marketing your own brand
- In the digital age, be careful with personal branding

Please rate your current overall level of success in Valuing Personal Brand Equity as a percentage score:

_____%

Chapter 17

Cherishing Relationships

"It is in the courageous encounter with others that we discover our personal path and purpose in life ..."

LOVEMORE MBIGI

Mother Teresa (1910-1997) was born Agnes Gonxha Bojaxhiu, the daughter of an ethnic Albanian grocer. She went to Ireland in 1928 to join the Sisters of Loretto at the Institute of the Blessed Virgin Mary. Six weeks later, she sailed to India, where she taught for 17 years at the order's school in Calcutta. She was the founder of the Order of the Missionaries of Charity, which is a Roman Catholic congregation of women who dedicated their lives to the poor, particularly those in India, where they opened numerous centres serving the blind, aged and disabled.

In 1962, the Indian government awarded Mother Teresa the Padma Shri, one of its highest civilian honours, for her services to the people of India. In 1979 she received the Nobel Peace Prize for her humanitarian work, and the following year the Indian government conferred on her the country's highest civilian honour, the Bharat Ratna. At the time of her death, Mother Teresa's order included hundreds of centres in more than 90 countries, with about 4 000 nuns and hundreds of thousands of lay workers.[183]

Some of Mother Teresa's quotes, which she also actively lived, include:
- "Intense love does not measure. It just gives."
- "If you judge people, you have no time to love them."
- "Let us always meet each other with a smile, for the smile is the beginning of love."
- "A life not lived for others is not a life."
- "God does not create poverty; we do, because we do not share."
- "One of the greatest diseases is to be nobody to anybody."
- "Do ordinary things with extraordinary love."

Remembering Mother Teresa, I think of her warmth, smile, humility, and how she stood up for what is right. But, above all, something else specifically stands out to me: Her love for people and how she cherished relationships. Her life epitomises the power of relationships and what is possible in this world if we value relationships. Aside from looking after our bodies, this is the one other area in our lives where we cannot afford to mess around if we are to be successful self-leaders. Our relationships are critical: Our relationship with God; our partners; spouses; children; friends; family; and the people around us, and ultimately, the most important relationship – with ourselves. Besides, our self-leadership efforts without the external support of those I have just mentioned, are less likely to succeed.[184]

Ubuntu – I am because we are

Africa is my home, and I have travelled sufficiently and seen enough of the world to know that this is where I want to be.

"If I have ever seen magic, it has been in Africa."

John Hemingway

Our continent has a distinctive philosophy called 'ubuntu', which particularly influences the way personal relationships are managed.

> **Ubuntu**: A view around humanity towards others that suggests that it is not through solitude that we discover who we are, but through relationships with other people. It is rooted in the belief that we can only find fulfilment within our extended family and community.[185]

The philosophy of ubuntu perfectly aligns with the rationale that relationships matter and that we need each other, and the support from one another, to be able to achieve our individual and collective goals. This should not only be an African way of life, though – it should be a global way of life that we all embrace.

Charity begins at home

If I had not had such a solid relationship with Marilé, there is no way I would have been able to complete a PhD and stay married. While I was spending time on my research and writing up my thesis, she took up various hobbies, some of which she mastered to the point of presenting classes in her field. She gave me nothing but incredible, unselfish love because she knew and respected how serious I was about achieving my personal goal.

"If you want to change the world, go home and love your family."
Mother Teresa

The way we love our family, and how we support each other, is a true testimony of who we are and of how much we value relationships. The value of having great relationships with everyone in our families can never, ever be overstated.

"The most significant work we will do in our whole life, in our whole world, is done within the four walls of our home."
Stephen Covey

What is needed to build these relationships is time, quality time. There is no better place to find this than around a table, enjoying a meal together. As a family, we spend what feels like hours around a dinner or Sunday lunch table, discussing stories, plans, events, news, or just having fun and talking nonsense. Spending quality time with your family is the best investment you will ever make.

CHAPTER 17: CHERISHING RELATIONSHIPS

"The greatest moments in life are not concerned with selfish achievements but rather with the things we do for the people we love and esteem."

Walt Disney

Time together as a family is vital, but it is equally important that we build one-on-one moments with different family members into our routines. The more time we spend in quality interactions, the stronger we will be as individuals and as a family. We should never underestimate how important this is. It all starts with our relationship with God and, as adults, with our spouse or partner. If the relationship between the parents in a family is on shaky ground, then the rest of the family will take strain, too. However, if we all have strong relationships and can support each other in achieving our individual and family goals, then life is a song.

Remember, we can never buy time later and make up for lost time – especially with our children.

Frederick Douglass was an American anti-slavery activist. Before he died in 1895, he was quoted as saying: *"It is easier to build strong children than to repair broken men."* Douglass was a wise man who understood the significance of building strong children by spending time with them and teaching them. Stephen Covey supported this when he said: *"If we do not teach our children, society will. And they, and we, will live with the results."* [186]

As successful self-leaders, our influence goes beyond just spending quality time with our family members. Part of cherishing our relationships at home and caring for our loved ones is teaching them things about life: Issues like finances, changing a flat tyre, what to look out for when travelling, how to do chores like ironing and cooking, to name just a few. But, if we really care for the people we love, we will not only sufficiently provide for them while we are alive, but also financially when we unexpectedly have to exchange this life for the life hereafter. Then, if we don't get the opportunity to achieve all of our personal goals, we can at least put them in a position to achieve their own.

The vulnerable

"Just because you're in the driver's seat, doesn't mean you have to run people over."

Randy Pausch

As self-leaders, our foundation of taking charge of our own lives does not give us the right to take charge of the lives of others. Yes, we sometimes need to help people to take charge of their own lives, but we cannot do it for them. This makes me think about those people who are vulnerable, like the young, the poor, the orphaned, the disempowered, the abused and the marginalised. Our relationship with them, and our kindness towards them, needs to be extra special and particularly gentle, because they need it more than anyone else does.

"I've learned that people will forget what you said, people will forget what you did, but people will never forget how you made them feel."

Maya Angelou

It is important that we leave every single person who intersects our path better, happier, and more engaged than we found them.[187]

"Live and let live," Dad taught me. Essentially, we have to tolerate the opinions and behaviour of others so that they will similarly tolerate our own.[188] In the context of self-leadership, I would like to put a twist on this definition and change it to: "Chase your personal goals and enable others to do the same." I think this is particularly applicable to people who are vulnerable because they don't necessarily have the means or skills to succeed without our help.

"The true measure of any society can be found in how it treats its most vulnerable members."

Mahatma Gandhi

Those who can do nothing for you ...

My dad also taught me that the true test of character is the way you treat your neighbour, specifically including the people you don't know, but with whom you interact. This should be applicable always – not only when they are nice to you or they can help you with something.

"Your true character is most accurately measured by how you treat those who can do 'nothing' for you."

Mother Teresa

If we believe that relationships matter, then other people, who cannot necessarily do anything for us, will experience and see this truth in how we treat and help them.

Kill rude people with kindness

As much as this counterintuitive statement may go against our very grain, it is something else that Mom and Dad always told me to do. Amazingly, I have found throughout my life that this works – not always, but most of the time. I am not suggesting that you need to sell your soul and cave into the demands of rude people, but if you are kind to them, then you usually catch them off guard. It confuses them, because they are often passionate people (in the wrong way), and kindness is the last thing they expect. They want to fight fire with fire, and your kindness is not a response they have considered. By being kind and fair, but firm, you'll build relationships with even those people who initially opted for rudeness as a default.

"As I think about the happiness I have experienced, it seems that it has come in its most acute and pleasing form when I have received kindness or when I have given kindness."

Norman Vincent Peale

People who are generally rude, contaminate relationships. People who are kind contribute to harmony in the workplace and other environments in which they find themselves. They build healthy relationships.

The value of networking

One of my friends at university would always say: "It's not what you know, but who you know." I think that is quite an extreme statement, but it highlights the value of networks and networking in all the different spheres of our lives.

"If you want to go fast, go alone. If you want to go far, go with others."
African proverb

The benefits of networking can be endless, and the beauty of it is that if we feel that others are gaining more from it than we are, we can either change that relationship or opt out of it. We can learn from one another, put people in contact with each other, and use the people in our network as a sounding board.

"Relationships are the currency of business."
Brian Basilico

If we understand how to manage our networks, we add to our resource pool. This automatically gives us an advantage in working towards our personal goal achievement – as long as we can reciprocally provide the same kinds of benefits to others in our network. I have found it useful to apply a little more science to network management by using a simple spreadsheet to track things, like people turnover in key organisational positions with which I deal, birthdays, preferences, a previous discussion summary, and outstanding actions.

"Every mind needs friendly contact with other minds for food of expansion and growth."
Napoleon Hill

If we have strong enough relationships – within our friendship circle, too – then nobody in such a network should in any way hesitate or feel scared to use the network for inspiration, or to provide the necessary support during times of serious challenge.

As a final word on networking: Dad always said that in any relationship, we need to keep our side clean. This means that we cannot owe anyone anything in any relationship. This includes forgiveness. It's a liberating feeling to be able to look someone in the eyes without having any regrets or feelings of guilt between you.

Discussing people harms relationships

Marilé once came across a quote: "Those who talk to you about people, talk about you to people." Talking about people without them being present and part of the conversation, destroys relationships. We, as successful self-leaders, cannot and do not entertain anything like this.

"Strong minds discuss ideas, average minds discuss events, weak minds discuss people."

Socrates

The wonderful gift of giving

"Service is the rent we pay for our space in life."

Dave Kraft

It took me a long time to realise how important service is in my life. If I had known that we got so much back simply by giving to others, I would have started doing this a long time ago … I'm not necessarily referring to money here, but to giving of our time, and having sincere, deep discussions with people whenever we get the opportunity to make a difference in their lives. In so doing, we are able to give back so much, in so many different ways, in the different communities in which we operate. We can do this simply by sharing our experiences, knowledge and wisdom with those who can benefit from it. I honestly believe that we cannot be genuinely happy if we are not willing to give something of ourselves to others …

"We exist temporarily through what we take, but we live forever through what we give."

Douglas A. Lawson

It is important to understand that the spirit in which we give to someone is as important as the act itself. We have so much to give, but we can probably make more use of this wonderful gift of giving with which we have been blessed. In the process, we can then build stronger relationships and bridges with other people. Our gifts to others don't have to be big, cost us money or take much of our time. I was once told that "encouragement creates life," and sometimes we only need to encourage someone to do the right thing, or to follow their dreams. That's enough.

"The time is always right to do what is right."

Martin Luther King Jr

Be willing to receive

I used to be someone who didn't like to receive, but I enjoyed being able to give something to someone. This included gift-giving. Over time, Marilé pointed out to me the unfairness of my view, and I slowly but surely started to change. At some point, I saw the light and realised that by only being willing to give, I was depriving others of the pleasure of giving something, too. Herein lies the heart of constructive relationships – those relationships that work both ways. In any relationship, we give, and we also receive. This allows us to create a bond with one another. If we are not willing to also receive, then this bond cannot be forged.

I am more interested in the colour of your soul

One day, after school, Refentse Morake, a 17-year-old Sesotho boy, was messing around with his guitar outside his parents' home in Vereeniging. A neighbour, Cecilia Marchionna, or Tannie Kleintjie, as she is known, heard him play. She asked him if she could take a video of him singing *De La Rey*, a traditionally white, Afrikaans song. She posted it on Facebook and within a couple of days, the video had gone viral and accumulated 160 000 views. Now, six years later, Refentse has established himself as a popular, black, Afrikaans music star.[189]

"You must be the change you wish to see in the world."
Mahatma Gandhi

Our world will be a much better place if we can all realise that the colour of someone's soul is more important than the colour of their skin ... Consider someone who has the same skin colour as you, but they are a rapist, murderer and menace to society. Compare that person to someone with a different skin colour or from a different culture from you. However, that person shares the same value system as you. They are caring, loving and a blessing to mankind. Who would you choose as a friend? It is more important than ever that we humans unite to embrace diversity and inclusion. Let's reach out to each other, despite our physical differences, as a sign of understanding that relationships matter, while working towards our common and personal life goals.

"There is no such thing as race. None. There is just a human race – scientifically, anthropologically."
Toni Morrison

Respect is the root of all good relationships

Mahatma Gandhi said that the first principle on which any relationship ought to be based is respect. We might not necessarily agree with someone or with their viewpoints, but if we respect them and their views, then at least we are opening our minds to different, exciting possibilities. We are then also able to engage in interesting and constructive conversations without denying ourselves the opportunity to explore further. Life would have been very boring and stale if we all held the same viewpoint and had the same skin colour, complexion, culture and interests. These differences spice up our lives and make it interesting – as long as we can respect each other.

On the topic of respect, we need to understand that religious or racist jokes, or jokes that discriminate against groups of people, do not exist – because they are not jokes. They are the ultimate sign of disrespect by those who make them. They destroy relationships. They go against the grain of working towards a diverse and inclusive society and can only do harm. As successful self-leaders who believe in building solid relationships, we cannot practise, condone or entertain such conduct.

You can't give what you don't have

There is a saying that goes: "You cannot pour from an empty cup." I cannot give to someone something that I don't have. If I am miserable, I can't give joy to another person in a relationship. If I am negative, then I can't expect someone with whom I engage on a daily basis to be positive. These are just a couple of examples of why it is so important to work on our successful self-leadership each day. I cannot teach someone else to be a successful self-leader if I am not successful as a self-leader. I can also not inspire, motivate or energise someone else if I am not inspired, motivated and energised …

If I am empty inside, then I cannot fill someone else's proverbial cup with something that is good and constructive. We therefore not only owe it to ourselves to become better at self-leadership to become the best we can possibly be, but also to benefit every single person with whom we have a relationship – to help them become the best they can be.

John Adair writes in the book *Confucius on Leadership*[190] that if we, as individuals, are not inspired, then we cannot possibly expect to inspire others. My interpretation of this is that we cannot give to others what we do not have. Let's make sure we have enough, and that our life batteries are sufficiently charged to be able to inspire others. Only if we are inspired can we positively influence and impact others.

Complimenting the chef

Leo Buscaglia tells the story of how he once complimented a big, burly chef, and how the seemingly rude man then morphed into the most pleasant person within a couple of seconds. From his story, I have learned to compliment the chef whenever I have an exceptional meal. I have done this in different parts of the world, and guess what? I always get the same pleasant response in the form of a big smile. Why? Because 99% of the time, the chef only receives moans or complaints from grumpy customers. To get a compliment, even that one percent of the time, makes a massive difference in their lives. If someone deserves a compliment, then give it to them. It does wonders to them and to you.

"I can live for two months on a good compliment."

Mark Twain

Complimenting the chef is an example of how small things in relationships can make meaningful differences. I used to be a much stricter dad. Chris, our youngest, is quite vocal about the fact that since I have been married to Marilé, I am a much more pleasant dad to be around. I obviously refute this and ascribe it purely to me becoming increasingly successful at self-leadership! However, Marilé definitely taught me that wherever I go in life, it is important to acknowledge people – even if it is just to look them in the eyes with a smile. I no longer stop at traffic lights without smiling and waving at someone standing there. Even if I am unable to give them money on a specific day, I do this because it makes them feel worthy, and it reminds me every single time that I am no better than anyone else on this Earth.

Tell and show others that they are good enough

Henri's Grade 0 teacher told him that he was stupid. Today, he is studying a course to which only 40 students get accepted each year from the whole of South Africa. He earned distinctions in all of his matric subjects and achieved a 90% average mark. I am not sharing this story because I am an upset father with a grudge against a teacher who made a bad judgement call. Rather, it is a reminder to us all not to make the same mistake. Earlier, we discussed how we all, at times, feel not good enough. When someone else then also tells us that we are not good enough, it is like being thrown off a cliff.

It is not only important to tell people that they are good enough, but also to show them that they are good enough by recognising their achievements, both privately and in the presence of others. We should celebrate their successes with them, too. For some reason, people are sometimes too shy or too scared to talk about their achievements, but if we have a close enough relationship with them, we will know when they have achieved something.

Recognising their achievements and celebrating with them gives us the opportunity to show them that they are good enough.

Telling and showing other people that they are good enough not only does them good, but it also makes us feel good. Then, where we live and work, we start to create a culture in which complimenting each other is encouraged. This gives relationships a healthy boost.

Don't let technology ruin relationships

I once read a suggestion that we should do more things that make us forget to check our phones. Technology is great, but only to a point. It is wonderful seeing my parents' joy during video calls with my sister and her family in Canada. This technological advancement is something that wasn't freely available a decade ago. Where technology is great for relationships in some ways, it can also be very damaging in others.

Whenever we, as a family, enjoy a meal together – at home or in public places – we play 'stack'. Basically, all of our cellphones are switched to flight mode and then stacked face down on top of each other on the far side of the table. If we don't do this, then we'll never get a chance to work on our relationships as a family by spending quality time together. If we don't manage technology, this great enabler will become cyanide to our relationships. It could even be a killer, when you drive into the back of that idling truck because you were texting someone while you were driving …

We are in this together

In the movie *Hunter Killer*, Commander Joe Glass (Gerard Butler) tries to convince the Russian Captain Sergei Andropov (Michael Nyqvist) to assist him and his crew on the USS Arkansas submarine to navigate through dangerous Russian waters to rescue the Russian president. He says: "It's not about your side or my side … This is about *our* future."[191]

These are insightful words, and if we can successfully adopt this approach in our families, careers, friendships and communities, it will go a long way to making a positive impact in this world.

There is a saying: "What if I told you that the left wing and the right wing belong to the same bird." My point is that we are all in this world together, and it is my hope that if there is one good thing that could come from the COVID pandemic, it is that all humans realise this.

REFLECTION ON THE CONTENT OF THIS CHAPTER – CHERISHING RELATIONSHIPS

Consider the topics that we have covered:

- Ubuntu – I am because we are
- Charity begins at home
- The vulnerable
- Those who can do nothing for you …
- Kill rude people with kindness
- The value of networking
- Discussing people harms relationships
- The wonderful gift of giving
- Be willing to receive
- I am more interested in the colour of your soul
- Respect is the root of all good relationships
- You can't give what you don't have
- Complimenting the chef
- Tell and show others that they are good enough
- Don't let technology ruin relationships
- We are in this together

Please rate your current overall level of success in Cherishing Relationships as a percentage score:

_____%

Chapter 18

Investing Time to Reflect

"Follow effective actions with quiet reflection. From the quiet reflection will come even more effective action."
PETER DRUCKER

One of my other passions is supply chain management. That is where my career roots lie. About 12 years ago, when I started thinking about doing my doctoral studies, I met with someone from the Council for Scientific and Industrial Research (CSIR) in Stellenbosch. I will call him Robert, for the sake of this anecdote. At that point, I was thinking of a research topic in an area on which Robert was focusing full-time at the CSIR.

I would guess that Robert was in his late 50s, and he struck me as a true gentleman and a caring person. We probably spent three hours together, during which time he patiently shared with me everything that occupied his time around my topic of interest. He seemed to be at peace and content and had just returned from a vacation in Europe with his wife – for the last time. At that point, Robert had a couple of months left to live. He had been diagnosed with terminal cancer.

Despite the fact that he was very ill, Robert still entertained my request to meet with a smile on his face. He had been told not to come to work any longer, but he insisted on doing so, because he said that it was part of his work ethic not to just give up for the sake of illness. Towards the end of our time together, Robert told me about Randy Pausch, who had then recently passed away at the age of 47. He had also battled terminal cancer.

Randy had published a book before he died, called *The Last Lecture*. That book had delivered a lasting message to his young children about the way he hoped they would live their lives when he would no longer be with them. At the time we met, Robert was reading Randy's book.

After my meeting with Robert, I bought and also read Randy's book, in which he touched on his life experiences and the lessons he had learned from those experiences. I was struck by a particularly important life lesson: No matter what challenges or obstacles try to get in the way of reaching our goals in life, never give up, and keep a positive attitude towards achieving these goals.[192] This was particularly profound from someone who had such a short time left to live.

Randy Pausch was an American educator and professor at Carnegie Mellon University (CMU) in Pittsburgh, Pennsylvania. On 27 November 2007, he gave his final lecture, with the important lesson that time is all we have.[193] This actual 'last lecture', which was expanded into a book, became a *New York Times* bestseller and sold millions of copies.

One of the important questions that Randy asked in his book, which we can all ask ourselves, is: "*Are you spending your time on the right things?*" He then also makes the following statement: "*Time is all you have. And you may find one day that you have less than you think ...*"[194]

Randy Pausch lived a full life until he died. He literally took advantage of every second.

So why would I tell you two stories of two guys who died from cancer? From what I have experienced first-hand, and from what I have read, they were both incredible individuals. It is also clear to me that both men accepted their fate with dignity and grace, although it could not have been easy. Both men were forced to invest time in reflecting on their lives, as their hourglasses were quickly running out. But here is the difference between them and, hopefully, us: Although they could reflect upon their lives and where they were in reaching their dreams and achieving their personal goals, they had one problem – they had no time left to do anything about their outstanding dreams and goals.

I can only speculate, but I am confident that if someone had told both Randy and Robert on their 30th birthdays that they were going to die at an early age, they would have reflected more and prioritised their dreams and personal goals differently. They would, in all probability, also have worked harder to achieve some of their dreams earlier in their lives.

Perhaps more than 99% of you reading this book won't have to face, at this point in time, what Robert and Randy had to face, but we owe it to ourselves to take their message seriously: Use your time wisely, reflect more, do more and achieve more. It is fair enough to say that we all have to die one day, and we don't know when that will happen. We have an option to ignore this fact and to live like death does not exist, or we can exercise the alternative option, in which we make time to reflect more on where we are in making our dreams and goals a reality. I choose to do the latter, and I trust that you will do the same.

"The journey into self-love and self-acceptance must begin with self-examination … until you take the journey of self-reflection, it is almost impossible to grow or learn in life."

Iyanla Vanzant

Why reflect?

> **Self-reflection**: Serious thought about one's character and actions.[195]

Self-reflection is a critical component of self-leadership, and it is vital if we are to learn and grow.[196]

Engaging in reflective thinking will influence our ability as leaders to learn about ourselves and about other people.[197] I think the benefit of investing in time to reflect upon and take stock of our lives, lies in the fact that it allows us to check whether we are on track to achieve what we want and aspire to in life. When we reflect, it should be for the right reasons. This should not be to take up the whip and regret, but to see how we, as self-leaders, have performed up to that point. We can then look to the future, take charge and, if necessary, change the course of our journey. Taking out the whip leads to self-doubt, which then leads to procrastination. Instead of propelling ourselves towards our personal goals, we then end up slowing down and battling to achieve these goals. Life is too short to spend it at war with ourselves.

One of the most amazing things about life is the fact that we have so much time and we can create so many opportunities to reflect and correct where we need to, yet so few of us make use of this most effective technique to improve our lives and circumstances … If more people made the time to deeply think about their lives and to identify what to improve, then less people would be unhappy or disappointed with themselves. Without reflection there can be no realisation, which is the first step to changing something for the good in our lives.

"Our souls need time to think, dream, and reflect."

Jo Ann Davis

> We need to stop and reflect on our lives. We need to make time for ourselves each week to, on our own, in a relaxed environment, ask ourselves these sorts of questions:
>
> - Am I living life right?
> - Do I have to make some changes?
> - What is stopping me from living to my full potential?
> - What is holding me back?
> - How am I doing, compared to the main personal goals and supporting goals that I set myself in my personal goals scorecard? What changes do I need to make to these?
> - If I continue on my current journey, will I one day look back on my life and smile with satisfaction?

It is important to note, though, that there are different ways to use reflection for personal improvement.

The self-leadership charter as a basis for reflection

We all have different schedules and routines, but we cannot underestimate the power of taking 20 minutes of 'me-time' – ideally once a day. We have spoken about the importance of routine and why routine matters in our lives, so to add a daily 20-minute self-reflection session into our routine will be another way to charge our life batteries.

If we are serious about achieving our dreams, then we need to use the power that such an appointment with ourselves gives us: To reflect on where we currently are, versus affirming and visualising what we can potentially achieve. There is no excuse why we cannot dedicate this amount of time to make one of the biggest and best investments ever – the investment in ourselves. This is an extremely important habit to learn and live.

"Time spent in self-reflection is never wasted – it is an intimate date with yourself."

Paul T.P. Wong

I believe that a key part of our self-reflection process should be the use of our individual self-leadership charter document to assess our progress. This is a way to check how you are performing against your own credo, your main personal goals and its supporting goals. Then you can work on making the necessary adjustments to your thoughts, feelings and behaviour in order to give yourself the best chance to achieve your dreams in the shortest possible time frame. During these reflection sessions, you will need to offer yourself as much honest and objective feedback as possible. Only when you can rely on your own feedback will it make a meaningful change in your life.

"Talk to yourself once in a day, otherwise you may miss meeting an excellent person in this world."

Swami Vivekananda

We learn, improve and grow through reflection, practice, and then reflection again. This deep reflection also gives us an opportunity to amend our goals and pull them in line with what we have already achieved as we progress. It's also possible that we might encounter something new that we would like to add to our personal continuous improvement journey. Reflection does not have to consume a significant amount of time, but it does require discipline to create a practice that supports our return to repeated reflection. That is how we grow and change.[198]

As a final note on this subject, we obviously don't want to use our self-leadership charter for menial personal objectives, because we then dilute its impact on our lives. It will also then take too long to work through it and to reflect on it on a daily basis. Besides, in addition to your own credo, it should only contain the goals that support your dreams. However, if upon self-reflection, you realise that you are really battling, perhaps on a daily basis, with something that has a profound impact on your life, like emotional intelligence or even depression, then I suggest that you add this to your self-leadership charter as part of your goal-setting process. This might then include, as a supporting goal, visiting or regularly seeing someone, like a coach, clinical psychologist or even a medical practitioner. They can assist you in achieving a new main personal goal of overcoming, or at least managing, this important area of your life.

The content of this book as a basis for reflection

Assuming that you agree with the content that I have shared with you in this book, you can use this as another tool to reflect on your life, chapter by chapter, in addition to using your own self-leadership charter. If you don't agree with some of the things that I have documented here, which worked for me but might not work for you, then simply exclude those areas from your reflection process and use the content with which you do agree. The content of this book is a good framework to use during reflection to help you significantly improve as a self-leader.

When using this book during your reflection process, it is important to not only use your own feedback, but to also consider the feedback of others. This assumes, of course, that they are reliable sources who will give you an accurate account of how you show up from, for example, a discipline or emotional intelligence point of view.

"Reflection is one of the most underused yet powerful tools for success."
Richard Carlson

In line with the basic definition of self-leadership, I have shared with you the goal-setting and achievement process from the point of view of the self-leadership charter. As far as the rest of the content of this book is concerned, my aim is to highlight those areas in feelings, thoughts and behaviour that helped me to chase my dreams and achieve my personal goals to support these dreams. This is an ongoing process. It is from this content that I suggest you pick two or three areas in which you feel you are weaker, to focus on improving daily. You can use the tools that I have shared with you, like affirmations, visualisation and self-talk, to improve in these areas – to such an extent that you can then replace them with new areas in which you feel the need for improvement.

Using a calendar for quick, daily reflection

I have an annual calendar in my garage that I use for self-reflection just after I park my car when I return from work in the afternoon, or simply at the end of the day if I have been working from home. Next to the calendar I have two highlighters – one green and one orange. Whenever I have had a good day, in which I have been proud of my thoughts, feelings and behaviour, I then highlight that day in green. Whenever I have had a day in which I didn't meet my own expectations in this regard, I mark that day in orange.

Regardless of the type of day I have had, I always ask myself: "Why? Why was it a good day?" or "Why was it less than a good day?" and "What can I learn from this or do better next time to help it become a green day?"

Using my calendar for quick reflection might sound weird, but it is incredible how I aspire, both consciously and I am sure unconsciously, to do whatever it takes to only see green days when I walk towards the calendar. It is a quick, one-page feedback tool that I use to check if my self-leadership journey is on track or not.

The power of: "From the next time"

Whenever we, as a result of our self-reflection, or just in the moment when we interact with someone, realise that we have made a mistake or have not done justice to ourselves, we can only learn from the experience to ensure that we don't repeat it. We can't rewind and undo what we have done wrong, but the least we can do is use affirmations, visualisation and self-talk to ensure that we don't repeat the same mistake from the next time.

If, for example, you allowed someone to upset you and you lost your cool, then simply affirm to yourself something like: "*But from the next time*, I am cool, calm and collected, because I am emotionally intelligent and everyone, including myself, will benefit as a result of my positive actions."

You can then add visualisation to this affirmation and already see how, if you encounter the same scenario in the future, you can act in an emotionally intelligent manner that will allow you to be proud of yourself afterwards. By quietly using self-talk while others are around, or out loud with passion and emotion when you are alone, you can then tell yourself in the moment, or before the moment, that you will not repeat the same mistake as before.

"In order to succeed you must fail, so that you know what not to do the next time."

Anthony J. D'Angelo

We can obviously not use 'from the next time' every time we repeat the same mistake, because then we are effectively saying it is acceptable to keep on doing an injustice to ourselves and to others. That is not something that we, as successful self-leaders, would entertain. Otherwise, we become like someone who repeats the same sin every day and expects to receive forgiveness for it every single day. No, we will use 'from the next time' once, or maybe twice, and then our thoughts, feelings and behaviour have to be aligned to who we are, and also aligned to our personal goals.

Reward yourself and celebrate your successes

Earlier I touched on the importance of celebrating our successes. Here I would like to remind you of the importance of recognising your achievements upon reflection and giving yourself a pat on the back. If you have achieved something significant, spoil both you and your family. Allow your successes, especially around goal achievement, to sink in properly. Appreciate them and celebrate them by rewarding yourself in some form or other. Remember, you are not here to impress anyone but yourself, as you are only accountable to yourself.

> "Rewarding yourself, helps to build rapport and give yourself that extra boost and determination to hit the next goal."
>
> James Fullerton

Even if it is something small, like swimming 50 continuous laps in the pool in preparation for the Midmar Mile, I celebrate my achievement through self-talk. I tell myself with some emotion: "Well done!" It is important to also reflect on the small things in life and to praise and reward ourselves for small victories. It is vital that we replace our reliance on the acknowledgement from other people with acknowledgement from ourselves. If we have to wait for acknowledgement from others, then we might have to wait for a long time.

Embrace your own process of evolution

If I do macro-reflection on my life, particularly over the past decade, I can see that I have changed so many of my perceptions, thoughts and approaches that I am certainly not the person I was back then. I believe, though, that these changes were mainly for the good and that they have made me a more successful self-leader. This is also because I consciously and continuously focus on working on my personal weaknesses. As developing self-leaders, we need to embrace and encourage the progress that we notice every time that we reflect on our lives. Embracing this positive change will lead to more positive change.

REFLECTION ON THE CONTENT OF THIS CHAPTER – INVESTING TIME TO REFLECT

Consider the topics that we have covered:

- Why reflect?
- The self-leadership charter as a basis for reflection
- The content of this book as a basis for reflection
- Using a calendar for quick, daily reflection
- The power of: "From the next time"
- Reward yourself and celebrate your successes
- Embrace your own process of evolution

Please rate your current overall level of success in Investing Time to Reflect as a percentage score:

_____%

Reflection Summary – Chapters 1-18

The first 18 chapters of this book cover the areas on which we should be focusing if we are to experience and enjoy self-leadership success. As a reflection summary, I would urge you to transfer all of your chapter percentage scores over to this page in order to get an overall self-leadership rating.

The intention is not to score a pass rate or a distinction, but to emphasise the significance of continuous improvement as self-leaders. Besides, self-leadership is a deliberate process with which each one of us chooses to engage, develop habits through experience, continually refine, and improve our processes along the way.[199]

"Champions keep playing until they get it right."

Billie Jean King

If you have read this far, then you are serious about improving as a self-leader, and about reaping the rewards and benefits associated with this process. So, do yourself a favour and diarise six months from now, so that you can rate yourself again then to get another overall score to compare to the one that you have just documented. I am not a clairvoyant, but I can almost guarantee that if you are serious and have committed to self-improvement, you would have improved your score.

Chapter 1	_____%	Chapter 10	_____%
Chapter 2	_____%	Chapter 11	_____%
Chapter 3	_____%	Chapter 12	_____%
Chapter 4	_____%	Chapter 13	_____%
Chapter 5	_____%	Chapter 14	_____%
Chapter 6	_____%	Chapter 15	_____%
Chapter 7	_____%	Chapter 16	_____%
Chapter 8	_____%	Chapter 17	_____%
Chapter 9	_____%	Chapter 18	_____%

TOTAL SCORE: (Adding up all 18 chapters) _____

AVERAGE SCORE: (Total score divided by 18) _____%

Another interesting perspective would be to ask someone close to you, who knows you well and whom you can trust, like your spouse or direct manager, to rate how successful they perceive you to be in each of the 18 chapters. Then compare their scores to yours. You will soon see if there are any big discrepancies between the two sets of scores. This will help you to double-check if *your reality* is a true reflection of the *real reality*. Nevertheless, this process will help you to identify the areas on which you should focus first to improve your self-leadership success.

When I personally reflect on how I am doing against all of the areas that we have covered in this book, then I am certainly doing much better than I did a couple of years ago. I do continuously strive towards improving every day, every week and every year. I have definitely not yet reached 100% as an overall subjective score – and I might never get there – but I am certainly working hard to try to master all of these areas in my life. Finally, I can attest to the fact that your mastery of these areas will make you a better self-leader with an increased chance of success and happiness in life.

Chapter 19

Embracing that it is Never too Late

"You can't go back and change the beginning, but you can start where you are and change the ending."

C.S. LEWIS

At the age of 16, Walt Disney served in the Red Cross Ambulance Corps in World War I. After falling victim to the global influenza pandemic, he went home to recover, before being reassigned to a new base in South Beach, Connecticut. There, Disney met the future founder of the McDonald's burger chain, Ray Kroc, who was only 15 years old at the time. Ray made the following observation of "Diz", as he nicknamed Disney. Kroc thought him to be a strange duck. "Whenever we went into town to chase girls, he stayed in camp, drawing pictures."[200]

Disney and Kroc had more in common than serving together in the army in 1918. On July 18, 1955, when Walt Disney was 53 years old, he opened Disneyland to the general public. Although Disneyland received a huge amount of publicity for the release, it did not perform as expected in the initial phase.[201]

In 1954, Ray Kroc visited a restaurant owned by brothers Dick and Mac McDonald in San Bernardino, California. He went into business with them, and the McDonald's franchise was launched on 15 April 1955,[202] when Ray was 52 years old. Neither Disney nor Kroc were successful in the early years of their lives. They were both late bloomers, and they certainly embraced the fact that it is *never* too late. Otherwise, they would not have kept on aiming for business and financial success, becoming famous in the process.

"It is never too late to be who you might have been."

George Eliot

As mentioned earlier, fame and fortune is only one measure of success. We can achieve success in so many other ways, but it's critical that we never think that it is too late to change our ways to achieve success, as we define it. It is never too late to tweak, or maybe even drastically change, a couple of things in our lives to become more successful self-leaders. This allows you and me to exponentially increase our chances of achieving success, simply because we will only then be able to live life to our full potential and lead other people in the best possible manner.

You can google all of the different reasons why people don't achieve their full potential as often as you like, but you might then discover, as I did when looking at these diverse opinions, that they are all nothing more than excuses that people like to use as reasons. The issue of age, and believing that we are too old for change, is one type of excuse.

You might say that you are 60 years old and that you have way less time than a 30-year-old. My response to this is that you might have another 25 productive years ahead of you. Randy Pausch only had another 17 years available to him when he was half of your current age …

"It's never too late for a new beginning in your life."

Joyce Meyer

At this point in our journey together, I would like to invite you to script your own success story, based on the assumption that it is never too late to start working on what you dream to achieve – also assuming that only excuses can stand between you and much more success.

Do the newspaper exercise that I shared with you earlier, and visualise what the cover page of your newspaper could potentially be five years from now. That would be a good starting point to accelerate your self-leaderhip journey.

It is critical to finish strong

In Dave Kraft's book, *Leaders Who Last*, he makes a seemingly controversial statement: "*Only 30% of leaders last.*"[203] Kraft focuses on the fact that it's not how you start the race, but how strongly you finish your individual leadership race that counts.

Steve Farrar writes in *Finishing Strong*[204] how so few leaders achieve this goal of a strong finish, and how crucial this is in our lives. Many people don't finish strong in life, and I believe this is mainly because somewhere along their self-leadership journey, they have steered and stayed off course. They have lost focus on personal leadership and, in the process, robbed themselves of the opportunity to become the best that they can possibly be.

"It's not where you start – It's where you finish that counts."

Zig Ziglar

One of my grandfathers died when I was four years old. He was only 46 at the time – four years younger than I am now. Sadly, my only recollection of him is that he was an alcoholic and an abusive man. He totally neglected his health and ultimately succumbed to emphysema and lung cancer. Sure, he probably had good points, too, but those are my only memories of him. That's it. My recollections are not that we played ball, or that I sat on his lap while he read me a story, or that he tickled me while we played on the carpet … I have no doubt that if he had realised at some point in his life that it was never too late to get his self-leadership journey back on track, he would have probably finished strong.

I am also convinced that in his dying moments, my grandfather was thinking of what he did to himself and, more importantly, what he did to other people, especially to those who were supposedly close to him. Finally, I am confident that, if he knew that the only legacy he would leave behind to his only grandson is what I am now sharing with you, he would have turned his life around and become a strong self-leader. I wish I could tell him that after the tender age of 46, there are so many great things that one can experience in life, but that you have to make the decision to take charge – but I can't.

Leave the past where it belongs and look to the future

"The past will be your teacher if you learn from it; your master if you live in it."

Steve Maraboli

If we live in the past, then we will never have a future, because our past will consume our lives. We cannot change the past and there is no reason why we have to dwell in it. We can learn from the past and from our mistakes and appreciate the fond memories that the past gave us. It lays the foundation for our future lives and forms us, but other than that, we can't afford to get stuck there. The sad reality is that so many people can't set their past free, or set themselves free from their past.

"The secret of change is to focus all of your energy not on fighting the old, but on building the new."

Socrates

Regardless of our age, we have to take charge of our future by scripting the lives that we would like to live. Even if you are 80 years old, you can set yourself free and enjoy the rest of your years as someone who focuses on being in control of what you do, think and feel, to the benefit of everyone, especially you.

Get rid of the guilt

"Guilt: An emotion that keeps you out of the moment where you are."

Kyra Sedgewick

If there is one incentive for embracing that it is never too late, it is to rid ourselves of guilt by getting our self-leadership process under control. At times, when mine was not under control, I would feel guilty. I felt that I should rather be in the pool exercising than in my bed, or I felt guilty that I was watching television rather than sitting in my study getting work done. Nowadays, there is hardly ever a time when I feel guilty because of what I should have done. I just do it! You have a choice to make the required changes to your life and to rid yourself of the guilt, or you can stay the same and forever live with the baggage.

"Forgiveness does not change the past, but it does enlarge the future."
Paul Boese

Another aspect of guilt is when we have not given or received forgiveness. Only you or I can take charge and work on making forgiveness happen. If you are the guilty party who is stubbornly refusing to forgive, then think about the amount of freedom that you will receive by forgiving. It is never too late – not for you or for the other person. Forgiving someone else might just be the key moment that you have both been waiting for so that you can really look to the future.

If a lack of forgiveness is holding you back, make peace with someone, or with yourself. Bury any regret that you might have, because regrets are leeches that sap your energy, slow you down and cause you to lose focus on achieving your personal goals. Life is too short to have any regrets.

It is never too late to follow your dreams

My business was registered on 19 May 2020. My decision to not go back to corporate life and to follow my dream of starting my own business is something that I am passionate about, but like all major life decisions, it obviously carries some risks. Someone might ask: "How on Earth do you start a business in the middle of a pandemic?" My answer would be: "There are many companies out there that will benefit from the input of an experienced businessman with a passion for, and a PhD in, leadership development." Besides, I am also telling myself that if I can be successful during a pandemic, who knows what the future could hold for my business?

CHAPTER 19: EMBRACING THAT IT IS NEVER TOO LATE

"I wake up every morning believing today is going to be better than yesterday."

Will Smith

I look to a bright future, focus on the positives, and get up every morning with a spring in my step. I work after hours and over weekends. I have always gone the extra mile, but now I am even going further. I am doing and experiencing all of these things with a smile, because I am following my dream, and I am thankful for all of these experiences. I have realised that if I don't follow my dream now, then I will never follow it, and I will regret it someday. Alternatively, I would have worked until the retirement age of 65 and then it would have been much more of a challenge to start a business from scratch.

I have shared my story to encourage you not to wait to follow your dreams. It is never too late. Yes, it could be risky, and you will have to plan properly. Your decisions may be criticised by some – and yes, there is even a possibility that you might fail. Weigh all of that up against the future regret you would feel if you didn't follow your dreams, and I would argue that possible failure is far less of a weight on your shoulders than the sorrow of not having lived your dreams, whatever they may be. Your dream might be to excel in your current career in the organisation for which you work, or to move to another functional area, which is also perfectly fine. It doesn't matter what your dreams are, as long as you make those dreams a reality.

It is NEVER too late.

Chapter 20

It is Ultimately Your Choice

> *"Your journey begins with a choice to get up, step out, and live fully."*
>
> OPRAH WINFREY

This is one of the shortest, but possibly the most important chapter in this book. I wish I could continue to share with you, but I don't want to be that guy who keeps talking after he has made his point, and I certainly don't want to overstay my welcome. My last story to you is one that had the biggest impact on my life: It is a story of how I made the biggest and most important choice I have ever made to get my self-leadership journey back on track after steering way off course.

After I had messed up two years at university, I received a formal letter from the University of Pretoria stating that I was not allowed to continue with any studies and that I needed to wait a year before I could apply again for possible conditional acceptance.

At that point, the letter did not faze me. I was done. I was done with my studies and I was extremely disappointed in myself and full of regret at what I had done to my parents.

CHAPTER 20: IT IS ULTIMATELY YOUR CHOICE

In January 1991, I climbed on to an army bus at the Fanie Botha Dam wall in Tzaneen, en route to complete my one-year compulsory military service. That was a safe option, because I had no clue what to do with the rest of my life.

The 450km trip to the army gymnasium in Heidelberg took about eight hours, but it felt more like 80 hours. There I was, driving into the unknown with a bunch of guys who had been in standard 8 when I was in matric. The only difference between me and them was that I had a slightly bigger liver and dirtier lungs as a result of two years of bad lifestyle choices – not to mention a R6 000 bursary and a R4 500 study loan that I needed to pay back.

When we arrived that night, we were met with much hostility. I had expected that, so it didn't bother me in the slightest. I had so much to reflect on in my life that I felt like a prisoner of war who was just going through the motions.

The next morning, after breakfast, we were issued with all of our kit, and then after lunch, while we were still in our civilian clothes, we were issued with a form to complete. That form would change the rest of my life … Still seriously disappointed in myself, I read the content of the form from top to bottom before putting pen to paper. Apart from all of the usual details required, the crux of the form could be found at the bottom – when it came to our army aspirations, we were given three options from which to choose: To stay 'troep' without rank, to become a corporal or to become a lieutenant.

At that point, standing on the lawn in front of the mess, I made the most important decision of my life. In that moment, I thought briefly about how my life would end up if I stayed my current course of no direction in life. Ticking the block to become an officer was not in any way a sign of me thinking that the other two options were inferior, but it was symbolic of me making the conscious decision to stop selling myself short and to change my mindset to one in which I started to live to my full potential. The fact that this decision took place at the beginning of my compulsory period in the army had nothing to do with the institution itself or what it stood for. It was simply a question of me drawing the line on that day, when I chose to start living a full life, to make use of every opportunity and to make a success of my life.

"I am not what happened to me, I am what I choose to become."
Carl Gustav Jung

The rest is history. I became a lieutenant, and then decided that I wanted to go back to Tuks to fix what I had messed up. I received conditional acceptance to study a B.Com degree, which I finished in three years, while also working like a trojan to pay for my own studies. The rest of my study and work career followed, and those are now things that I look back on with much satisfaction.

Since the day that I left Tuks under a cloud of uncertainty in 1990, I never failed a university subject again. Why? Because I chose not to fail anything.

I believe that most things in life boil down to our choices, and that is why I am ending our self-leadership journey together by discussing this most important topic. Making the right choices in our lives is such an important part of our story. Choices define our lives and what we become: To choose God or not; to choose our life partner; to choose our career; to choose what we study; to choose to love; to choose to let live; to choose to make a meaningful difference in this world, and to choose to at least consider the content of this book as part of becoming a better self-leader … The list of our choices is infinite, but each option could make a profound impact on our lives.

With choices come consequences and accountability

"It's your road, and yours alone. Others may walk it with you, but no one can walk it for you."
Rumi

I am reminded again of what my teacher told us in matric: "If we make a decision, we have to carry the consequences."

To me, this quote is also a great tool to assess different options when we have to exercise our choice. It allows us to pause before we make a choice by first reviewing the available options and their pros and cons. Taking the time to properly consider the consequences of different options, although there are no guarantees, guides us towards the right choices. Accountability comes down to choices, which are the only things we truly own.[205]

Success relies mostly on choice

Success in life comes down to the choices that we make. We might find ourselves at a crossroads. We have to make the following choice every single minute of our lives: "Do I want to lead myself in a way that allows me to be really proud of myself, or really disappointed in myself?" It is our choice whether or not to seriously focus on those areas that lead to the sustainable positive changes that self-leadership brings.

We don't always stick to the basic principles in life and choices that will bring us what we define as success. A good starting point though, is to make the choice to continuously focus on what is required to make a success of your self-leadership. This will bring permanent, positive change to your life.

"Success emerges from the quality of the decisions we make and the quantity of luck we receive. We can't control luck. But we can control the way we make choices."

Chip Heath

Unfortunately, there are no quick fixes in life, so when we choose to focus on becoming a better self-leader, there is no light switch we can flip to allow everything to fall into place. It takes time and hard work, but the results are really rewarding. You have to believe in the content, though, and you have to trust the process. It all starts with you believing in the benefits of self-leadership and exercising the choice to continuously become a better self-leader.

The process of improving as self-leaders requires us to exercise self-leadership on a daily basis.[206] Lasting change can only occur when it takes place in the spirit of the mind.[207] You need to consciously make the decision in your own mind to want to experience change, otherwise it won't happen.

Why not postpone the choice?

There are numerous examples of sisters or brothers – even twins – who have experienced different outcomes in life. How is it possible that children from the same gene pool and the same household, with the same upbringing and education, can end up so differently in life? One could be happy and successful and the other, miserable and unsuccessful. I am not a trained psychologist, but I can say quite confidently that it usually boils down to the different choices they make and their different responses to their environments.

"No one gets out of this world alive, so the time to live, learn, care, share, celebrate, and love is now."

Leo Buscaglia

Let's expand a bit on the idea of two siblings. Let's assume that Susan is the sibling who is not successful. She decides to accept the status quo for now and to postpone the choice to do something about her state of mind and circumstances until a later stage in her life. Since it is her life, it's exactly that ... her rightful choice to make. But here's the thing: What if she falls terminally ill and she only has three months to live? Would she then regret the fact that she did not get her life back on track to achieve her full potential? To me, the obvious answer is that anyone in her shoes must have regrets, because she would not have time to fix her life. This is one of the reasons why I love the earlier quote by Leo Buscaglia. He urges us to choose NOW to make the best of this one life that we have been given. Then, and only then, can we enjoy the fruits of living a fulfilled life.

Privately and professionally

During our journey together, I have often used the phrase 'privately and professionally'. I have done this simply because self-leadership transcends all spheres of our lives. If you make the important choice to be serious about self-leadership, then not only you and your family and friends will benefit from you achieving your full potential, but your colleagues at work and the organisation for which you work will, too. If you are a successful self-leader, you cannot underestimate the increased value that you can add to the lives of the people at work and to the performance of your organisation.

Becoming successful at self-leadership does not necessarily imply that you now have to make a career change. On the contrary, it implies that there where you are, you are living a life in which you do justice to yourself and to others by being the best possible version of you. You realise that, frankly, the second-best version of yourself is not good enough. This allows you to not only better lead yourself, but to also be the best possible leader to others in your organisation.

If, as I did, you have a really strong desire and dream to make a career change to something that you feel is your calling, and you believe that both you and others will benefit from your success as a self-leader in that new setting, that is a different story and also perfectly acceptable. My encouragement to you is this: Follow your dreams, both privately and professionally – the dreams that you are convinced are real dreams and not just impulsive, in-the-moment, pseudo-dreams.

Our legacy

I'd like to finish this, the last formal chapter of my message to you, with a topic that is very dear to me: Our legacy. We all have fears, and one of my biggest fears is that one day, when I change my address from this life to the next, my legacy will not be what it could have been. If I have to summarise my own credo in one sentence, it would be: "Leave behind a great legacy."

> **Legacy**: Something that somebody has done successfully and that has positive effects even after they retire or die.[208]

If the inscription one day on my tombstone reads: "He left behind a great legacy," then I would be satisfied.

In the movie, *Gladiator*,[209] Maximus (Russell Crowe) tells his men before battle: "What we do in life echoes in eternity …"

What is the legacy that you want to leave behind, and will it echo in eternity? You can't answer this important question on my behalf, and I can't answer it on yours. We can only answer this question for our own lives. So, do we or don't we want our *only* life story to be an epic one? I would suggest that we can only choose it to be an epic one, because any other answer would not do us justice. You can only choose to leave behind a legacy that will one day prompt people to look back on your life with fondness.

Of course, we cannot always determine the outcome of every aspect of our lives, and there are no guarantees, but I can assure you that if you take charge of your life and decide what it is you want, then the probability is high that you will one day leave behind an epic legacy. A legacy is not built in one day, just as we don't become successful self-leaders in one day. We build these things over time, which could just start *today*.

"The greatest thing you can leave behind is the example of a life well lived. If you leave that to your kids, then you've left them 'everything.'"
Steve Farrar

For me, the crux of the legacy that we leave behind is that it can never be changed afterwards. If you have a great legacy right now, then you have nothing to worry about, but if you have an average or poor legacy, then you might be in trouble. You won't do yourself justice if your time on Earth ends today. Your legacy is partly a product of your thoughts, behaviours and feelings, aligned with the objectives that you set for yourself in life. So, you can choose to neglect self-leadership and think that you might only get serious about it next year, but in truth, there might not be a next year. The life that you live now *is* your legacy. Each one of us has this choice.

"It's the events in our life that shape us, but it's our choices that define us."
Unknown

Conclusion

> *"There is no passion to be found in settling for a life that is less than the one you are capable of living."*
> NELSON MANDELA

> "Greatness is not a function of circumstance. Greatness, it turns out, is largely a matter of conscious choice, and discipline."
> James C. Collins

If I were asked for two words to summarise the essence of self-leadership, they would be: *Choice* and *discipline*. Making the right choices will help us to achieve our personal goals, and discipline will help us to consistently live the correct thoughts, feelings and behaviours in support of this achievement. I believe that this is what differentiates successful people from unsuccessful people, and happy people from unhappy people ... Although these two words encapsulate the essence of self-leadership, there is so much more to it. Each area that I have shared with you in this book will help you to become a better self-leader – working from the assumption that you master these areas by working hard on them on a consistent basis.

I was told once that wisdom helps us to live the detail of life correctly. I trust that the stepping stones I have shared with you will help you to make a success of your self-leadership journey and to live the detail of life correctly, while staying on the right course. You might want to add some additional stepping stones that work for you that I have not included.

Using the outlined stepping stones each day allowed me to become a better self-leader and to conquer my ne*m*esis – me. For too long in my life

I had been my own ne*m*esis, allowing the follower in me to be stubborn and not follow the leader within me. In fact, to top it all off, the leader in me was not the best leader and became confused at times about the right thing to do. These stepping stones played a critical role in transforming the confused leader within me into a good, strong leader.

Finally, after conquering myself and using these stepping stones in a disciplined manner, the follower in me started to align with the strong leader in me. I am now listening to my inner voice, which tells me the right thing to do, and I am experiencing all of the resulting physical and psychological benefits.

I am completely aware of the fact that when I score myself, like you did at the end of Chapter 18, that I do not yet score 100% in all areas that I deem important to successful self-leadership. I realise though, as I hope you do, too, that our efforts to master these areas are part of our ongoing quest for continuous improvement as individuals. Therefore, ongoing focus is required to ensure that we are always moving closer to becoming the best person that we can possibly be, to achieve our full potential …

"Great men are not born great, they grow great."

Mario Puzo

Of course, the above quote could equally read: "Great women are not born great, they grow great." May you use the content of this book to take control of your self-leadership story and to grow great.

One of my best friends was killed in an armed robbery a couple of weeks before he turned 40. He was not given the years or opportunity to finish strong. We don't know when it's our time, but in the context of our self-leadership journey, this doesn't matter. If, in the unlikely yet possible event that you or I die prematurely, then we would have achieved and experienced so much more than if we had not dedicated ourselves to this process. So, committing to self-leadership and beginning to use the stepping stones is a win-win.

"You only live once, but if you do it right, once is enough."

Mae West

Working through this book provides an opportunity to take stock of your life, and to identify and work on the aspects in which you recognise that you can improve. It is a great way for you to reflect on your self-leadership success. Your self-leadership journey is not only life-long, but it requires your attention every single day.

Robin Sharma emphasised this point when he wrote: "*Success is created through the performance of a few small daily disciplines that stack up over time to produce achievements far beyond anything you could have ever planned for.*"[210]

> I would like to end this book by asking you these questions:
>
> - What amazing results could you see in your life if you could master self-leadership and those areas that we have covered in this book?
> - What would your lasting legacy and positive impact be on this world and its people, if you had your self-leadership journey under control?

I would encourage you to reflect upon these two questions and to then take action to ensure that you increasingly develop positive responses to them. I believe that when you make a success of your self-leadership, you will be able to be the best that you can be, for yourself and for others.

"Mastering others is strength. Mastering yourself is true power."

Lao Tzu

If I have managed to get you thinking about your life and how you can improve it to become a better self-leader, then I have achieved all I set out to do in writing this book. If you gained more value from the book than that, it's the proverbial cherry on the cake and it gives me great satisfaction. In the movie, *Tin Cup*[211], Roy McAvoy (Kevin Costner) tells his caddy: "When a defining moment comes along, you can do one of two things: Define the moment, or let the moment define you."

Maybe, just maybe, reading this book is a defining moment in your life, when you make the right choice by starting to put real effort into leading yourself as best as you possibly can.

I'd like to leave you with two final quotes on which to reflect deeply. I wish you all of the best in becoming the greatest self-leader that you can possibly be. My wish is also that you give yourself the best possible chance to make this happen.

"The will to win, the desire to succeed, the urge to reach your full potential … these are the keys that will unlock the door to personal excellence."

Confucius

"One day, or day one. You decide."

Paolo Coelhos

References

1. Peale, N.V. *The Power of Positive Thinking*. (1952) Prentice Hall.
2. Peale, N.V. *Why Some Positive Thinkers get Positive Results*. (1986) Ballantine.
3. www.iol.co.za/news/south-africa/tears-for-inspirational-mr-harley-davidson-357735 (Accessed: 12 February 2021).
4. Covey, F. (2012) *The Wisdom and Teachings of Stephen R Covey.* Simon & Schuster.
5. www.oxfordlearnersdictionaries.com (Accessed repeatedly).
6. Browning, M. (2018) Self-Leadership: Why it matters. *International Journal of Business and Social Science*, 9(2), 14-18.
7. Manz, C.C. (1983) *The Art of Self-leadership: Strategies for Personal Effectiveness in your Life and Work*. Prentice Hall.
8. Bryant, A. & Kazan, A.L. (2013) *Self-Leadership – How to become a more successful, efficient, and effective leader from the inside out*. McGraw Hill Publications.
9. Browning, M. (2018) Self-Leadership: Why it matters. *International Journal of Business and Social Science*, 9(2), 14-18.
10. Bendell, B.L., Sullivan, D.M. & Marvel, M.R. (2019) A gender-aware study of self-leadership strategies among high-growth entrepreneurs. *Journal of Small Business Management*, 57(1), 110-130.
11. Browning, M. (2018) Self-leadership: Why it matters. *International Journal of Business and Social Science*, 9(2), 14-18.
12. Bryant, A. & Kazan, A.L. (2013) *Self-Leadership – How to become a more successful, efficient, and effective leader from the inside out*. McGraw Hill Publications.
13. Na-Nan, K. & Saribut, S. (2020) Validation of employees' self-leadership using exploratory and confirmatory factor analysis. *International Journal of Quality & Reliability Management*, 37(4), 552-574.
14. Stewart, G.L., Courtright, S.H. & Manz, C.C. (2019) Self-leadership: A paradoxical core of organizational behavior. *Annual Review of Organizational Psychology and Organizational Behavior*, 6, 47-67.
15. Napiersky, U. & Woods, S.A. (2018) From the workplace to the classroom: Examining the impact of self-leadership learning strategies on higher educational

attainment and success. *Innovations in Education and Teaching international*, 55(4), 441-449.
16. Browning, M. (2018) Self-leadership: Why it matters. *International Journal of Business and Social Science*, 9(2), 14-18.
17. Stewart, G.L., Courtright, S.H. & Manz, C.C. (2019) Self-leadership: A paradoxical core of organizational behavior. *Annual Review of Organizational Psychology and Organizational Behavior*, 6, 47-67.
18. www.lexico.com (Accessed repeatedly).
19. Gibson, M., Ladd, A. Jr, Davey, B. (producers) & Gibson, M. (director) (1995) *Braveheart*.[Motion Picture]. United States: Paramount Pictures & 20th Century Fox.
20. www.poetryfoundation.org/poems/51642/invictus (Accessed: 23 March 2021).
21. www.businessinsider.com/rags-to-riches-story-of-oprah-winfrey-2015-5?IR=T (Accessed: 12 February 2021).
22. www.theguardian.com/tv-and-radio/2018/jan/12/oprah-winfrey-unlikely-to-run-for-us-president-but-could-win-if-she-did (Accessed: 12 February 2021).
23. www.forbes.com/profile/oprah-winfrey/?sh=6c9c334d5745 (Accessed 12 February 2021).
24. Sharma, R. (2010) *The Leader Who Had No Title – A modern fable on real success in business and in life*. Simon & Schuster.
25. Kraft, D. (2011) *Leaders who Last – Only 30% of leaders last*. Good News Publishers (Crossway).
26. https://spartacus-educational.com/Jgrimshaw.htm (Accessed: 10 March 2021).
27. Munroe, M. (2005) *The Spirit of Leadership – Cultivating the attitudes that influence human action*. Whitaker House.
28. Peterson, J.B. (2018) *12 Rules for Life – An antidote to chaos*. Allen Lane.
29. Carnegie, D. (1998) *How to Stop Worrying and Start Living*. Penguin Random House.
30. www.lexico.com
31. Bryant, A. & Kazan, A.L. (2013) *Self-leadership – How to become a more successful, efficient, and effective leader from the inside out*. McGraw Hill Publications.
32. www.lexico.com
33. www.history.com/news/5-famous-wwii-covert-operations (Accessed: 13 February 2021).
34. www.lexico.com
35. Maxwell, J.C. (2008) *Mentoring 101 – What every leader needs to know*. HarperCollins Leadership.
36. Deming, V.K. (2004) *The Big Book of Leadership Games*. McGraw-Hill.
37. Kraft, D. (2011) *Leaders who Last – Only 30% of leaders last*. Good News Publishers (Crossway).
38. www.lexico.com
39. www.lexico.com
40. Sharma, R. (2010) *The Leader Who Had No Title – A modern fable on real success in business and in life*. Simon & Schuster.
41. Kraft, D. (2011) *Leaders who Last – Only 30% of leaders last*. Good News Publishers (Crossway).

REFERENCES

42 Fuda, P. (2013) *Leadership Transformed – How ordinary managers become extraordinary leaders*. Profile Books.
43 www.merriam-webster.com/dictionary/aspiration (Accessed: 16 March 2021).
44 www.entrepreneur.com/article/315161 (Accessed: 15 February 2021).
45 Bruckheimer, J. (Producer), & West, S. (Director). (1997). Con Air [Motion Picture]. United States: Buena Vista Pictures.
46 https://voxeu.org/article/effect-age-willingness-take-risks (Accessed: 14 March 2021).
47 www.billboard.com/articles/news/8490429/toby-keith-clint-eastwood-inspired-dont-let-the-old-man-in-the-mule-interview (Accessed: 14 March 2021).
48 www.entrepreneur.com/article/241346 (Accessed: 14 March 2021).
49 https://global.kfc.com/our-locations/ (Accessed: 14 March 2021).
50 www.collinsdictionary.com/dictionary/english/charter (Accessed: 13 March 2021).
51 www.lexico.com
52 www.lexico.com
53 https://hbr.org/1992/01/the-balanced-scorecard-measures-that-drive-performance-2 (Accessed: 15 March 2021).
54 www.lexico.com
55 www.peoplegoal.com/blog/smarter-goals-setting (Accessed: 16 March 2021).
56 www.merriam-webster.com/dictionary/affirm (Accessed: 16 March 2021).
57 Sharma, R. (2010) *The Leader Who Had No Title – A modern fable on real success in business and in life*. Simon & Schuster.
58 www.mindtools.com/pages/article/affirmations.htm (Accessed: 17 March 2021).
59 www.mindtools.com/pages/article/affirmations.htm (Accessed: 17 March 2021).
60 www.mindtools.com/pages/article/affirmations.htm (Accessed: 17 March 2021).
61 https://briefly.co.za/89563-what-spoken-language-south-africa-top-11-sa-languages.html (Accessed: 16 March 2021).
62 https://garyplayer.com/the-legend/ (Accessed: 15 February 2021).
63 https://garyplayer.com/the-legend/ (Accessed: 15 February 2021).
64 www.lexico.com
65 Rowling, J.K. (2000) *Harry Potter and the Goblet of Fire*. Bloomsbury.
66 www.urbandictionary.com/define.php?term=Zombie%20Mode (Accessed: 16 February 2021).
67 www.speakersinstitute.com/online/how-jon-morrow-built-a-personal-brand-by-blogging-without-using-his-real-name/ (Accessed: 18 February 2021).
68 https://citizenaffiliate.com/the-extraordinary-story-of-jon-morrow/ (Accessed: 17 February 2021).
69 https://www.speakersinstitute.com/online/how-jon-morrow-built-a-personal-brand-by-blogging-without-using-his-real-name/ (Accessed: 18 February 2021).
70 https://citizenaffiliate.com/the-extraordinary-story-of-jon-morrow/ (Accessed: 17 February 2021).
71 www.lexico.com
72 Silverstein, S. (2010) *No More Excuses – The five accountabilities for personal and organizational growth*. John Wiley & Sons, Inc.

73. Altman, S. www.brainyquote.com/quotes/sam_altman_714789 (Accessed: 1 June 2021).
74. George Washington's letter to his niece, Harriet Washington, Sunday, October 30, 1791, www.mountvernon.org/ (Accessed: 2 May 2020).
75. Sharma, R. (2010) *The Leader Who Had No Title – A modern fable on real success in business and in life*. Simon & Schuster.
76. https://us.macmillan.com/author/brettarchibald/ (Accessed: 18 February 2021).
77. www.bbc.com/news/world-africa-37645201 (Accessed: 4 February 2021).
78. Archibald, B. (2016) *Alone – The Search for Brett Archibald*, Burnet Media.
79. Butler, G., Siegel, A., O'Toole, M., Thompson, J., Weldon, L. & Lerner, Y. (producers) & Waugh, R. (director) (2019) *Angel Has Fallen*. [Motion Picture]. United States: Lionsgate.
80. www.mindtools.com/pages/article/newTMC_5W.htm#:~:text=The%20method%20is%20remarkably%20simple,prevent%20the%20issue%20from%20recurring (Accessed: 19 February 2021).
81. www.lexico.com
82. Williams, M. & Penman, D. (2011) *Mindfulness – A practical guide to finding peace in a frantic world*. Piatkus.
83. www.lexico.com
84. www.sportskeeda.com/athletics/the-story-of-alex-zanardi-a-remarkable-man (Accessed: 17 February 2021).
85. Peale, N.V. (1982) *The Power of Positive Thinking*. Ballantine Books.
86. www.olympic.org/news/derek-redmond-on-the-power-of-perseverance-what-defines-you-in-life (Accessed: 20 February 2021).
87. www.vuca-world.org/ (Accessed: 20 February 2021).
88. www.medicalnewstoday.com/articles/317950 (Accessed: 20 February 2021).
89. www.abrahamlincolnonline.org/lincoln/education/failures.htm (Accessed: 20 February 2021).
90. https://news.harvard.edu/gazette/story/2008/06/text-of-j-k-rowling-speech/ (Accessed: 25 January 2021).
91. Bryant, A. & Kazan, A.L. (2013) *Self-leadership – How to become a more successful, efficient, and effective leader from the inside out*. McGraw Hill Publications.
92. www.lexico.com
93. Williams, M. & Penman, D. (2011) *Mindfulness – A practical guide to finding peace in a frantic world*. Piatkus.
94. https://thehappinessindex.com/employee-engagement/importance-of-work-life-balance/ (Accessed: 21 February 2021).
95. Covey, S.R. (2004) *The 7 Habits of Highly Effective People – Powerful lessons in personal change*. Simon & Schuster.
96. https://elitefeet.com/the-legend-of-cliff-young/#An_Unlikely_Competitor (Accessed: 20 February 2021).
97. Stengel, R. (2010) *Mandela's Way – Lessons in life*. Virgin Books.
98. www.lexico.com

99 Maxwell, J.C. (2008) *Mentoring 101 – What every leader needs to know.* HarperCollins Leadership.
100 www.lexico.com
101 Soria, M. (producer) & Darnell, E. & McGrath, T. (directors) (2005) *Madagascar* [Motion Picture]. United States: DreamWorks Pictures.
102 www.lexico.com
103 www.lexico.com
104 Farrar, S. (1995) *Finishing Strong – Going the distance for your family.* Multnomah Publishers.
105 Sandler, A., Giarraputo, J., Moritz, N., Koren, S. & O'Keefe, M. (producers), & Coraci, F. (director). (2006) *Click* [Motion Picture]. United States: Sony Pictures Releasing.
106 www.lexico.com
107 Palmer, W. & Crawford, J. (2013) *Leadership Embodiment – How the way we sit and stand can change the way we think and speak.* CreateSpace.
108 https://growmindfulness.com/mindfulness-as-self-observation/ (Accessed: 11 January 2021).
109 Bryant, A. & Kazan, A.L. (2013) *Self-Leadership – How to become a more successful, efficient, and effective leader from the inside out.* McGraw Hill Publications.
110 Na-Nan, K. & Saribut, S. (2020) Validation of employees' self-leadership using exploratory and confirmatory factor analysis. *International Journal of Quality & Reliability Management,* 37(4), 552-574.
111 Williams, M. & Penman, D. (2011) *Mindfulness – A practical guide to finding peace in a frantic world.* Piatkus.
112 Williams, M. & Penman, D. (2011) *Mindfulness – A practical guide to finding peace in a frantic world.* Piatkus.
113 Williams, M. & Penman, D. (2011). *Mindfulness – A practical guide to finding peace in a frantic world.* Piatkus.
114 www.lexico.com
115 https://dictionary.apa.org/meditation (Accessed: 15 February 2021).
116 Williams, M. & Penman, D. (2011). *Mindfulness – A practical guide to finding peace in a frantic world.* Piatkus.
117 Bryant, A. & Kazan, A.L. (2013) *Self-leadership – How to become a more successful, efficient, and effective leader from the inside out.* McGraw Hill Publications.
118 Bryant, A. & Kazan, A.L. (2013) *Self-leadership – How to become a more successful, efficient, and effective leader from the inside out.* McGraw Hill Publications.
119 www.more-selfesteem.com/self-motivation-and-self-esteem.htm (Accessed: 18 January 2021).
120 www.express.co.uk/news/world/1226660/michael-schumacher-health-skiing-french-alps-grenoble-formula-one-ferrari-accident-spt (Accessed: 25 February 2021).
121 https://holocaustmemorialmiamibeach.org/Henry_Flescher_Memoir.pdf (Accessed: 26 February 2021).
122 www.abc.net.au/news/2016-04-07/holocaust-survivor-does-reddit-ama/7302244 (Accessed: 26 February 2021).

123 https://holocaustmemorialmiamibeach.org/Henry_Flescher_Memoir.pdf (Accessed: 26 February 2021).
124 www.abc.net.au/news/2016-04-07/holocaust-survivor-does-reddit-ama/7302244 (Accessed: 26 February 2021).
125 https://www.dignitymemorial.com/obituaries/north-miami-beach-fl/henry-flescher-7976854 (Accessed: 31 March 2021).
126 Bryant, A. & Kazan, A.L. (2013) *Self-Leadership – How to become a more successful, efficient, and effective leader from the inside out.* McGraw Hill Publications.
127 Covey, F. (2012) *The Wisdom and Teachings of Stephen R. Covey.* Simon & Schuster.
128 Maxwell, J.C. (2008) *Mentoring 101 – What every leader needs to know.* HarperCollins Leadership.
129 Kraft, D. (2011) *Leaders who last – Only 30% of leaders last.* Good News Publishers (Crossway).
130 https://issafrica.org/iss-today/what-is-the-future-of-poverty-in-africa (Accessed 26 February 2021).
131 Munroe, M. (2005) *The Spirit of Leadership – Cultivating the attitudes that influence human action.* Whitaker House.
132 Peale, N.V. (1986) *Why Some Positive Thinkers get Powerful Results.* Ballantine Books.
133 Munroe, M. (2005) *The Spirit of Leadership – Cultivating the attitudes that influence human action.* Whitaker House.
134 Covey, F. (2012) *The Wisdom and Teachings of Stephen R. Covey.* Simon & Schuster.
135 www.britannica.com/science/gold-chemical-element (Accessed: 27 February 2021).
136 https://edition.cnn.com/2015/07/15/africa/patrice-motsepe-to-know/index.html (Accessed: 28 February 2021).
137 Haft, S., Witt, P.J. & Thomas, T. (producers) & Weir, P. (director) (1989) *Dead Poets Society* [Motion Picture]. United States: Buena Vista Pictures.
138 www.the-numbers.com (Accessed: 28 February 2021).
139 www.thecharactercompany.co.za/what-we-do (Accessed: 15 February 2021).
140 Sharma, R. (2010) *The Leader Who Had No Title – A modern fable on real success in business and in life.* Simon & Schuster.
141 Munroe, M. (2005) *The Spirit of Leadership – Cultivating the attitudes that influence human action.* Whitaker House.
142 Covey, S.R. (1991) *Principle-centered Leadership.* Simon & Schuster.
143 Kraft, D. (2011) *Leaders who Last – Only 30% of leaders last.* Good News Publishers (Crossway).
144 Patterson, K., Grenny, J., McMillan, R. & Switzler, A. (2002) *Crucial Conversations – Tools for talking when the stakes are high.* McGraw Hill Publications.
145 www.lexico.com
146 www.oxfam.org/en/press-releases/worlds-billionaires-have-more-wealth-46-billion-people (Accessed: 2 March 2021).
147 www.health.harvard.edu/heart-health/top-five-habits-that-harm-the-heart (Accessed: 2 March 2021).
148 https://careersinpsychology.org/ten-worst-habits-mental-health/ (Accessed: 2 March 2021).

REFERENCES

149 www.healthline.com/health/how-long-does-it-take-to-form-a-habit#takeaway (Accessed: 2 March 2021).
150 https://www.skilledatlife.com/18-reasons-why-a-daily-routine-is-so-important/ (Accessed: 3 March 2021).
151 https://www.verywellmind.com/the-importance-of-keeping-a-routine-during-stressful-times-4802638 (Accessed: 3 March 2021).
152 www.nm.org/healthbeat/healthy-tips/health-benefits-of-having-a-routine (Accessed: 3 March 2021).
153 Farrar, S. (1995) *Finishing Strong – Going the distance for your family*. Multnomah Publishers.
154 www.bbc.com/news/magazine-17631595 (Accessed: 7 March 2021).
155 Palmer, W. & Crawford, J. (2013) *Leadership Embodiment – How the way we sit and stand can change the way we think and speak*. CreateSpace.
156 Covey, S.R. (2004) *The 7 Habits of Highly Effective People – Powerful lessons in personal change*. Simon & Schuster.
157 Bryant, A. & Kazan, A.L. (2013) *Self-leadership – How to become a more successful, efficient, and effective leader from the inside out*. McGraw Hill Publications.
158 Palmer, W. & Crawford, J. (2013) *Leadership Embodiment – How the way we sit and stand can change the way we think and speak*. CreateSpace.
159 https://blog.smarp.com/top-5-communication-skills-and-how-to-improve-them (Accessed: 7 March 2021).
160 www.oxfordlearnersdictionaries.com
161 Stewart, G.L., Courtright, S.H. & Manz, C.C. (2019) Self-leadership: A paradoxical core of organizational behavior. Annual Review of Organizational Psychology and Organizational Behavior, 6, 47-67.
162 Carnegie, D. (1998) *How to Stop Worrying and Start Living*. Penguin Random House.
163 Carnegie, D. (1998) *How to Stop Worrying and Start Living*. Penguin Random House.
164 Carnegie, D. (1998) *How to Stop Worrying and Start Living*. Penguin Random House.
165 www.marketwatch.com/story/half-of-americans-are-just-one-paycheck-away-from-financial-disaster-2019-05-16 (Accessed: 8 March 2021).
166 www.northeastern.edu/graduate/blog/tips-for-building-your-personal-brand/ (Accessed: 9 March 2021).
167 www.fastcompany.com/3052350/7-traits-that-make-or-break-your-personal-brand (Accessed: 10 March 2021).
168 www.sixpixels.com/articles/archives/the_10_core_values_of_a_winning_personal_brand/ (Accessed: 10 March 2021); https://medium.com/@malcolmlemmons/top-5-characteristics-you-need-to-have-when-building-your-personal-brand-63d51d5091d3 (Accessed: 10 March 2021).
169 www.cio.com/article/3525151/five-things-that-will-damage-your-personal-brand.html (Accessed 10 March 2021).
170 https://keydifferences.com/difference-between-ethics-and-values.html (Accessed: 12 March 2021).
171 Covey, S.R. (1991) *Principle-centered Leadership*. Simon & Schuster.

172 Sharma, R. (2010) *The Leader Who Had No Title – A modern fable on real success in business and in life*. Simon & Schuster.
173 Covey, F. (2012) *The Wisdom and Teachings of Stephen R. Covey*. Simon & Schuster.
174 www.lexico.com
175 www.forbes.com/sites/kathycaprino/2019/12/21/the-top-3-reasons-new-years-resolutions-fail-and-how-yours-can-succeed/?sh=1c874b646992 (Accessed: 13 March 20210).
176 www.lexico.com
177 Munroe, M. (2005) *The Spirit of Leadership – Cultivating the attitudes that influence human action*. Whitaker House.
178 www.forbes.com/powerful-brands/list/ (Accessed: 12 March 2021).
179 www.forbes.com/2010/07/28/apple-google-microsoft-ibm-nike-disney-bmw-forbes-cmo-network-most-valuable-brands_slide.html?sh=616e472138f3 (Accessed: 12 March 2021).
180 https://medium.com/seedx-digital-marketing-guru/why-apple-spends-1-8-billion-on-advertising-38d3940270bf (Accessed: 12 March 2021).
181 https://digitalmarketinginstitute.com/blog/7-steps-to-build-your-personal-brand (Accessed: 12 March 2021).
182 www.northeastern.edu/graduate/blog/tips-for-building-your-personal-brand/ (Accessed: 9 March 2021).
183 www.britannica.com/biography/Mother-Teresa (Accessed: 9 March 2021).
184 Stewart, G.L., Courtright, S.H. & Manz, C.C. (2019) Self-Leadership: A paradoxical core of organizational behavior. *Annual Review of Organizational Psychology and Organizational Behavior*, 6, 47-67.
185 Mbigi, L. (2005) *The Spirit of African Leadership*. Knowres Publishing.
186 Covey, S.R. (1997) *The 7 Habits of Highly Effective Families*. St. Martin's Griffin.
187 Sharma, R. (2010) *The Leader Who Had No Title – A modern fable on real success in business and in life*. Simon & Schuster.
188 www.lexico.com
189 www.ozy.com/around-the-world/the-first-black-afrikaans-music-star-has-arrived/247070/ (Accessed: 9 March 2021).
190 Adair, J. (2013) *Confucius on Leadership*. MacMillan Publishers.
191 Moritz, N.H. et al. (producers), & Marsh, D. (director) (2018) *Hunter Killer* [Motion Picture]. United States: Lionsgate.
192 https://thelastlectureestebez.weebly.com/theme-analysis.html (Accessed: 19 March 2021).
193 www.chicagotribune.com/suburbs/post-tribune/opinion/ct-ct-ptb-davich-time-management-wisdom-randy-pausch-st-0421-story.html (Accessed: 18 March 2021).
194 Pausch, R. & Zaslow, J. (2008) *The Last Lecture*. Hyperion.
195 www.lexico.com
196 Sidwell, A.J. (2019) Psychological Hardiness and Self-leadership: Leading yourself to effective stress coping. *International Journal of Existential Positive Psychology*, 8(1), 1-12.

197 Browning, M. (2018) Self-Leadership: Why it matters. *International Journal of Business and Social Science*, 9(2), 14-18.
198 McLean, P. (2019) *Self as Coach, Self as Leader: Developing the Best in You to develop the Best in Others*. John Wiley & Sons.
199 Sidwell, A.J. (2019) Psychological Hardiness and Self-leadership: Leading yourself to effective stress coping. *International Journal of Existential Positive Psychology*, 8(1), 1-12.
200 http://disneybythenumbers.com/walt-disney-and-the-ambulance-corps/ (Accessed: 19 March 2021).
201 https://brandriddle.com/walt-disney-success-story/ (Accessed: 19 March 2021).
202 www.biography.com/business-figure/ray-kroc (Accessed: 19 March 2021).
203 Kraft, D. (2011) *Leaders who last – Only 30% of leaders last*. Good News Publishers (Crossway).
204 Farrar, S. (1995) *Finishing Strong – Going the distance for your family*. Multnomah Publishers.
205 Silverstein, S. (2010) *No More Excuses – The five accountabilities for personal and organizational growth*. John Wiley & Sons, Inc.
206 Stewart, G.L., Courtright, S.H., & Manz, C.C. (2019) Self-leadership: A paradoxical core of organizational behavior. *Annual Review of Organizational Psychology and Organizational Behavior*, 6, 47-67.
207 Munroe, M. (2005) *The Spirit of Leadership – Cultivating the attitudes that influence human action*. Whitaker House.
208 www.oxfordlearnersdictionaries.com
209 Wick, D., Franzoni, D. & Lustig, B. (producers) & Scott, R. (director) (2000) *Gladiator* [Motion Picture]. United States: DreamWorks Pictures.
210 Sharma, R. (2010) *The Leader Who Had No Title – A modern fable on real success in business and in life*. Simon & Schuster.
211 Foster, G. (producer) & Shelton, R. (director) (1996) *Tin Cup* [Motion Picture]. United States: Warner Bros.

About the Author

Hekkie van der Westhuizen grew up in the small citrus farming community town of Letsitele in Limpopo Province and comes from a family of teachers. After completing his military service, he graduated with a B.Com (Hons) degree in Finance from the University of Pretoria. Although he started out in finance as a financial accountant at Heckett Multiserv and then became a management accountant at Nampak Tissue, his career quickly branched out to managing various functional areas in the supply chain field.

Hekkie joined the Polyoak Packaging Group in 2004, where he held various executive positions in sales, supply chain management and operations, before being promoted to General Manager for the Dairypack division in Gauteng, and finally to the National Executive for that part of the group's business.

Hekkie graduated with an MBA from Wits Business School in 2005, and in 2008 he received Certified Supply Chain Professional (CSCP) accreditation from Apics (ASCM) in the United States. After serving the manufacturing industry for 22 years, Hekkie was given the opportunity to join the retail industry as General Manager of Tile Africa, part of the Norcros Group of companies.

Throughout his career, Hekkie has been involved in various leadership development programmes and projects, ranging from lecturing to guest-lecturing MBA classes; speaking at conferences; developing corporate business school curricula, and acting as an accredited facilitator and assessor.

In 2020, Hekkie left the corporate world to focus full-time on completing his PhD in leadership development at the University of Johannesburg. His research topic was: "Development and validation of a measure of organisational leadership development process maturity". Leadership and people development have always been dear to him, and parallel to completing his studies, Hekkie started his own full-time business focusing in this area. The Southern African Leadership Development and Training Institute (www.saldati.com) partners with organisations to help grow their leaders, to positively impact on their personal lives and organisational results.

Apart from consulting, developing and facilitating leadership development programmes for organisations, Hekkie also acts as an accredited moderator and Masters student supervisor for various business schools. His areas of expertise and interest in leadership development include self-leadership, organisational leadership development process maturity, and youth leadership.

Outside of his full-time profession, Hekkie focuses on his lifetime commitment to personal development. He is also a passionate family man who loves spending time in the African bush. He enjoys open-water swimming and motorcycling and lends his support to various community upliftment projects.

Contact Hekkie at hekkie@saldati.com